979.4004924
L

Levinson
The Jews in the California Gold Rush

8011986

Skokie Public Library
Skokie, Ill.
Telephone OR3-7774

The Jews in the California Gold Rush

LANDMARKS OF WESTERN JEWISH HISTORY
PUBLICATION 1

The Jews in the California Gold Rush

BY

ROBERT E. LEVINSON

KTAV PUBLISHING HOUSE, INC.
NEW YORK
COMMISSION FOR THE PRESERVATION OF PIONEER
JEWISH CEMETERIES AND LANDMARKS OF THE
JUDAH L. MAGNES MEMORIAL MUSEUM
BERKELEY, CALIFORNIA
1978

© Copyright 1978, 1968
Robert E. Levinson

Library of Congress Cataloging in Publication Data

Levinson, Robert E.
  The Jews in the California Gold Rush.

  (Landmarks of Western Jewish history; publication 1)
  Bibliography: p.
  Includes index.
  1. Jews in California—History.   2. California—
Gold discoveries.   3. California—History—1850-1950.
I. Title. II. Series.
F870 J5L38   979.4'004'924   77-10474
ISBN 0-87068-436-1

Manufactured in the United States of America

CONTENTS

ACKNOWLEDGMENTS ix

PREFACE xv

·1· "GOLD!" 1

·2· THE MINING ECONOMY 13

·3· JEWISH BUSINESSMEN IN THE WEST 23

·4· THE GOLD RUSH MERCHANTS 37

·5· JEWS IN THE COMMUNITY 61

·6· JEWS AND JUDAISM 87

·7· DECLINE 125

NOTES 139

BIBLIOGRAPHY 191

INDEX 211

ILLUSTRATIONS

1. The Mother Lode and Northern Mines
2. Sonora, January 1853
3. The Volcano Diggings
4. Present-day Mokelumne Hill. Store-front of L. Mayer & Son on the left
5. Entrance to W. Y. O. D. ("Work Your Own Diggings") Mine in Grass Valley, owned by Jacob and Joseph Weissbein
6. Levinsky Brothers Store, Jackson, 1857
7. A. Wolf & Brothers, Sonora
8. Henry Silvester & Co., Grass Valley, 1858
9. Fred Auerbach & Bro., Rabbit Creek, 1862
10. Block & Furth, North San Juan, 1858
11. Aaron Baruh
12. Moses Dinkelspiel
13. Lewis Gerstle
14. Henry Greenberg
15. Oser Meyer
16. Jacob Schweitzer
17. Sigmund Steinhart
18. Joseph Weissbein
19. Anthony Zellerbach
20. The family of Kaufman and Fanny Mayer Hexter of Mokelumne Hill in San Francisco about 1885 for the wedding of Louis Hexter
21. Gravestone of Rachel Levinsky in Jackson

Illustrations

22. Gravestone of Isaac Peiser in Jackson
23. Gravestone of Herman Landecker in Placerville
24. Gravestone of Kalonymos ben Natan in Jackson
25. Gravestone of Jacob Reeb in Sonora
26. Home of Aaron and Rosalie Wolf Baruh, Nevada City
27. Congregation Ryhim Ahoovim, Stockton, now known as Temple Israel
28. Big Oak Flat and Yosemite Stage Company of Chinese Camp
29. A portion of the gravestone of Isaac Lurch, in the Mokelumne Hill Jewish Cemetery
30. Gravestone of Charles Brownstein, Shasta Jewish Cemetery
31. Grass Valley Jewish Cemetery, in process of restoration, 1970
32. The first synagogue building of Congregation B'nai Israel, Sacramento, 1852, destroyed by fire
33. Israel Joseph Benjamin II
34. Washington Street, Sonora, looking toward the north, in the early 1860's. The store of A. Mock is visible in the right foreground.
35. Title-page of Yom Kippur prayer book used in Sonora
36. Ketubah (marriage contract) printed in San Francisco and executed in Sonora in 1860
37. Newspaper advertisements from the Placerville *Mountain Democrat*, 1864
38. United States Internal Revenue receipt from Anthony Zellerbach, 1863
    Bill-heads of S. & H. Levy, Columbia, 1868, and A. Block & Co., Nevada City, 1858
39. Nineteenth century bill-heads
40. Survey of the Hebrew Societys "Shaar Zedek" or Cemetery in Grass Valley, 1856

ACKNOWLEDGMENTS

    The Commission for the Preservation of Pioneer Jewish Cemeteries and Landmarks expresses its profound appreciation to the following contributors whose generosity has made the publication of this volume possible.

"HONOR HISTORIANS"
The Zellerbach Family Fund

PATRONS

Mrs. Edith Friedlaender Bondi
Jack & Lea Cohen
Mr. & Mrs. Melvin K. Cotton
First National Mortgage Co.
Al & Barbara Frank
Mr. & Mrs. Alfred Fromm
Judge Emil Gumpert
Estate of Harry H. Hilp
Mrs. Samuel Kahn
Dr. & Mrs. Judah Landes
Lulu & Albert Levy
Edmond Michel
Mr. & Mrs. Jacques Reutlinger
Dr. Martin & Edis Robinson
Mrs. Samuel Roland
Mr. & Mrs. Israel S. Shainsky
Mrs. Louis Shenson
Dr. Ben Shenson
Dr. A. Jess Shenson
Sinai Memorial Chapel
Jacqueline Morris Slater
Dr. & Mrs. Marvin S. Weinreb
Dr. & Mrs. Saul Winchell
Harold L. Zellerbach
Stephen Zellerbach

Acknowledgments

SPONSORS

Mr. & Mrs. B. Alter
Mrs. Lillian Altman
Gerald B. Ames
Armin Baron
Mr. & Mrs. Ezra M. Battat
Mr. & Mrs. Alex S. Bauer
Howard & Estelle Bern
Marlene, Phil, David & Steven Bernstein
Nogah & Rhoda Bethlahmy
Margaret & Carl Bregman
Mr. & Mrs. B. Bresler
Barbara, Abe, Daniel, Elise, Marsha & Sara Bromberg
M. A. Bunow
Mrs. William Coffill
Cong. Beth David, Saratoga, CA.
Cong. Emanu-El, San Francisco, CA.
Jay Darwin
David & Elizabeth Davis
Mr. & Mrs. Richard S. Dinner
Conrad & Sandra Donner
Israel Drabkin
Philip S. & Frances S. Ehrlich
Sam & Miriam Engel
Laurence Fabian
John Felstiner
Martin & Sandra Gandel
Dr. & Mrs. Matthew B. Ganz
Mr. & Mrs. Melvin S. Gerton
Anita & Brian Gold
Drs. Vivian & Sherman Golub
Alma Son Goodman
Mr. & Mrs. Robert Guggenheim
The Gutterman Family
James D. Hart
Dr. & Mrs. I. A. Herman
Hartwig & Helen Heymann
Ed & Faye Hirschberg
Dr. & Mrs. Reuben Hoffman
Dr. Burton B. Jacknow & Florence S. Jacknow
Dr. Selna Kaplan
Herman & Dorothy Katz
Rina & Simon Katzen
Mrs. J. M. Kaye
Raymond Kimeldorf
Dr. & Mrs. Edward Kiss
Susan Lee Klawansky
Rabbi Allen Krause

Moshe Jesse Kushman, in memory of Abraham Kushman
Mr. & Mrs. Sol Kutner
Al & Fredda Lampell
David & Anita Lapin
Judge Leland J. Lazarus
Roger Levenson
Steven Paul Levin
Florence Levinson
Helene Baer Maneval
Audrey & Fred Marcus
Charles & Miriam Marr
Leonard & Sylvia Metz
Drs. Dorothy & Charles Miller
David Monasch, III
Mr. & Mrs. Mark Morris
Frederica & Monroe Postman
Rabbi's Discretionary Fund, Temple Beth Sholom, San Leandro, CA.
Mr. & Mrs. Bernard Reiner
Mark & Analee Reutlinger
Rabbi & Mrs. Bernard J. Robinson
Natanya & Avidan Rose
Rosalind Bernheim Rosen
Mr. & Mrs. A. Rubnitz
Mildred R. Sabath
Ed & Fritzi Schoen
Natalie & Richard Schriger
Mrs. Beatrice L. Schwartz
Ursula F. Sherman
Mr. & Mrs. Sy Siegel
Mr. & Mrs. Sol Silverman
Philip & Donna Solin
Mr. & Mrs. Melvin Sosnick
Maureen Starr
Dr. & Mrs. Lee Stone
Barbara & Charles Taubman
Temple Beth Hillel, Richmond, CA.
Richard Thalheimer
Mr. & Mrs. Harry H. Tonkin
William & Aline Usim
Mel Wacks & Family
Mrs. Matt Wahrhaftig
Dr. & Mrs. Edwin J. Whitman
Virginia H. Williams
Lynn Wolff
Jeanie Wright
Ellis & Rosalie Youdovitch

To Fay

PREFACE

The news of the discovery of gold in California was greeted with enthusiasm all over the world. To the western United States came many people of different backgrounds, races, religions, and nationalities, all eager to become rich from a discovery of gold or from some occupation related to the gold-mining economy.

Jews constituted one of the more prominent ethnic and religious groups in the California gold rush. The present study concerns the region of the gold rush from 1849 to approximately 1880. Because gold mining in California became a big business during this era, the region remained well populated until the 1880s. The Jews, for the most part merchants, assimilated into the general community and became important businessmen and valued citizens of the towns and cities in which they lived. To a lesser extent, they were involved in mining and other enterprises related to the mining industry. Additionally, they formed Jewish communities and organizations, conducted worship services, and established and maintained separate cemeteries.

I have used several tests to determine whether a particular person was Jewish. Gravestones in Jewish cemeteries offered almost indisputable proof, as did public documents in county courthouses that involved transfers of property to or from a Jewish organization in which the officers were named. In addition, the probate records of certain individuals revealed that they were buried in Jewish cemeteries in other cities or that their widowed or orphaned heirs were being maintained by Jewish organizations. The newspapers of the region occasionally printed lists of newly elected officers of local Jewish organizations and also noted whose stores were closed for the High Holidays and the weddings and funerals that rabbis conducted. The Jewish newspapers that were published in San Francisco regularly printed vital statistics and, occasionally, letters from the Mother Lode. Finally, it was my privilege to interview or correspond with literally hundreds of descendants of pioneers in the gold rush who informed me that their ancestors were Jews. In several cases a Jewish ancestor was a source of pride to a family that is no longer Jewish by religion. Every effort was made to avoid references to a Gentile in a particular place where a Jew of the same name resided.

This study could never have been undertaken or written without the aid and cooperation of many people. In the first two years during which I devoted my efforts to the Jews in the California gold rush, my family and I were maintained by generous grants from the National Foundation for Jewish Culture in New York and the Commission for the Preservation of Pioneer Jewish Cemeteries and Landmarks of the Judah L. Magnes Memorial Museum in Berkeley. I am also grateful to all the clerks and recorders of the counties of Amador, Calaveras, El Dorado, Mariposa, Nevada, Placer, Sierra, and Tuolumne, and their deputies, for allowing me the unrestricted freedom to search through numerous record books. The Bancroft Library on the campus of University of California, Berkeley, provided me with study space and many research materials, and I wish to acknowledge the aid given to me by Professor James D. Hart, Robert H. Becker, John Barr Tompkins, Cecil L. Chase, Irene Moran, Linda Schieber, Frederick Lynden, the late Helen Bretnor, Alma Compton, Willa Baum, and the library pages.

The following individuals were most helpful in making suggestions to me and in sharing their knowledge of the subject and their personal papers: James de T. Abajian, Julius E. Baer, Professor Gunther Barth, William R. Blumenthal, Dr. Stanley F. Chyet, Sara G. Cogan, Dr. William Newell Davis, Jr., Carlo M.

DeFerrari, Barbara Eastman, Dr. Elliot Evans, Helen Giffen, Rabbi Joseph B. Glaser, Mr. and Mrs. Robert Guggenheim, Carroll D. Hall, Harvey Horowitz, Dr. Nathan M. Kaganoff, Edgar M. Kahn, Joseph W. Kahn, William J. Keough, Sidney Kluger, Dr. Bertram W. Korn, Rabbi Paul S. Laderman, Dr. Jacob R. Marcus, Dr. Isidore S. Meyer, Irene Simpson Neasham, Ruth Ann Newport, Allan R. Ottley, Bob Paine, Ruth Rafael, Dr. Bernard D. Rosenberg, Mr. and Mrs. Jerome Salomon, Mrs. David Schwartz, Donald I. Segerstrom, Norman Simon, Norton B. Stern, Professor and Mrs. John Stone, James Sweeney, Maude K. Swingle, Dr. Max Vorspan, Lyle White, Dr. David Winston, Herbert Zafren, Harold L. Zellerbach, Stephen A. Zellerbach, the officers and trustees of the Commission for the Preservation of Pioneer Jewish Cemeteries and Landmarks, and all the interviewees and correspondents who are individually acknowledged in the bibliography.

The late Hal Altman suggested this topic to me. I am grateful for his many favors. Seymour Fromer, director of the Judah L. Magnes Memorial Museum in Berkeley, expressed a constant interest in my work and placed all the facilities of the Magnes Museum at my disposal. I also wish to acknowledge the support and friendship of Dr. Gerald E. Wheeler, Dean of the School of Social Sciences, and Dr. Charles B. Burdick, Chairperson of the Department of History, San Jose State University.

Professors Edwin R. Bingham, Earl Pomeroy, Kenneth W. Porter, and Martin Schmitt, and Mr. Jeffrey D. Salzman read the manuscript while it was in the form of a doctoral dissertation. Mr. David L. Gitin, Professor Billie Barnes Jensen, and Rabbi Allen Krause read the revised manuscript. Lisa Wasserman, Diane Solomon and Dan Levy assisted me with proofreading.

My wife, Fay, patiently aided me in my research and the writing of early drafts of the manuscript and also assisted with the proofreading. It is to her, with love, that this book is dedicated.

R. E. L.

San Jose, California
November 1976

1. The Mother Lode and Northern Mines.

Courtesy of The Bancroft Library, University of California, Berkeley

·1·

"GOLD!"

When the reports of the discovery of gold in California in 1848 were published[1] and received in the East, a feeling of excitement spread over the eastern United States. Later that same year, when the news reports were verified by President Polk in his annual message to Congress,[2] gold-seekers and adventurers were already on their way to California or making plans to go there.[3] To this American possession on the Pacific Coast, recently acquired from Mexico, came people of all colors, castes, nationalities, and religions. They came by every conceivable means, by ship around Cape Horn, by a combined land and water route that included passage across the Isthmus of Panama or Nicaragua, by wagon or on foot across mainland North America.[4] They were lured to California by reports that slowly filtered back to the eastern states—reports that did not emphasize that the gold fields were over one hundred miles inland, or that mining was a very hazardous occupation. Rather, the books that appeared during this period fanned the flames of desire for gold by describing the riches that could be found with a minimum of labor. Ray Billington states that "Guide-books appeared as if by magic; during the winter of 1848–49 some thirty were published, most of them by hack writers who employed imagination rather than knowledge to inflame their readers."[5] These books appeared in English and several foreign languages.[6] Thousands of immigrants came to California to share in the wealth that they believed the gold would bring them, often not realizing that the metal was not simply waiting on the ground to be picked up.

In the year after 1848, the dream of instant wealth drew people from nearly all of the world's nations to this western American possession. Moreover, the spirit of Manifest Destiny urged that Americans take control of the continent. The war with Mexico was over, and now there were new territories to be settled. The population of the republic had increased during the previous decade as a result of an influx of Irish immigrants and the beginnings of immigration from continental Europe. Americans in the South, it was generally believed, were searching for new regions to extend the peculiar institution of slavery. Also, there was the feeling that the inventive genius of the 1840s would soon result in the growth of manufacturing, the need for new markets, and in more improved means of transportation and communication.

To California, then, came tens of thousands of people, all bent upon acquiring wealth by exploiting the new economy. Included in this migration to California were many Jews, the majority of whom were recent arrivals from Germany and Central Europe.[7] Events in Europe in 1848 had led to their immigration to the United States. The Jews of Central Europe had been freed from restrictive ghetto communities for about a half century. They were enjoying civil rights, receiving liberal educations, and engaging in occupations and professions formerly forbidden to them. Although the revolutions of 1848 were not led by Jews and did not have religious overtones, many Jews still feared economic and political persecution in the wake of the reaction to these revolutions, so they came to the United States.[8]

Marcus Lee Hansen noted: "What . . . people wanted was freedom from laws and customs that curbed individual economic enterprise. . . . They wanted the freedom to buy, sell and bargain, to work or loaf, to become rich or poor."[9]

Many thousands of Jews left their European countries of origin and traveled westward. Once again there occurred a great

Jewish migration. This time, the dislocation terminated in the United States. The Jews came to America believing there would be better opportunities for them there. They settled in all parts of the country. Generally, they did not regard the added distance from the Atlantic coast to some interior city or town as a hardship.

Because of the gold rush to California, jobs for the newcomers were plentiful. Marcus Lee Hansen observed:

> In even greater numbers [than the Europeans] the Americans thronged to California, trekking across the plains or struggling through the jungles of Panama or sailing around Cape Horn. For every one who departed, business and industry in the older parts of the country had to discover a substitute; and the able-bodied European, no matter what his trade or tongue, found a place awaiting him. Factories, shipyards and labor contractors hung out the sign, "Help Wanted"; and if the immigrant disliked the city and its slums, he could obtain employment in the household of a farmer whose "hired hand" had slipped off to California.[10]

Some Jews went almost directly from Europe to California without stopping long in the East. Others remained in the East for varying periods of time, to learn the English language and adjust themselves to American culture, to save money for their westward journey or for the voyages of other European relatives, or, in the case of a fortunate few, to live with and work for relatives who had preceded them to America and were already established in business.

These immigrants finally broke with civilization, as they had known it, when they felt ready and sufficiently prosperous to journey to California. Many ships plied the waters between the major ports of the East and South, from Boston to New Orleans, and San Francisco. But there were many hazards the traveler faced on the long voyage to California. In addition to inclement weather, from which there was scant protection, some ships, hastily built, were often unseaworthy. As gales and squalls rocked the vessels about, passengers and freight rocked from side to side involuntarily.

Moreover, the length of the early voyages around the Horn, or at least to Panama, could not be determined with exact accuracy, because the ships were dependent entirely upon the wind for their motive power. And, with regard to the human cargo, on occasion California-bound gold-seekers passed upwards of two months without any sight of land. Landings were occasionally made at various ports in South America, however, that afforded the passengers the opportunity of going ashore for short periods of time.[11]

Many regarded the voyage to California, via the Horn, as too great an investment of time. They feared the gold would be gone within the five to eight months that a sailing ship required to round South America. Some believed the Panama route would save them some time, and indeed it did when steam-powered ships began the New York–Panama run. The popularity of the Panama route also led to the introduction of competitive companies, the lowering of ship fares, and the eventual construction of the Panama railroad in 1855.[12]

For the most part, there was a certain sameness to ship voyages to California, whether around South America or via Panama. The passengers were wealthy enough to pay the relatively high rates that were demanded by the private ship companies, or they formed companies of their own that outfitted a ship in which they shared common ownership. Along the way, there was, at the outset, a feeling of exhilaration to be out on the open sea headed for California. This exultant spirit soon descended into boredom as day followed day with little to alter the routine. Those would-be gold-seekers who took the time to pen memoirs or diaries of their trip to California by sea repeated these problems of seafaring time and time again.[13]

But it was an undisputed fact that the trip to California by sea was more preferred than the overland trip. This was especially so for the Jewish immigrants to California, who were numbered in the thousands on ships' passenger lists but only by the scant handful among recollections of overland trips. They were among the 22,086 people who arrived in San Francisco between July 1 and December 31, 1849.[14] And they must have been well-to-do because the ship fare for the New York–to–California trip, via Panama, in December 1849, was $380 for first-class cabins and $200 for steerage.[15]

By the end of 1849, the news of James W. Marshall's discovery of gold on the American River had reached around the world. Thousands of people on both sides of the Atlantic prepared to join in the search for gold. The first to arrive on the scene usually tried to find gold where the original discoveries had been made. Others, however, sought unexplored areas, and some of them, too, uncovered traces of the element all through the region that was soon called the Mother Lode and, farther to the north, the Northern Mines. Defined geologically, "The Mother Lode belt of California is a strip a mile or so wide extending for 120 miles along the lower western flank of the Sierra Nevada. It begins near Georgetown, in El Dorado County, and extends to Mormon Bar—two miles south of Mariposa, in Mariposa County."[16]

The region of the Northern Mines, however, is less clearly defined than the Mother Lode. One writer, a journalist and local historian, suggests that the area is not a specific one but rather extends from the American to the Feather River and from the plain of the Sacramento River to the Sierras.[17]

Another historian, Rodman W. Paul, prefers to describe the region as consisting of three parts, with the Northern Mines as "northwestern . . . [from] the head of the Sacramento Valley, centering in Shasta City, and a thin line of camps that lay beyond the northern and northwestern walls of the valley," and the "central" and "southern" sections as the northern and southern parts of the Mother Lode, respectively. "Of these three sections, the northernmost one was first in size and the last in economic value."[18]

This region was the mecca for thousands of gold-seekers after 1848 and is a popular tourist attraction today. The present-day traveler passes through the Mother Lode and Northern Mines on State Highway 49, from Sattley to Mormon Bar, through the counties of Sierra, Nevada, Placer, El Dorado, Amador, Calaveras, Tuolumne, and Mariposa.

The authors of the exaggerated travel guides and books describing the riches that were available did their work well. As each new group of immigrants arrived and found that the gold fields were overpopulated, they set out on their own and, oftentimes accidentally, made discoveries of fabulous deposits of gold. When such news was circulated, miners and prospectors immediately converged on the new discovery in order to stake a claim. Each new discovery, each new recording of a claim, each letter written to the East, and each edition of a mining camp newspaper added to the notion that anyone could get rich with a minimum of effort.

People searching for wealth, primarily through the discovery of gold, but also in related occupations, such as freighting or merchandising, poured into California from all over the world. By 1852, Governor Peter Burnett reported that 264,435 people resided in California, of whom 47 percent, or 123,822, were in the region of the Mother Lode and Northern Mines.[19] French and German Jews were among the thousands who took part in this gold rush. Some Jews also came from Great Britain, Russia, Prussian Poland, and the Netherlands.[20]

The California gold rush was an odyssey into an unknown land for everybody, but the Jewish immigration to California at this time was a unique phenomenon. Jews had migrated to new lands before, but, for the most part, they had settled in metropolitan areas or in smaller towns where there were good prospects of earning a livelihood. They did not know what to expect when they reached California. The claims of travel guides proved to be exaggerated. In 1849, there were no large cities at the mines, only a few small towns; means of transportation from San Francisco to the mountains were poor; and the gold was usually not easily obtained. But the Jews came in large numbers to this unknown land on the strength of the same rumors that motivated the Gentiles. Statistics for the early years are not available, but there are indications that by 1860 there were possibly as many as 962 Jewish males in San Francisco.[21]

Most of the Jews who came to California during the gold rush were tradesmen. They brought goods to sell in California or money with which to buy goods in San Francisco to sell in the mining camps. Charles Peters, long a resident of the gold country, reminisced about how a Jewish merchant discovered possibilities of trading in a newly established mining camp.

> It is stated that on hearing of a rush to a new mining excitement in the interior, a Jewish merchant in San Francisco sent a relative to view the prospect and advise on the proposition of opening a store. A few days afterward he received a telegram from his relative, sent from a telegraph office, the nearest to the new diggings, reading: "Come. It was richness."

As more and more merchants followed the example of the merchant Peters described, Jewish businessmen in the towns and mining camps soon became numerous. Peters recalled:

> A well known showman of that time was used to often remark, he could easily gauge the prosperity of a mining town by the number of Jewish shopkeepers it maintained and the size of its Chinatown.[22]

San Francisco, noted earlier, was the first port of call in California for these adventurous Jews, and many remained there. They became retail and wholesale merchants and grew prosperous from trading in the city and from supplying merchants in the mountains with goods.[23] Since Jews were in San Francisco from the beginning of the gold rush period, and helped to build the city, there was little anti-Semitism in the metropolis by the bay at that time. And the Jews who settled permanently in San Francisco organized congregations and benevolent societies from the earliest years of their arrival.[24]

San Francisco underwent a very rapid growth during the 1850s as the world port of entry to the gold mines. At first deserted when local citizens tried to cash in on the original discoveries of gold,[25] the city expanded as tens of thousands of immigrants passed through the Golden Gate. Buildings appeared overnight, housing merchandise stores, forwarding firms, residences, and saloons.[26] With the boom also came an influx of lawless men that resulted in the formation of an extralegal law-enforcement group, the Committee of Vigilance, when the normal channels of law failed to keep order.[27]

The city grew from a couple of hundred before the American occupation to 56,000 in 1860. Fires frequently leveled most of the downtown section in this decade, but San Franciscans began to build anew before the ashes of each previous fire had cooled.[28]

However, even in San Francisco during the hectic decade of the 1850s, life was too complacent for many of the newly arrived Jews. A large number of them, therefore, traveled 150 miles into the interior, to the mines. The only restrictions a traveler had were the few ships that were available. The ships that brought the gold-seekers to California were too large for the inland waterways of the Sacramento and San Joaquin Rivers. Those who wished to travel to the mines immediately had to transfer in San Francisco to a smaller ship that could reach Marysville, the head of navigation of the Sacramento River, for example, in about twenty-four hours.[29]

Others were more inclined to go to the mines overland in the company of friends and with horses and wagons that could carry provisions and merchandise. Although it was necessary to look for an overnight camping site and to cross an occasional river or stream, this method of transportation was regarded as more favorable by those who had the means to afford the expense of purchasing a horse and wagon and the goods the party carried.[30]

For the most part, however, as long as the weather did not interfere, those who were destined for the mines reached their goal by a combination of passage by water and by land—by water to the head of navigation of a river or some other convenient landing place, and then by horse- or mule-back to the Sierra foothills located to the east of Sacramento and Stockton.[31]

The Jewish argonauts found life in California much different from anything in their past culture and experiences. Whether they had lived in isolated, self-reliant ghetto communities or in free cities, one notable characteristic of Jews in Europe was the closeness of the family. In the early years of the gold rush, families and legal institutions, as they were known in the East, were almost nonexistent. Fortunately, this isolation from public-supported forms of law-enforcement did not lead to lawlessness. In the mining camps, the miners, Gentiles and Jews, ruled themselves.[32]

Mining camps, in the earliest years of the gold rush, were collections of crude, hastily constructed buildings that gave no semblance of plan or permanence. Little more than one main street, some wood and tent structures, such camps were, nevertheless, beehives of activity and served as supply centers for miners and prospectors. Since mining was the *raison d'être* of the camp, the miners themselves paid scant attention to, and invested as little time as possible in, cooking, housing themselves, or washing their clothing.[33]

Charles Shinn observed:

> The mines put all men for once upon a level. Clothes, money, manners, family connections, letters of introduction, never before counted for so little. . . . Social and financial inequalities between man and man were together swept out of sight.[34]

William Perkins's description of Sonora upon his arrival there in mid-1849 was typical of other contemporary recollections.

> When I arrived . . . the habitations were constructed of canvas, cotton cloth, or of upright unhewn sticks with green branches and leaves and vines interwoven, and decorated with gaudy hangings. . . .
> On either side of the street were ranged the gambling tables, generally covered with a rich scarlet gold embroidered cloth.[35]

This unique setting soon became the home of hundreds of transplanted mid-nineteenth-century European Jews. They proved to their eastern and European brethren that they were capable of settling and succeeding in a region that had been a wilderness only a short time before. They opened stores and sold goods from all over the world. They prospered from the very earliest years and were among the leading citizens of their communities. And they also remembered their religion and established benevolent societies, cemeteries, and congregations.

Some Jews in the Mother Lode also participated in the dominant industry of the region, gold mining. In this way, they carried on a tradition among American Jews who engaged in general merchandising wherever they were located and invested in the local economy as well.[36] Whether the Jews did this to convince the local population that they had a genuine interest in the industry of the immediate region can never be known. Perhaps they became involved in the mining economy involuntarily by accepting deeds to mining claims in return for the extension of credit. Whatever it was that motivated them, the Jews, in new surroundings, participated, together with the local population, in the local economy. All over the West, they were interested in investing in some new enterprise, any unique enterprise, that would return a good profit. And, in the West, gold mining was that endeavor.

Floyd S. Fierman, who has studied the Jews of the American Southwest quite extensively, concludes that the pioneer Jews in that region were almost compelled by necessity to find new lands and to engage in whatever occupations would promise a good return.

> Whether the transportation companies or the laudatory literature served as a magnetic pull we cannot be certain. But of this we can be definite: The material at hand discloses that the typical Jewish settler was a young man without opportunity in his homeland, who had a compulsion to find a new prosperous life. He was a treasure hunter and nothing else.[37]

The same may be said of the earliest Jews in the Mother Lode and those who came to California in the 1850s.

In the Far West, the chronicle of Jewish participation in many phases of the mining industry is an example of such an interest on their part. In rural areas, such as the Pacific Northwest or the Old South,[38] or in the gold regions of California, the Jews were interested in whatever occupations and investments would provide the most comfort for them and their families. To this extent, they were treasure hunters and followed the local economy with a great deal of interest and participation.

·2·

THE MINING ECONOMY

Following the Jewish immigration of the 1850s, anti-Semitism in the United States reached a climax during the Civil War.[1] In the 1850s and 1860s, there were persons in California, too, with anti-Jewish prejudices. Among some of the more transient visitors to the gold rush country were writers whose anti-Semitism colored what they saw. Because of the prejudice of these writers, students of the early years of California's American period have been exposed to half-truths concerning the role of Jews as miners or participants in the mining economy. Four authors are most responsible for the image of the Jew as one who shunned the exertion necessary for mining,[2] and later historians accepted these observations on Jews that were based on incomplete and one-sided evidence. These writers perpetuated the myth of the miner as a hero who helped to populate and civilize the newly obtained land. Not only did these writers disparage the Jews for engaging in the very necessary occupation of merchandising, but they were so impressed by the number of Jewish merchants that they were unwilling to admit that some Jews occupied themselves in mining and prospecting.

For example, Hinton Rowan Helper, whose tract, *The Impending Crisis of the South,* would soon crystallize opinions concerning slavery, was as vociferous in his claims of Jewish laziness in the gold rush as he was in condemnation of the southern slaveholder. With regard to Jews as miners, he wrote:

> Mining, the cultivation of the soil, in a word, any occupation that requires exposure to the weather, is too fatiguing and intolerable for them. The law requiring man to get bread by the sweat of his brow is an injunction with which they refuse to comply.³

The contemporary writer J. D. Borthwick generalized concerning the Jews he encountered.

> In travelling through the mines from one end to the other, I never saw a Jew lift a pick or shovel to do a single stroke of work, or, in fact, occupy himself in any other way than in selling slops. While men of other classes and of every nation showed such versatility in betaking themselves to whatever business or occupation appeared at the time to be most advisable, without reference to their antecedents, and in a country where no man, to whatever class of society he belonged, was in the least degree ashamed to roll up his sleeves and dig in the mines for gold, or to engage in any other kind of manual labour, it was a very remarkable fact that the Jews were the only people among whom this was not observable.⁴

The writings of Helper and others seemed to indicate that no Jews ever prospected or recorded gold-mining claims in the Mother Lode. But there are evidences of Jewish miners and claimants all through the region in the period before 1880. A few Jews became prospectors for a time;⁵ some others were numbered among the miners who staked their own claims, individually or in groups.

The Jewish miners in California were much like the Gentile argonauts who came to California; they also resembled their fellow Jews around the country who participated in varying degrees in the dominant economy of the region and also engaged in retail merchandising. Exactly how long mining by Jews remained a factor in the overall economy of the region is not known. Many soon turned to trading, to be sure, but some made the greater portions of their incomes from mining.

There were Jews in the Mother Lode who were listed on the decennial census records as miners. When the Great Register of voters was established in 1866, many men also indicated their occupation as miner. For example, miners whose names appeared on the Tuolumne County Great Register included Albert Jacobi, Herman Jacobs, Bernhard Marks, and Herman Wolfe.[6]

Further documentation of the presence of Jews in the mining economy appears in the records of the mining claims. In addition to recording their own claims as miners, Jews often underwrote mining enterprises as individuals or as members of corporations, and they received title to mining claims in payment for debts owed to them as merchants.

Jews recorded claims from the earliest days of gold discovery through the entire region of the Mother Lode. In El Dorado County, from December 4, 1850 to November 21, 1881, Jews recorded ninety-one mining claims.[7] In Amador County, for the period September 22, 1862 to January 3, 1882, forty-nine mining claims by Jews were recorded.[8] In Calaveras County, 128 claims owned in part or wholly by Jews were recorded from April 30, 1852 to September 4, 1880.[9]

An early Jewish prospector in Murphys, Calaveras County, was Lewis Gerstle, who in 1851 appended his name to a public letter that charged a gold-mining company with prejudice against foreigners.[10] Gerstle later moved to Sacramento and San Francisco and became associated in business with Louis Sloss, with whom he organized the Alaska Commercial Company.[11]

Along the Sierra, gold was likely to be found anywhere, and the distance to be traveled or the ruggedness of the terrain did not deter prospectors. Fortunately, for some, gold might be found in a town, on one's own property, as in Mariposa in 1853.

> ... Be it known, that I, *A. Blumenthal* ... claim by right of possession purchase & location, a *certain piece or parcel of land*, situate, lying & being *in the town of Mariposa* on the south west side of Charles Street & fronting on said Street 45 feet ... being the same premises which I have occupied as a Store house for the last two years. ...[12]

Another miner panned gold in downtown Columbia in 1866.

> Good Dirt.—On a vacant lot on State street, immediately

opposite the Citizen office, Mr. A. Levy washed out eighteen pans of dirt, on Thursday last, and obtained $6.50 in gold, being an average of a fraction over thirty-six cents to the pan. A few acres of such dirt as this, and a good hydraulic, ought to be sufficient to satisfy any reasonable man. There's lots of it "lying around loose."[13]

Gold mines and mining claims were usually named after a nearby geographical or geological area, but a refreshing example of originality was one mining claim that was named for a member of the claimant's family.

> ... this Ledge is situated on Rocky Ravine Nevada Township Nevada County State of California. I do intend to work this Ledge according to the Laws of this State and also according to the Laws of the United States, this Ledge is to be known as the Jenny Ledge. A. Baruh.[14]

Occasionally, mining claims made the news columns of the local newspapers because of the richness of the discovery. For example, in 1872,

> The ... Cohen claim at Vallecito has made another "whopping clean up." Thirteen pounds of pure gold was the result. In addition to this several "chispas," weighing from an ounce to six ounces, were picked up.[15]

An important investor and mine operator in El Dorado County was Nathan Rhine, who was also a merchant in the city of El Dorado and charter member of the "Shaurey Shomagin" [sic, i.e., Shaarey Shomayim, Gates of Heaven] Cemetery Association of Diamond Springs and El Dorado. A correspondent in El Dorado wrote to the Placerville *Mountain Democrat* in 1865:

> ... Nathan Rhine has one of the best ledges I have seen. He has expended about $8,000 to develop it, and has a shaft 132 feet in depth, and at the depth of 100 feet he has drifted north and south, following the vein both ways. He has sufficient quartz already on

the surface to run a twenty stamp mill for one year, and it will pay $40 a ton. . . .[16]

Jews also invested in enterprises related to gold mining.

> In very early days the "Vallecito Flat" was very rich [the Mokelumne Hill *Weekly Calaveras Chronicle* recalled in 1866]. During the first five or six years it was being worked, many lucky *hombres* went to the States with their thousands of dollars obtained from the flat. And although eight years ago it was believed to be worked out, it is not so, as will be demonstrated by the "Vallecito Tunnel and Mining Company," when their tunnel is completed, which will enable races to be cut in their tunnel, thereby carrying off at a rapid rate everything run into their main flume. The tunnel is owned by Morris Cohen & Co., and from the continued perseverance of Mr. Cohen, under whose superintendence the entire work has been entrusted since its commencement, (three years,) by next Fall it will reach sufficiently into the flat to enable a portion of the owners of claims adjacent to commence work. The present length of the tunnel is 750 feet, 7 feet high, and 5½ feet wide, the entire distance being through very hard rock, and costing about $40,000. Mr. Cohen is entitled to much credit for his patience and perseverance in the management of this great piece of work. . . .[17]

In 1872, when gold was no longer as readily available as it once had been, the news of a new mineral discovery in Nevada County attracted a great deal of attention.

> A Very Rich Discovery.—Simon Furth, Esq., brought to our office, on Thursday last, a beautiful specimen of Cinnibar [*sic*], taken from a ledge near Eureka, in this county. The parties locating it represent that the ledge is visible for a distance of five hundred feet. Some of the rock has been forwarded to San Francisco for assay. Should it turn out to be as rich as anticipated by the owners, it will be the greatest discovery ever made in the mountains of California.[18]

Once, in 1852, a report of trespass disclosed a Jewish miner.

> Riot at Grass Valley.... A Jew named Heyman, and several others, have held and worked for some weeks some claims on the new lead. These claims were jumped by a man named Moore and some others. A suit brought for the recovery of the claims was decided on Friday last, and a writ of restitution issued. Heyman and his party were put in possession of his claims by Constable Humiston. On the same day Moore and others went to the claims, knocked down Heyman, considerably bruising him on the face and breast, and again took possession. A new writ of restitution was issued and placed in the hands of the Sheriff on Wednesday last, and the Sheriff put Heyman's party again in possession. Moore was also arrested on a charge of riot.[19]

Jews also helped to organize partnerships, companies, and corporations to dig gold on a large scale. On November 6, 1863, in Mariposa County, twenty men, including Moses Schwab, Reuben and Jacob Bernheim, Henry Weil, Hiram C. Simons, Henry Blum, and F. Nieman, recorded the claim of the Piny Hill Quartz Ledge or Vein.[20]

On July 1, 1874, Marks Zellerbach of San Francisco registered his firm, to be known as Marks and Company, and stated that the purpose of the business was "banking, buying and selling mining claims and working the same, Moores Flat."[21] Two years later, on June 8, 1876, Zellerbach, now of New York, and Henry Cohn, Herman Stursberg, and Herman Marcuse incorporated the Eureka Lake and Yuba Canal Company Consolidated, to purchase mining claims and mining lands. The corporation was capitalized at $2,250,000.[22]

It was necessary to form partnerships and corporations with great financial backing because, within a few years, costly methods had to be employed in order to extract the gold from beneath the surface. Several corporations underwritten by Jews for this purpose were based in San Francisco; one, organized in New York, operated in Mariposa County. Known as the Yosemite Mining Company, it was capitalized at $600,000. One of the incorporators and a trustee was Julius Bien, then president of the Independent Order of B'nai B'rith.[23]

Apparently, the ownership of mining property by Jews was

reasonably widespread. I. J. Benjamin visited Placerville in 1860 and noted: "The Israelites here are well off. They do a great and good business and several have interests in the neighboring gold and silver mines from which they receive handsome dividends."[24]

Unfortunately, it has not been possible to discover whether any Jewish miners were forced to pay the tax legislated against foreign miners by the state on April 3, 1850 and May 4, 1852. The only surviving records on this subject in the county court houses from this period are whole amounts receipted by county auditors upon collection from various individuals around the county assigned to collect the tax. It is generally known, however, that this tax was rarely levied upon northern and central Europeans who had declared their intention to become American citizens.[25]

In some areas, Jews formed companies to deal with many phases of the mining industry, as in Sonora, in 1851.

> Quartz Mines and Intelligence Office.
> THE undersigned have opened in the city of Sonora, an office under the above title.... We will attend to the purchase and sale of shares in Mining Companies, receive orders for the purchase of tools and machinery for the working of Quartz.
> We will keep a record and diagram of all the different claims that are being, and may be worked, in the Southern Mines.
> Connected with this office will be an agency for the most approved machinery for crushing Quartz....
> E[manuel] LINOBERG & CO....[26]

One month following the publication of the above advertisement, the *Herald* announced that Linoberg had purchased a four-fifths interest in the Louisiana Company's quartz claim at Sandias for $4,000.[27]

In another region, the sale of mining property and a mill was noted by the local newspaper.

> *Volcano Correspondence.* Volcano, March 23d, 1858.
> ... Dr. Perham has disposed of his interest in the Buckeye quartz lode and mill to ... H. Kaufman.... The mill is now

running, and we hope to hear of our enterprising townsmen reaping a rich reward for their untiring energy and perseverance.[28]

Those Jews who preferred merchandising rather than mining also filled important positions in the mining economy. Merchants whose stores were located close to a newly discovered strike became recorders of the new mining district. In addition, certain merchants who were also the owners of mining stock, whether by a voluntary purchase or because they were involuntary creditors of luckless prospectors, served as officers of mining companies. In the first part of 1852, Henry Rothschild served as secretary of the Phoenix Quartz Mining Company, the Tehama Quartz Mining Company, and the North California Mining Company. Stockholders of the companies were reminded in the meeting notices that appeared in the local newspapers that meetings would be held at Rothschild's Empire Clothing Depot in Nevada City.[29] In the Placerville area, Samuel Harris served as secretary of the Argare Copper Mining Company.[30]

Jews were also stockholders in many mining enterprises. All through the region and period, the newspapers carried notices of unpaid assessments on stockholders for improvements to mining company equipment or for the acquisition of additional land upon which to mine. A public notice was required before a mining company was permitted to conduct a sale of stock that became defaulted owing to an unpaid assessment. For example, in 1868, the Cosumnes Copper Mining Company of El Dorado County advertised unpaid assessments on the three and one-third shares owned by B. M. Fleishman, two shares of Mrs. E. Berg, and eleven shares of Isaac Levy.[31]

Since most of these delinquent assessments were for amounts of less than $50, it was possible that the Jewish stockholders whose assessments went unpaid were not active participants in the affairs of the companies, but rather were merchants to whom deeds or shares in mining property were given by miners in exchange for the extension of credit for food, clothing, and mining equipment. Once the owners of a piece of mining land went about seeking additional funds for more extensive prospecting or new mining equipment, a merchant-stockholder would decide carefully whether to contribute to the new venture or let his reluctant participation lapse. The merchant Bernhart Miller of Nevada City, who operated a men's furnishings establishment, was one who accepted many deeds to mining property in exchange for outfitting miners, but few of the claims he accepted paid off.[32]

Miller was only one of many merchants whose clothing business depended heavily on the gold economy, because many potential customers had nothing but worthless mining deeds with which to pay for their purchases. Many merchants, themselves credit customers of San Francisco wholesalers, were often hard pressed to make payments on their purchases and were, at times, forced into bankruptcy.[33]

The discovery of gold in the mountains of California was only the first of many such discoveries that occurred all over the West during the next generation. Numerous gold deposits were located in Nevada, Idaho, Montana, and British Columbia and, to a lesser extent, in Oregon, Washington, Colorado, Arizona, and New Mexico. In addition, silver was found in abundance in Nevada and Colorado.[34] A glance at any newspaper published in these mining centers during the nineteenth century would reveal the advertisements of many Jewish clothing and drygoods merchants.

However, the role of Jews as miners and participants in the mining economy of the West is also noteworthy. Unfortunately, it is not easy to determine the amount of participation by the Jews in the mining industry, because the principal documents that verify such participation are the books of claims in the offices of county recorders, not all of which are still extant. But Jews joined in gold mining to help supplement their incomes from merchandising. Some Jews did participate in the mining economy as miners and prospectors but soon left this phase of the industry and turned to merchandising almost exclusively. It is noteworthy that they did not leave the mining economy altogether; they merely took part in it from another vantage point. By the end of the 1850s, it was less likely that an individual miner would strike it rich. The Jews left mining because it involved a greater personal risk than merchandising and because they preferred to live together with their wives and children in cities and towns.

Moreover, mining was unknown in the medieval and post-emancipation eras of Europe's Jewish communities. The Jews who came to California were businessmen. Their families had engaged in various businesses in the ghetto and after emancipation, and this was the occupation that Jews knew best. In California they were stockholders and passive participants in the mining economy, but it was as drygoods merchants and sellers of general-store items to miners, prospectors, farmers, and city dwellers that they supported themselves and their families. And, as will be seen, the places throughout the West where they traveled, and the problems that they faced, made merchandising just as difficult an undertaking as mining. Throughout western America, the Jews who moved into towns and opened mercantile businesses helped in the rise of urban society and the growth of cities in the gold region. To a significant degree, the credit for the settlement of urban areas in the mining regions of the West belongs to the Jewish merchants and not to the romantic miner or transient prospector.

·3·

JEWISH BUSINESSMEN IN THE WEST

THE MERCHANT.

Tare and Tret, Gross and net,
Box and hogshead, dry and wet,
Ready made, Of every grade,
Wholesale, retail, will you trade?

Goods for sale, Roll or bale,
Ell or quarter, yard or nail,
Every dye, Will you buy?
None can sell as cheap as I!

Thus each day Wears away,
And his hair is turning gray!
O'er his books, Still he looks,
Counts his gain and bolts his locks.

By and by He will die—
But the ledger book on high
Shall unfold How he sold,
How he got and used his gold.[1]

There was no assurance of wealth for anyone from prospecting or gold mining. But profiting on their experiences elsewhere, Jews succeeded at merchandising in California and the West. They entered this occupation for the profits that it offered and because they wanted to save enough money to bring close relatives still in Europe to America.[2]

Some Jews came west with some merchandise to sell immediately upon their arrival, intending to use the profits to expand their business.[3] Others worked for a time with a firm in San Francisco owned by a Jew; they learned the business, obtained credit, and moved to the mountains with a stock of merchandise, whether only a backpack load or enough to outfit a store.

Some Jews in the gold rush country were peddlers, but the exact number is not known. They walked from town to town, mining camp to mining camp, and farmhouse to farmhouse with their wares strapped to their backs. Detailed records concerning peddlers for any extended period of time in the early years of the gold rush are not extant, but the Great Register, a compilation of registered voters that began in 1866, reveals only six Jewish peddlers in seven counties.[4] There may have been many more who were either not registered voters or who gave their occupation as trader. One of the six was Theodore Levy (or Levey), who resided in Jackson, Amador County, from at least the time of his registration, August 17, 1867, until he moved from the county, August 29, 1873. On August 18, 1875, he registered as a voter in El Dorado County.[5]

An early peddler advertised in a newspaper in 1853:

PROCLAMATION
Of Simon Prager, the Pedlar
KNOW all the FAIR LADIES of this good city of Nevada, that I am able and willing to *Sell cheaper Dry and Fancy Goods* than any store keeper, all their self-praise and blowing notwithstanding, and I will prove it with the following reasons:

    1st; I do not pay any store rent, and I need not put a percentage on my goods, which you, Fair Ladies, have to pay.

    2d; I dress according to my business, and therefore do not make you pay for expensive clothes.

    3d; I receive every week a fresh assortment from my brother....

    I'll always try to sell as cheap as I can, although I never use those honeyed words to bribe you, fair ladies, in the belief that dear is cheap and cheap is dear.[6]

A pack peddler who later established a settled business and, eventually, a branch in another city, was Bernard Schweitzer, who came to Mokelumne Hill from Altdorf, Baden, in 1848 or 1849. He was joined shortly thereafter by a brother, Sam, with whom he established a small store. Occasionally, the brothers sewed buttons on miners' clothing. A branch of the firm was later opened in Campo Seco. By the 1860s Bernard Schweitzer had settled in San Francisco. Sam returned to Altdorf.[7]

The federal census records for California enumerated only a few peddlers, Jewish or Gentile. For example, the only Jewish peddler listed in Mariposa County for the four federal censuses 1850–80 was Joseph Rosenthal of Hornitos.[8]

In spite of the scantiness of documentation, there were apparently many itinerant peddlers in California, both Jewish and Gentile, in the early years of the gold rush. The legislation that was enacted against them, beginning in 1851, was probably sufficient to discourage peddling a decade or two later, as is shown by the small number of peddlers after 1866. In the early days, when there were probably more peddlers in the state, both newly established governments and local merchants felt that peddlers were not contributing a fair share to the expense of local governments. Several counties and cities passed legislation regulating peddling. The ordinance of Sonora required "Every person engaged in the business of hawking, or peddling or in the itinerant vending of any goods, wares, or merchandise . . . [to] pay . . . twenty-five dollars per quarter."[9] The fine for violating the above ordinance was up to three times the license fee for each day of violation.

The state also enacted two laws regulating peddlers. The law passed April 25, 1851 set the license fee at $15 per month and the clerk's fee for issuing the license at $2 per month. The fine for conviction following a first offense was not less than $10 or more than $50; for the second offense, the fine was from $20 to $200; a jail sentence was provided in either case until the fine was paid.[10]

The second law, enacted May 1, 1851, stated that "Each travelling merchant, hawker, and pedlar, shall pay the sum of fifty dollars per annum under such rules and regulations as the Court of Sessions may determine."[11]

In order to resolve what appeared to be a conflict of three laws (one city ordinance and two state laws, the latter to be administered through the counties), the Tuolumne County clerk advertised in the *Sonora Herald* that all the laws regulating peddlers by a license tax remained on the books and were to be enforced.[12]

In addition to the prohibitive license fees, the risks involved in peddling soon discouraged Jews from entering that occupation. A robbery of a peddler in 1857 reached the pages of the local newspaper.

> Robbery.—As a Mr. Jacobson a peddler was on his way from Grass Valley to Nevada [City], at about 5 o'clock on Sunday morning last, he was accosted about a mile this side of the former place by two robbers with masks on, who compelled him to surrender three hundred and eighty dollars in money and his pack worth about as much more. The villains then tied him to a tree and threatened him with death should he endeavor to escape, or hail the Marysville stage which was shortly expected to pass.[13]

Thus, only a few Jews entered the occupation of peddling in the gold rush.[14] The majority of the Jews in this region lived in cities and towns with their families and became clerks, salesmen, managers, and owners and operators of retail and some wholesale clothing establishments.

Historians of this period, both scholarly and popular, overlooked the dominance by Jewish businessmen of the retail economy in practically every mining camp and town in the Mother Lode and Northern Mines of California and in every other mineral discovery region in the American and Canadian West. Those writers who noted the presence of Jews but criticized them because they were not miners also criticized them because they were merchants. The romantic writers of this period wrote in favor of the miner, and any class of people, such as merchants, who took money from miners was regarded as exploitative. The observation of William Perkins on the Jewish merchandisers of Sonora may have been colored by the fact that Perkins himself was in competition with these Jewish merchants. On March 12, 1852, Perkins wrote:

> The Jews have built large numbers of small swindling shops in the broad bed of the *arroyo,* as the ground was unocupied [*sic*], and being "miners property" belongs to every one. ... The Jews receive very little sympathy from the community, for as their hand is against all men's pockets, their misfortunes only excite the mockery and risible faculties of the crowd.[15]

Eleven days later, Perkins had occasion to mention his Jewish competitors once again.

> I know not what we are coming to. What with peaceable citizens, picayunish yankees, Jew clothing shops and down-East strong-minded women, Sonora will soon be unbearable, and all the old settlers will have to move off and seek more congenial shades.[16]

J. D. Borthwick, too, had his opinions concerning Jews and their businesses.

> The Jew slop-shops were generally rattle-trap erections about the size of a bathing machine, so small that one half of the stock had to be displayed suspended from projecting sticks outside. They were filled with red and blue flannel shirts, thick boots, and other articles suited to the wants of the miners, along with Colt's revolvers and bowie-knives, brass jewellery, and diamonds like young koh-i-Noors. ... In their appearance there was nothing whatever at all suggestive of California; they were exactly the same unwashed-looking, slobbery, slippery individuals that one sees in every seaport town.[17]

Charles Elmer Upton wrote thus concerning the Jewish merchants and peddlers he remembered in the Placerville area:

During the summer and fall of 1849, Jewish peddlers frequently came into the foothills with merchandise to sell to the Americans and the Indians. Their goods were usually strapped across their backs, while the necessary provisions were carried on mules. These peddlers, like most of their countrymen, were expert tradesmen. Reaching a settlement, they would pitch their camp and immediately set out a tempting display of their wares, consisting, as a rule, of gaudy-colored shirts, socks, cheap jewelry and similar articles. A blue or red shirt would sell for at least half an ounce of gold dust and the Jewish trader would invariably get the better part of the bargain, as the settlers had no means of weighing their gold. The peddler would put the desired article of purchase in one side of his scale and insist upon the buyer's pouring sufficient gold-dust into the other side to balance the goods. But, while the Americans were invariably cheated in all these transactions, it was the poor, ignorant Indians who suffered the worst in their dealings with those rascally traffickers. Doubtless my readers can readily understand how so many of these self-same Jews afterward became wealthy and prominent merchants in various California towns.[18]

However, observations of Jewish business dealings in this region were not all negative. There was one recollection of miners treating a Jewish merchant's business dealings as entertainment.

Amongst our population of that golden day, we had *one* Jew. The old miners will ever remember Dutch [Deutsch?, i.e., German] John. When I arrived in the diggings, old friends hailed from every side, and an invitation was soon given all hands to go down to Dutch John's and take a *big drink.* As John's store was about a fair sample of the trading establishments of the day, a short description may not be uninteresting:

The *building,* like all others then used, consisted of brush cut from the closest trees; his stock of goods, two boxes of crckers [*sic*], a few boxes of sardines, a few knives, (samples of every pattern ever made,) a half box of tobacco, and two barrels of the *youngest* whiskey I had ever tasted. The counter was the head of an empty barrel, set off with a broken tumbler, tin cup, and a junk bottle of the ardent. Scales and weights were not much then in use, and John's store had none. A drink was paid for by his taking a *pinch* of gold dust with his thumb and fore-finger from the miner's bag, or sorting out a lump the size and value of a dollar, according to Jewish ideas of such things. Before taking the pinch from the bag, John's finger and thumb could be seen sliding down his throat (as far as the balance of the hand would permit) for the purpose of covering them with saliva, to make the gold stick, and he then thrust it into the miners *pile*. The amonut [sic] of such a pinch was from four to eight dollars! *"Got and* [sic] *Himmel,"* John: if we have accounts to settle in the next world, wont [sic] the clerks have a time of it with yours! This mode of settling was looked upon rather as a source of fun for the miners, than as an imposition.[19]

Jewish merchants were everywhere in the gold rush country from the remotest mining camps to the largest towns. They settled in the California county seats: Nevada City, Placerville, Sonora, and others. They were also found in out-of-the-way places with picturesque names. From time to time, there were Jewish merchants in Big Oak Flat (Tuolumne County), North San Juan and Rough and Ready (Nevada County), Agua Fria (Mariposa County), and Fiddletown (Amador County). The commercial stream of the settled communities during the gold rush was kept open by the Jewish merchants who sold their wares to miners, prospectors, and farmers and their families as well as to those who lived and worked in cities. The city directories of the day make it plain that the retail sale of general merchandise, drygoods and clothing, and tobacco in the Mother Lode and Northern Mines was almost entirely in the hands of Jews.

Brown and Dallison's directory enumerated merchants by occupation in Nevada City and listed sixteen Jewish clothing and drygoods merchants to five Gentiles in the same field, eleven Jewish cigar and tobacco dealers to two Gentiles, and two Jewish jewelers and watchmakers out of three.[20]

In the Nevada City and Grass Valley directory for 1861, the proportions were similar, with fourteen of the seventeen clothing and drygoods merchants in Nevada City being Jewish, as well as all six cigar and tobacco sellers. In 1867, thirteen of the fifteen clothing and drygoods merchants and all eight of the cigar and tobacco dealers in Nevada City were Jewish.[21]

In nearby Grass Valley, in 1861, only two of the nineteen clothing and drygoods merchants were not Jewish; all five of the cigar and tobacco merchants were Jewish.[22] Four years later, proportions were similar, with twenty Jewish and four Gentile clothing merchants.[23]

The only Placerville directory from this period (1862) recorded twenty-three Jewish clothing merchants and three who were not Jewish, and four Jewish cigar and tobacco sellers out of six.[24]

Even though ample evidence exists that some Jews were miners and farmers,[25] the majority of the Jews were not so much interested in these occupations as they were in the more familiar and profitable life of the merchant. This occupation had been pursued by Jews in the United States as far back as the earliest American Jewish communities in New York and Newport in the late seventeenth and early eighteenth centuries. There were Jewish investors in the Dutch West India Company and in many trading ventures on the islands of the Caribbean.[26] Whole families were engaged in the same trade, and it was relatively easy for a younger man to enter the family occupation, especially if agents were needed whose honesty would not be questioned. In the early years of Jewish settlement in the New World, "the Jew in New York had relatives in Amsterdam, Brazil and London. The Jew of Newport was acquainted with the Jews of Barbados, Constantinople or Italy."[27]

When the great migration of Jews from Central Europe to the United States began after the mid-1830s, it followed the same pattern as that of the Sephardic period. Merchants who had started in seaports or in small interior towns eventually settled in major business centers and established social and economic solidarity through marriage, which led to interlocking business connections and the control of an entire trade or commercial region. In New York, for example, marriages were contracted among the Lehman, Kuhn, Loeb, Schiff, Warburg, Seligman, Hellman, Guggenheim, Straus, and Rosenwald families.[28] And in San Francisco, which became the trading capital of the American West, marriages among the first Jewish families—

Sloss, Gerstle, Greenebaum, Lilienthal, Hecht, Levison, Fleishhacker, Brandenstein, and Moses Dinkelspiel—resulted in many business connections and interrelated firms.[29]

Once these first families had gained business experience and saved some money, they left the regions of the gold discovery for San Francisco. They maintained their branch businesses in the interior, however, by bringing over relatives from Europe, who were assigned to stores in the mountains until they, too, learned English and were ready to work in the family's wholesale houses in San Francisco. In this way, a few Jewish families in the West expanded their businesses and established large numbers of Jews in most of the commercial centers of the American West. In the late 1870s, the estimated number of Jews in San Francisco was 16,000; Stockton, 200; Santa Cruz, 100; Portland, 625; Helena, 112; Salt Lake City, 180; Virginia City, Nevada, 305; Denver, 260.[30] A descendant of a merchant family in Sacramento noted in his memoirs:

> I have never seen it in Print but the Jewish merchant had lots in the opening of this Coast. Every town, village, city had retail or wholesalers, carried large stocks, gave liberal credit. It was observed where there were *no* Jews, Gamblers, Fast sports, there were no business.[31]

A large number of Jewish merchants in the Mother Lode of California operated stores that were branches or affiliates of firms based in San Francisco. In this way, the merchant in the mountains did not have to undertake the arduous trip to San Francisco to purchase goods for himself; instead, he could remain in town and keep his store open. Samuel Haas, the "Cheap John" of Nevada City, advertised a branch in San Francisco.[32]

The variety store firm of Kohlberg, Rosenbaum and Company, of San Andreas, served as an agency of A. S. Rosenbaum and Company, of San Francisco.[33] One gold rush firm with a supplier in Sacramento, instead of San Francisco, was Abraham Klauber, of Volcano, whose partner in Sacramento was Francis Mandelbaum. The firm, A. Klauber and Company, sold

> Groceries, Provisions, Liquors, Crockery, Glassware, Hardware, Mining Tools, Clothing, Boots and Shoes, Domestic Dry Goods....
> Goods purchased at our Store, will be delivered *Free of Charge* at any of the mining camps in this vicinity.[34]

Many merchants in the Mother Lode and Northern Mines who operated branches of San Francisco firms were related by blood or marriage to their counterparts in San Francisco. Occasionally, the merchant in the mountains advertised his business as a branch of the firm of the same name that was headquartered in San Francisco. The local newspapers of the Mother Lode announced from time to time that a merchant had gone to San Francisco for a vacation to visit his relatives and bring back a new stock of goods from their wholesale house. In addition, when some merchants in the mountains died,[35] relatives were located in San Francisco and the orphaned children were sent to them to be raised.

The reminiscences of Harriet Lane Levy furnish examples of mountain-bay marriages. She recalled her childhood in San Francisco in the 1870s and the plight of her as-yet-unmarried relatives and friends.

> I knew that there were old maids; a cousin was fast becoming one. I heard my mother reproach her on her twenty-first birthday, but that did not mean that a girl would not eventually marry; it meant only that she would have to go to the country to live, to the interior. The interior was the market for all marriageable material that could not be advantageously disposed of in the city.
>
> Shopkeepers came to the city from the interior, from towns of the San Joaquin or Sacramento valleys, or from the mining towns, Grass Valley, Calaveras, or Mokelumne Hill to buy goods. Their quest often included a sentimental hope, confided to a downtown wholesale merchant. If a man's appearance was agreeable and his credit good, he would be invited to the merchant's home to dine and meet the unmarried daughters.[36]

On the occasion of the wedding of one of Harriet Levy's sisters, the family received telegrams from friends and relatives all over the gold rush country, indicating a more than passing relationship between the Jewish business communities.[37]

In addition to supplying Mother Lode merchants with goods at this time, San Francisco dominated the trade of the entire American West.[38] Prior to the advent of the railroad, the cheapest means of transporting freight was by ship. Most goods from the East destined for western trade were shipped to San Francisco; from there they were distributed throughout the West.

North of San Francisco, the father and brothers of Sam Aaron had general stores in Yreka and Cottonwood in the early 1850s. They sent all the gold they accumulated through trade to S. W. Rosenstock of San Francisco for deposit. They would accumulate $100,000 to $150,000 in gold dust before making such a shipment.[39] Farther to the north, when a gold strike in 1851 created an important trading center in Jacksonville, Oregon, the entire Jewish merchant community was totally dependent upon San Francisco for its merchandise. One firm, operated by the Sachs brothers, was a branch of the Sachs family firm in San Francisco.[40] Even the major metropolises of trade in the Northwest, Portland and Victoria, preferred to buy from San Francisco rather than rely on direct shipments from the East. Adventurous Jewish merchants all along the Pacific coast in what became the states of Oregon and Washington and the province of British Columbia depended on Jewish wholesalers in San Francisco for their goods.[41]

When gold was discovered along Canada's Fraser River in 1858, many Jewish merchants went to Victoria. Some had previously been merchants in the interior of California, such as Lewis Lewis and Nathan Koshland of Sacramento, Emil and Gustave Sutro and Abraham Blackman of Stockton, and David and Herman Shirpser and J. S. Landecker of Nevada City. When they moved north of the border, they naturally continued their business relationships with the same wholesalers in San Francisco.[42]

A local newspaper told of the departure of one such merchant, John Levinsky of Jackson, the second president of

Congregation B'nai Israel, to the new gold discoveries in the north.

> Gone to Frazer.—John Levinsky started for Frazer River yesterday morning. Mr. Levinsky, until recently, was one of our most prominent merchants, and highly esteemed citizens. We wish him good health and abundant prosperity.[43]

Perhaps the greatest Jewish venture into trading and merchandising in the Northwest was the Alaska Commercial Company of Louis Sloss and Lewis Gerstle, which dealt in furs and sealskins from 1870 and supplied the miners in the Klondike gold strike in 1897. The firm was under the direct management of Sloss and Gerstle at 310 Sansome Street, San Francisco. Gerstle had been a prospector in the Mother Lode in 1851.[44] He moved to Sacramento late in 1851 and there joined the firm of Louis Sloss and Company, ultimately the Alaska Commercial Company.

There was also a time when San Francisco's merchant community served as the general supplier of merchandise to Los Angeles.[45] The American Southwest was also economically dependent upon the shippers and wholesalers of San Francisco. Tobias and Max Oberfelder of San Francisco had branches of their hardware, mining supply, and farm implement business in Tucson and Tombstone, Arizona.[46]

After Michael (or Michel) Goldwater, formerly of Sonora, moved to Arizona, he planned his purchasing expeditions in San Francisco to coincide with the High Holidays. The Prescott *Weekly Arizona Miner* reported in 1877:

> Mr. Michel Goldwater, one of our successful merchants, we learn from a telegram received of Morris, his son, arrived in San Francisco today, where he plans to remain four or five weeks and be present during the Jewish New Year and participate in the festivities thereto. He will also purchase a large stock of goods for the company's stores at Ehrenberg and Prescott.[47]

Jewish merchants connected with the California gold rush

who later lived in Utah and may have retained connections with their original wholesalers in San Francisco included Conrad Prag, formerly of San Andreas[48] and later a member of the N. S. Ransohoff and Company firm of Salt Lake City; the three Auerbach brothers, Frederick, Samuel H., and Theodore, whose first store in the United States was a tent at Rabbit Creek, Sierra County; [49] and the brothers Louis and Alexander Cohn, originally in Poker Flat, Sierra County.[50]

The Auerbachs were in Austin, Nevada, for a time before they moved east. Frederick H. Auerbach later recalled:

> We came to Salt Lake City [in May 1864] from Austin Nevada, where we had met with considerable losses, and were largely in debt to creditors in San Francisco, whom we have paid in gold coin when we might have paid them in currency—Levi Strauss and others. We met all our engagements in gold coin . . . which enabled us to go on the eastern markets with all the recommendations that men could ask for.[51]

Although it may have been natural for most of the Jews who came to California and the West to enter the general merchandise and clothing businesses, it is strange that only a few Gentiles did so. Perhaps they had no training for it in the East before they came to California or believed that they could not compete with the close-knit Jewish families who were so prominent in merchandising. Most of the Jews in the gold rush region sold clothing and general merchandise, but some were also hotel-keepers, farmers, saloon-keepers, teamsters, bakers, butchers, auctioneers, daguerreotypists, and hay and barley merchants.[52] Emanuel Linoberg of Sonora, mentioned previously as a buyer and seller of gold-mining property and equipment, was also a farm owner, auctioneer, the owner and operator of a mule train, the proprietor of the Tienda Mexicana store in Sonora, and the proprietor of the Russian Steam Baths, located at his ranch one-half mile from Sonora. For $3 one could enjoy this "panacea in the eradication of some of the most stubborn diseases—such as Rheumatism, Gout, Contractions, Scrofula, Chronic Nervous and Pulmonic diseases, &c."[53]

One remarkable characteristic of the Jews of this period was their mobility. Moreover, those who felt adventurous enough to leave the civilization of Europe or the eastern United States for San Francisco and then to leave San Francisco for the interior took with them to their new homes a knowledge of merchandising that their families had acquired in Europe. Wherever Jews traveled in the West, they put their knowledge of retail and wholesale selling to work. In the region of the California gold rush, the first great American mining rush, Jews dominated the merchandising community and achieved outstanding success and a permanent place in the history of the region.

·4·

THE GOLD RUSH MERCHANTS

Jewish merchants who came to California in the earliest years of the gold rush and settled in the regions of the Mother Lode and Northern Mines became not only permanent fixtures in the business community but civic leaders as well. Many of them remained long after gold was no longer the dominant economy. Because of their connections with the large mercantile firms of San Francisco, they provided an unceasing supply of goods for the local population. The Jewish merchants, as a group, were responsible for bringing to this remote area the latest fashions, the newest books, and the most recent news from the outside world. Moreover, they brought to the region a willingness to work, a desire to win the friendship of the other national and religious groups, and a very advanced knowledge of business practices that would aid them in securing large numbers of regular customers.

   One of the means they used to inform the community of their business was the local newspaper. Jewish merchants in the gold rush used newspaper advertising far more than the Gentiles. It was not unusual to see at least ten advertisements from Jewish clothing and tobacco merchants and general merchandisemen in every edition of the weekly and daily newspapers in the major towns and perhaps one from a Gentile. Jews frequently advertised their entire inventory; Gentiles rarely did. One is led to conjecture that Jews may have advertised to a greater extent because their enterprises, including their advertising budgets, may have been underwritten by their relatives in San Francisco who were their suppliers.

The results of the hard work and long hours put in by these merchants were quite rewarding. The merchants became some of the richest men in the gold rush region. To serve the public better, they carried large inventories, and their county taxes were among the highest, comparable with those of an occasional water-ditch proprietor or large mine owner. Though not all the counties have retained their old assessment rolls, sufficient rolls have been preserved to demonstrate Jewish wealth.

Two instances in the year 1860 are particularly noteworthy. In Calaveras County, Jewish taxpayers constituted only 3.1 percent of all taxpayers in the county and 0.34 percent of the total population. Yet these fifty-five taxpayers declared themselves to be owners of 7.8 percent of all the real and personal property in the county and accounted for 7.2 percent of the total tax assessment that year.[1] In adjacent Tuolumne County, eighty-three Jewish taxpayers made up 3.6 percent of the taxpayers and 0.51 percent of the total population, but owned 6.67 percent of the real and personal property and were assessed for 8.43 percent of the total tax.[2]

The Jewish merchants set the tone for the annual collection of taxes by paying promptly and in full. The delinquent Jewish taxpayer was an exception. Only rarely was the property of Jews sold at public auction for unpaid taxes. Even after destructive fires, the Jewish merchants managed to pay their property taxes on time.

In the gold rush region, most of the retail customers of the Jewish merchants were Americans by birth; a large number of them were recent arrivals from the New England states.[3] They were not willing to settle for goods inferior to those to which they were accustomed. The merchants did their best to supply large quantities of up-to-date clothing, as well as clothing for miners and prospectors.

In the early 1850s, the bulk of the clothing destined for California was manufactured in New York and taken west by ship. Soon afterward, merchants in California began to purchase from the London and Paris markets as well. Finally, clothing was produced in San Francisco, from cloth brought in from all parts of the world or manufactured within the state. Eventually, the finished clothing or, for the more enterprising housewife, bolts of cloth, reached merchants in Downieville, Mariposa, and all points between, for sale to the general public.

The Levinsky brothers of Jackson included in one of their advertisements in 1857 an announcement that they relied on the world at large as their source of supply.

> Particular Notice.
> We are in receipt of New Goods, direct from N. York and Europe, by every *Ocean Steamer*. One of the firm resides in San Francisco, so that our facilities for keeping up a constant supply of fresh and fashionable goods are unsurpassed.[4]

One merchant in 1856 directed notice to his merchandise by naming the ship that brought his goods, as if to prove he had taken pains to shop for his customers at a great distance from California.

> Simon Rosenthal & Brother Ahead. . . .
> The Largest Stock Ever Brought To Nevada [City]! Just received by the last Nicaragua steamer, the Uncle Sam, direct from Paris, the largest and most desirable assortment of French Goods ever bro't North of Sacramento. . . .
> Ladies, remember that we shall receive monthly by steamer new stocks of goods directly from Paris which we promise to sell cheaper than can be bought this side of San Francisco.[5]

Another merchant, not wishing to be outdone by any of his competitors, announced that he had personally traveled to Europe in 1852–53 to purchase goods for sale in the gold rush.

> Western Clothing Depot.
> By Henry Rothschild. Formerly of the firm of M. Lewis & Co., The subscriber having sold out his entire interest in the Empire Clothing Depot last fall and having been absent on business since

that time, begs leave to announce to his friends and to the public, that he has purchased in the Atlantic Cities and in Europe, And is receiving constantly, direct, the largest and best selected assortment of Clothing, Boots, Shoes, Hats, Shirts, and Fancy Goods, And all articles belonging to a well-assorted Purchasing Store.[6]

Not all the trade that these merchants conducted with the public was on a cash-and-carry basis. In fact, business was conducted largely on credit. The merchants themselves were credit customers of their wholesalers in San Francisco,[7] and wholesale houses in San Francisco sent goods to mountain merchants in return for payment in gold coin. The latter, too, were liberal in extending credit. Occasionally, merchants would advertise in the newspapers, when a new stock of goods arrived, that they were requesting their credit customers to come forward to settle their past-due accounts.

There were, however, merchants who were not inclined to extend credit to retail customers. Charles Steckler of Jackson was only one of many merchants who advertised: "I Sell Cheap for Cash Only."[8]

A merchant took a risk when he sold goods on credit.[9] Often miners and prospectors did not have cash or gold dust to pay for their purchases. Occasionally, too, a retail merchant in the mountains fell behind in his payments to his wholesalers, by design or by poor management, and was the target of lawsuits. The merchant N. Solomon of Amador County was such an unfortunate man. In June 1860, he confessed judgments to six plaintiffs, four of them from San Francisco, who had extended credit to him in the amount of $3,282.83.[10]

San Francisco wholesale merchants advertised in mountain newspapers that they were prepared to send goods to retail dealers. Among such wholesalers were Israel Woolf, proprietor of Woolf's Shirt Depot, southwest corner California and Sansome Streets,[11] and Goodman and Company, 50 Front Street, who sold groceries and provisions.[12]

One factor that severely hampered further research describing relationships between San Francisco wholesale merchants and their retail customers in the mountains and throughout the West was the San Francisco earthquake and fire. On the morning of April 18, 1906, San Francisco and surrounding towns suffered from an earthquake caused by the periodic slippage along the San Andreas fault; a catastrophe ensued when fires broke out and could not be extinguished because the earthquake had also broken the city's water mains.

By the time the flames subsided, a few days later, twenty-eight thousand buildings, located in four square miles of the city's business district (primarily east of Van Ness Avenue) lay in ashes. More than four hundred people lost their lives, and although the city was rebuilt to such an extent that, nine years later, it played host to nine million visitors to the Panama-Pacific Exposition, the city was not the same as it once had been.

Because the earthquake and fire destroyed so much of the business section of San Francisco, no records of the firms that dealt with mountain merchants survive there. One is forced, then, to examine probate records in the several county courthouses, because these records comprise the largest extant repository of billheads from San Francisco merchants. They indicate the thriving credit business mountain merchants maintained with the wholesale houses of San Francisco. The estate of Charles Steckler of Jackson was typical; it included claims from forty-six parties, forty of whom were San Francisco firms; of the forty, twenty-four were Jewish merchants.[13]

Merchants in towns closer to the Mother Lode than San Francisco advertised in mountain newspapers that they would supply interior merchants with goods and wares. William Price, J. Benhayon, and J. Levison, of William Price and Company, 44 K Street, Sacramento, advertised in 1871 as "Importers and Wholesale Dealers in Brandies, Wines and Liquors. . . . Orders from the interior solicited and promptly attended to."[14]

Jacob and Charles Levy, of Marysville and San Francisco respectively, urged merchants in the Northern Mines not to travel the great distance to San Francisco.

To Mountain Merchants. We are ready to sell you your Fall Goods, in Marysville, at San Francisco prices! Wholesale Warehouse! Furnished in part, with a large assortment of Clothing, especially adapted to the wants of the Mountain Merchants, which we are now selling at San Francisco prices! . . .

Now, Merchants of the Hills, for your own goods, call and examine for yourselves before purchasing elsewhere, and you will find that we undersell any house in Marysville.[15]

Eventually, the mountain merchants themselves entered wholesaling. In the early days of Nevada City, at least three merchants thus occupied themselves, in addition to their regular retail trade. Henry Hershman (or Hirschman) advertised: "All Orders from the Country will be promptly attended to."[16]

Two years later, A. Block and Company laid in a large supply of men's clothing, which they offered for sale to merchants in the surrounding camps.

> . . . We can and will offer great inducements to wholesale or retail customers.
> Country Dealers Will find it to their advantage to give us a call before going to the Bay or Sacramento as we can supply them in quantities to suit at a small advance over San Francisco prices.[17]

Samuel Haas, an auctioneer and commission merchant and dealer in clothing, boots, and shoes, announced that he would attend to sales in any part of the county.[18]

The high prices of manufactured goods reflected the difficulty of moving merchandise from San Francisco to the Sierra foothills. Pack trains were the usual method of transporting bulk goods. The packer needed extra animals to carry feed for those carrying the goods, which added to the costs. Other factors that raised the price of goods were inclement weather, which sometimes caused a longer journey, and the occasional bandit.

An early merchant, Emanuel Linoberg of Sonora, solved his transportation problems by maintaining his own mule train; his brand, "44," was the first recorded in Tuolumne County, September 7, 1850.[19]

Stockton merchants also saw the potential profit in freighting, and a number of them advertised this aspect of their business in Mother Lode newspapers. One example was:

> A. KOHLBERG, Freighter & Commission Merchant (Centre Street, near Wells, Fargo & Co's.) Stockton, Cal., Takes pleasure in announcing to the merchants of Sonora and vicinity that he will run his own teams after this, and deliver merchandise by regular teamsters only, with the quickest dispatch and at the lowest rates of freight. All damages promptly paid.[20]

Rain often delayed goods destined for mountain merchants. The editor of the Columbia *Weekly Columbian* once apologized to his readers for late publication, explaining that rains delayed his newsprint seventeen days on the road from Stockton.[21]

The great distances from San Francisco, Sacramento, and Stockton to the towns of the Mother Lode not only raised freight costs but also increased the danger of theft.

> Teamster Robbed.—On Friday last a teamster came into town with a load of goods for D. Shirpser about three hundred dollars of which were missing,—The teamster reported that he stopped over night at a house below Grass Valley, and that his wagon was robbed during the night.[22]

Improved methods of transportation soon lowered costs. Steamboats plied the San Joaquin River to Stockton and the Sacramento River to Sacramento. These two cities served as economic appendages of San Francisco and as supply centers to the mining camps and rising towns of the southern and northern mines.[23] Some mountain merchants, such as Shirpser of Nevada City, had their inventories hauled in by wagon, which could carry a greater amount of merchandise more safely than a team of pack animals.

Eventually, railroads were constructed in the region and merchants were able to order large quantities of goods at low prices. In 1864, the Placerville and Sacramento Valley Rail Road advertised:

On and after September 19th, 1864, ordinary Freight will be received at Freeport and forwarded to Latrobe without charge for transhipping, drayage or forwarding.

Goods shipped by steamers of the California Steam Navigation Company, leaving San Francisco at 4, P. M., daily, can be delivered in **Latrobe** at 9 o'clock next morning. Freight shipped by sailing vessels will be forwarded with dispatch. No charge on ordinary freight per sailing vessels for levee dues, transhipping, drayage or forwarding. . . .

Prices of Freighting: Freight, from Freeport to Latrobe, $4 per ton.[24]

Whatever the mode of transportation, merchants were able to obtain large inventories of goods. Philip Schwartz of Columbia was

determined, that no other store in his business
shall get ahead of him, in the way of keeping
up his stock—
for he has got—
All manner of things that a woman can put
On the crown of her head or the sole of her foot,
Or wrap round her shoulders, or fit round her waist,
Or that can be sewed on, or pinned on, or laced,
Or tied with a string, or stitched on with a bow,
In front or behind, above or below;
For bonnets, mantillas, caps, collars and shawls;
Dresses for breakfasts, and dinners, and balls;
Dresses to sit in, and stand in, and walk in;
Dresses to dance in, and flirt in, and talk in;
Dresses in which to do nothing at all;
Dresses for winter, spring, summer and fall;
All of them different in color and pattern,
Silk, muslin, and lace, crape [sic], velvet and satin,
Brocade and broadcloth, and other material
Quite as expensive and much more ethereal;
In short for all things that could ever be thought of
Or milliner, or modiste, or tradesman be bought of.[25]

Other merchants, less poetically inclined, advertised week in and week out, year after year, through the entire period of the gold rush and after. At that time, newspaper advertising was the major means of publicizing one's goods. Advertising rates averaged $3 per insertion for a "square" one column wide and ten lines long. Discounts were generally given for long-run advertising.

Edward and Philip Elias of Columbia advertised according to the season of the year and the approaching holidays. One December the Elias brothers announced the arrival of a new stock of toys and gifts from San Francisco and New York and concluded their advertisement by declaring:

> Persons desirous of purchasing Christmas and New Years' Presents, would do well to call at the splendid store of the undersigned, and examine, their large stock of Goods before purchasing elsewhere, as they have the only Wholesale Fancy Toy Store in Tuolumne County.[26]

The Fourth of July offered similar opportunities.

> Fire Works.—The largest stock of Fire works ever brought into the mountains, can be found at the Store of that patriotic gentleman, E. Elias, who will sell at very low prices. Let every man and boy have a rocket for the glorious Fourth.[27]

The Jewish merchants in the Mother Lode and Northern Mines were primarily clothing merchants, and their inventories, as advertised in the local newspapers, were generally similar. For example, the advertisements of A. Selig and Company, of Volcano, "Clothing, Dry Goods, Boots, Shoes, Hats, Caps," were nearly the same as those of Rosenheim and Brother and Jacob Kohlman, both of Nevada City, and A. Blumenthal of Mariposa.[28] Louis Seldner of San Andreas advertised his varied collection of wares in 1863 thus:

> Fancy and Staple Dry Goods, Clothing, Boots, Shoes, Hats and Caps, Cutlery, Yankee Notions, Paper Hangings, Window Shades, Carpets, Oil-cloths and Matting, Main Street, (Brick Building), opposite the Post Office, San Andreas.

Goods received daily from San Francisco. Office in San Francisco, 410 Sacramento Street.[29]

Some merchants specialized in providing durable miner's clothing. Wolf Brothers of Sonora advertised "well selected stock of Miners' Supplies, India Rubber Coats, d[itto]. Boots Oil Cloth Suits."[30]

Several noticeable changes in the general merchandise and clothing businesses occurred in this region during the thirty years after 1849. Improvements in methods of transportation from pack animal and freight wagon to railroad made the shipment of goods more regular and less dependent on the weather, and thereby increased a merchant's stock.[31] But while the Jewish merchants maintained their clothing and drygoods stores, Gentile merchants became specialists in other lines. As time passed, a trend developed among Gentile merchants away from general merchandising toward the selling of specific items: furniture or hardware or farm equipment or drugs and notions.

With regard to the Jewish clothing merchant, as the population increased in the cities and towns, and as employment, tastes, and desires changed, there was a definite trend from a general line of ready-to-wear and miner's clothing toward an inventory of fine clothing. Such goods did not appeal to the city dweller alone; they also caught the fancy of the numerous miners and prospectors who frequented the towns for provisions and entertainment, and the ever-increasing numbers of farmers and their families, for whom fine clothing for fancy-dress balls and church services was a necessity.

As early as 1853, when the means of freight transportation from the bay were still primitive, some merchants were already carrying fine clothing. In Nevada City, Simon Rosenthal and Brothers advertised a stock that included

> ... Black and colored silks, French and English Merinos, Black and colored Alapacas [sic], Gloves, Sewed Muslin Collars, Family Blankets, Matting, Damask and Table Linens, Bleached and brown Sheetings, Ginghams, Prints, White and colored Flannels, Tweed and Satinetts, Fine square and long Shawls, Jaconette and Swiss Muslins.[32]

A decade later, when the means of transportation had improved and goods could be moved in greater quantities, merchants were able to stock fine grades of clothing with little difficulty. Levy Brothers of Jackson

> ... CONTINUE to keep two Stores, and will constantly have on hand the largest and most varied stocks of Goods in Amador County; consisting of FALL & WINTER GOODS of every description ... Silks, Satins, Velvets, Flannels, Linnens [sic], Delains, Alpaccas [sic].[33]

In Placerville, P. Silbermann and Henry D. Raphael of P. Silbermann and Company, "at the old stand of A[aron]Kahn, Main st." sold

> ... the best quality of custom-made Fashionable Dress Coats; Black Doeskin Pants; Cassimere Business Suits; Beaver Suits and Overcoats; Blue Flannel Suits; Benkert's Boots and Shoes; Fall Style Silk and Cass[imere] Hats; Davis and Jones' Shirts; Silk, Velvet and Plush Vests.[34]

Jews also entered other occupations closely related to the clothing business. Moses Reeb and Brother of Sonora, "at Cohen's Old Stand—Opposite the 'Long Tom'" saloon, specialized in the sale of shoes and maintained a large inventory, including "the finest quality BOOTS, SHOES, AND GAITERS. Benkert's Celebrated Boots, Miles & Son's Philadelphia Gaiters, India Rubber Boots, Gaiters, Slippers, Shoes."[35]

In addition to carrying full lines of clothing, A. Rosenthal of Nevada City and I. Peyser of Jackson advertised as "Merchant Tailor."[36] And, to accommodate those interested in making their own clothing, S. Levy of Jackson sold "The Late World Renowned Gold Medal Sewing Machine. Price $65 00 to $150 00."[37]

Except for the thousands of newspaper advertisements describing the Jewish merchants' wares, the only other contemporary evidence concerning inventories is found in the probate records of deceased merchants. The latter source of information is especially important because it is the one place where the itemized value of a merchant's inventory is found. Since the appraisers of the estate left by a Jewish merchant were, for the most part, Jewish merchants themselves, their valuation of the goods in a store was likely to be close to actual current prices.

The earliest known estate of a Jewish merchant that includes a stock of goods is that of Marcus Abraham of Grizzly Flat, who died October 11, 1856. The inventory of his merchandise, which consisted almost entirely of clothing, totaled $1,845.87. There was an even distribution between men's and women's clothing, including fancy goods as well as mining outfits. Bolts of material were also available. The going rate for a cloth mantilla was $5. Gingham was 14 cents per yard. Silk cravats ranged from 50 cents to one dollar each. A black silk vest was appraised at $3.50. The value of the merchandise in the store, however, represented only about one-third of the total value of Abraham's estate, which was over $5,000. Abraham must have extended liberal credit, for he left $790.52 owed to him in promissory notes and $1,473.60 in accounts receivable, divided among eighty-three debtors.[38]

Ten years after the death of Abraham, Elias Levi (or Levy), also a merchant, died in Amador County. The inventory of his store consisted of clothing for every member of the family, as well as some general merchandise, and was appraised by H. Harris, T. Leiser, and H. Zerker at $8,371.47½. Clothing prices in Jackson a century ago included corsets for $1, toothbrushes at $1 per dozen, business coats from $6 to $15 each, and silk vests at $3.[39]

Michael Abels (or Abel) died in Calaveras County about the same time as Elias Levi. His store's inventory, which was entirely clothing, was appraised in excess of $2,400, and included black frock coats at $12 each, undershirts and drawers at $1.25 apiece, and calf boots from $2.50 to $4.00 per pair.[40]

Many Jews sold goods other than clothing. The next most numerous group of Jewish merchants in the gold rush country, after the clothing merchants, were the tobacconists. They were in every town and carried a wide range of tobacco products.

Theirs was a lucrative business, since all kinds of tobacco were in demand. Tobacco was lightweight merchandise, easy to transport as long as due precautions were taken to prevent it from getting wet. A tobacconist did not restrict himself solely to the sale of tobacco. But he would advertise tobacco most frequently because it sold more readily than other goods he carried.

In Nevada City, Newbauer and Company advertised eleven brands of cigars and also had "constantly on hand a supply of Figs, Oranges, Raisins, nuts, Confectionary, etc."[41]

L. and J. Oppenheimer, of San Andreas, benefited primarily from the sale of "Domestic Cigars . . . All kinds of Chewing and Smoking Tobacco" and secondarily from "Green and Dry Fruit, Candies, Nuts, Cutlery, Matches, Playing Cards."[42] Marks and Jessel, of Grass Valley, sold "tip top segars" and also watermelons.[43] H. Oppenheimer, located "One Door North of 'Riffle' Saloon," Sonora,

> Calls the attention of the public to his well assorted stock of the finest HAVANA CIGARS and best brands of VIRGINIA SMOKEING [sic] and CHEWING TOBACCO. Also to his GENUINE MEERSHAUM [sic] PIPES and other qualities too numerous to mention.
>
> Also to his unsurpassed stock of Fruits and Candies, Perfumes, Toys and Yankee Notions; and also all kinds of Oils, Paints, Glassware, Lucine Fluid, and Lamps and Chimneys, Collins' Patent Sun-Burners. . . . Genuine Italian Violin & Guitar Strings always on hand. Limes, Lemons and Oranges fresh every week.[44]

More than any other group, the Jewish tobacco merchants contributed toward the distribution of the printed word in this isolated region. They were the dealers in foreign and domestic newspapers and the local retail outlets for books and magazines. They provided local newspaper editors with exchange copies from the Atlantic states and received editorial mention for this service. From the tobacco shops came newspapers that were published around the world, grammars and spellers for children, and stationery.

As with the clothing men, the overwhelming majority of

tobacco merchant–book dealers were Jewish. Their advertisements, too, appeared in the local newspapers from the beginning of the gold rush until after mining was no longer profitable.

T. Ehrenberg, of Columbia, in addition to carrying "fifteen different Brands of Chewing Tobacco," announced: "We also have a fine assortment of European, States and California Papers, Stationery, &c."[45]

When A. Rosenfield purchased S. Guthrie's newspaper and periodical agency in Mokelumne Hill, he advertised that he would sell "the latest California and Atlantic papers, Illustrations, Magazines, Steamer Novels, and standard works; together with a large assortment of Fancy articles, best brands of Cigars and Tobacco, etc."[46]

Three Jewish merchants in Nevada City contributed to entertainment and learning by operating circulating libraries in their stores; M. Michelsen sold musical instruments as well as books and stationery; W. M. Cohen carried a similar line and also cutlery;[47] and A. Peyser sold tobacco and also advertised:

> Particular attention is likewise called to the Circulating Library, Connected with the establishment, and comprising about two thousand volumes of the best and most popular English and German works. The public is respectfully invited to call and examine the stock.[48]

Another occupation in this region in which Jews were as conspicuous as Gentiles, or more so, was that of jeweler and watchmaker. The amount of business in this line in any one town was never large, but, at times, the only watchmaker in town was Jewish. Robert Sachs was a jeweler in Mariposa and advertised his ability to "make all kinds of Rich Jewelry and Specimen Work, to order: Repair and Clean Watches, Melt and Refine Gold, &c."[49]

Nevada City also had Jewish watchmakers and jewelers, M. and A. S. Rosenheim, who operated in their clothing store.[50] J. Straus, a jeweler in Downieville, advertised his ability to converse with customers not only in French, his native tongue, but also in German, Spanish, and English.[51]

Merchandising by Jews in the gold rush was not always confined to clothing, hardware, groceries, or jewelry. Nor was merchandising limited to men. An advertisement of the Bruml family of Jackson placed them in a class all their own.

> Bruml's Celebrated BOHEMIAN BITTERS Manufactured by M. & S. Bruml, Jackson, Cal.
> These bitters are made from Purely Vegetable articles, procured only in the forests of Bohemia, and have been very highly recommended as a Tonic, by some of the most eminent physicians of Europe.
> A small wine glass full, taken before meals, will be found very beneficial in preventing any serious sickness.[52]

Wives of merchants, too, entered business in their own name, usually when a husband was ill or the property in his name was involved in litigation or bankruptcy proceedings. The greatest participation of wives in business occurred in Tuolumne County, where eleven of 131 documents declaring sole ownership between January 22, 1852 and November 16, 1870 were by wives of Jewish merchants.[53] The majority of them engaged in occupations that were also characteristic of the Jewish males of Sonora and vicinity: selling liquor, tobacco, groceries, and drygoods.

One woman who entered business in her own name in an occupation other than her husband's was Sarah Goldwater. In the same year, 1855, that her husband's name M[ichel] Goldwater, appeared on the Tuolumne County assessment rolls as a fruit dealer in Sonora,[54] she recorded her intention with the county "to carry on and transact in my own name and on my own account, the business of tailoring and merchandizeing [sic] . . . and that I will be personally responsible for all debts contracted by me in Said business."[55]

Her entry into the business world was a by-product of her husband's financial difficulties because the next year Michael (or Michel) Goldwater declared himself an insolvent debtor.[56] The following year the Goldwater family moved to Los Angeles, where again Michael Goldwater declared bankruptcy.[57] A short time later, he moved to Arizona to begin anew.

Bankruptcies and declarations of insolvency by Jewish merchants occurred for such reasons as an uninsured loss of goods in a fire, an overextension of credit to retail customers, or a tightening of credit by San Francisco wholesalers.[58] When such misfortunes occurred, local newspaper editors were quick to seize upon the event as an opportunity for a combination news item and message of sympathy. The loss of a town's leading merchant was cause for concern to an editor because of the loss in advertising.

> Business Suspension.—It is with sincere regret that we learn that financial embarrassment has caused the temporary suspension from business of Mr. A. S. Haxter of this place. Mr. Haxter is one of our earliest and most esteemed of resident merchants, and has ever been regarded as a gentleman of unexceptionable probity, at once honorable in his dealings and enterprising in his business. We are pleased to be informed that the difficulties in which he is involved will meet with a speedy arrangement, and that he receives as he so justly merits the unfeigned sympathy of the whole community.[59]

Occasionally, a sudden tightening of credit in San Francisco led to bankruptcy, and when this occurred, the newspaper editor's sympathy was for the local merchants rather than for the San Francisco wholesalers.

> Attached.—We are sorry to learn that the store of Henry and Moses Hirschman was attached yesterday by the Sheriff and closed up. The Messrs. Hirschman suffered heavily in the fire of a year ago [July 19, 1856—a loss of $15,000], losing all their property which was considerable, and leaving a debt in San Francisco, every dollar of which they have discharged like honest and honorable gentlemen as they are. . . . Foul play has been the cause of their present troubles—the attachment being for goods barely received from San Francisco.[60]

A merchant could get out of debt by one of several means. He might return the goods to his wholesaler. If his debts were many, he could declare himself bankrupt and lose his remaining assets at an auction. Such an act, however, might result in an impairment of future credit. An extreme method of escape from debt was the suicide by hanging of the Sonora merchant Selig Ritzwoller in 1869. M. Kaufman, a witness before the coroner's inquest, read a letter left by the victim:

> Dear God pardon and forgive me—my poor wife and poor children, pardon and forgive me—my heart is broken—the Hebrew Benevolent Society in San Francisco take pity on my poor wife and children—do not let them starve—to my kind brothers in law Rosner I owe a great deal of money—Dear God into thy hands I recommend my soul amen—Joel Levy and Kaufman take care of my wife and children.[61]

Other merchants were more fortunate. They prospered and remained in one town for decades. They used this permanence and their reputation for honesty to good advantage by offering to their customers the added service of banking. When a miner brought an excess amount of gold to a merchant with which to make his purchases, the merchant kept the gold in his safe and gave a receipt to the miner for the difference. Thus Jewish merchants became bankers. The merchant either kept the money left with him or deposited it in his personal bank account and then always returned the amount to the depositor upon demand. In Placerville, such a business was conducted by the brothers-in-law Augustus Mierson and Godfrey Jewell, whose clothing establishment, Mierson and Jewell, became the A. Mierson Banking Company and, later, A. Mierson and Sons.[62]

The brothers Jacob and Joseph Weissbein of Grass Valley organized the banking and brokerage firm of Weissbein Brothers and Company on October 28, 1878, with $700 capital they had saved from their wages in the store of their brother-in-law, Jacob Heyman.[63] A previous banking establishment had failed, and the Weissbeins purchased, on installment, the bank fixtures, counters, and assaying equipment. To instill confidence, the brothers borrowed wooden spools from their

brother-in-law, wrapped them so that they appeared to be coins, and placed them in the safe to impress potential customers. In addition to banking, they bought gold, sold life insurance, real estate, stocks, and bonds, and bought and sold gold mines.[64] Joseph Weissbein conducted the mining business, while Jacob operated the other business of the bank. The brothers struggled to win the confidence of the townspeople, and eventually the bank emerged on a solid foundation.[65] The firm was incorporated as the Weissbein Brothers and Company Broking and Business Corporation on June 12, 1880. Its stated objects included:

> Buying and selling exchange, Buying and selling gold dust, bullion and other precious metals, Buying and selling, bonding and leasing mines and other real property, Buying and selling stocks and other securities, Discounting notes and other commercial paper, and Loaning money.[66]

The stockholders and directors of the corporation, which was capitalized at $20,000, included Jacob and Joseph Weissbein, their brother-in-law Jacob Heyman, William Goldberg of Grass Valley, and Moritz Hendelsohn of San Francisco, who was chosen to replace Benjamin Cohn, also of San Francisco.[67] Heyman was the majority stockholder, owning 180 of the 200 shares.

Other Jewish banking firms, for which only a very few records survive, were Marks and Company of Moore's Flat, Nevada County, organized by Marks Zellerbach;[68] Block and Furth of Nevada City and North San Juan, Nevada County;[69] and Julius Beer, who advertised in the *Columbia Gazette* from October 23, 1852 (its first edition) until February 26, 1853:

> Julius Beer, Agent for B. Davidson of the Messrs. Rothschild. Office: Main Street, one door Below the Italian Saloon. Gold Dust purchased at the highest rates. Drafts on the Messrs. Rothschild, and their Agencies.[70]

D. W. Lubeck, formerly a merchant in Nevada City, was

vice-president of the Placer County Bank in Auburn in the 1890s.[71]

When Aaron Kahn of Placerville sold his clothing business to P. Silbermann and Henry D. Raphael in 1864, the local paper noted that Kahn would remain in town and "continue to purchase county warrants and gold dust."[72] Kahn was only one of many Jewish merchants who learned how to determine the fineness and value of gold dust. Although Charles Peters, recalling his younger days as a miner, spoke disdainfully of Jews because none of them seemed to be miners,[73] he expressed the highest admiration for a Jewish merchant who solved a robbery of fine gold dust mined at Iowa Hill when it turned up in the possession of a miner who had mixed it with a coarser variety of El Dorado County dust.[74]

Some merchants came to the Mother Lode not intending to settle permanently. They came either with a stock of goods or with credit from an eastern merchant, sold their goods as quickly as possible, and returned east or to San Francisco with the profits. Others, however, came to the gold fields and settled there. Merchants who are especially remembered for their long careers in the area sometimes got their start by purchasing the goods of Jewish merchants who left. A. Barlow enlarged his boot and shoe firm by his purchase of A. Cohen's inventory.[75] Moses Hanauer, one of the earliest Jewish merchants of Sonora, sold his stock to Mayer Baer in 1868[76] and the store building in 1870.[77] Barlow was a merchant in Sonora for decades, and Mayer Baer's descendants still manage the business that Baer started in 1851.

In Placerville, one store retained its name while changing its ownership several times. The Round Tent Store, a clothing store which is still open in the same location after over 120 years of operation, was successively owned in the early days by several Jewish merchants.[78]

Several early advertisements, however, announced the departure of a firm's proprietor from the region. In Bear Valley, B. Oppenheim advertised:

> The undersigned, determined to close out . . . offer their entire large and fine stock of Goods at San Francisco cost. . . .

> We must also call the attention of those indebted to us to call and settle by cash or due bill immediately or legal steps will be taken to collect the same.[79]

Many times, a merchant merely tired of a particular business or arrangement and sought a change in the same town. In Jackson, Moses Bruml, Charles Steckler, and P. Vertimer were in partnership as M. Bruml and Company until 1858, when the firm was dissolved, Steckler continuing the grocery and provision business "at the old stand," and Bruml becoming proprietor of the New York Bakery and Saloon.[80] In Placerville, in 1864, the newspaper editor announced the termination of a business agreement in language as affectionate as if the partners were members of his own family.

> NEW FIRM.—Our old friend, Aaron Kahn, has sold his clothing business to Messrs. P. Silbermann and Henry D. Raphael, who will continue the business at the old stand, under the style of P. Silbermann & Co. The new firm, we doubt not, will do a fine business, as both gentlemen are well-known and deservedly popular, and withal thorough men of business and devilish good fellows. They start off with a magnificent stock of goods, and an exhaustless supply of perseverance and energy. Uncle Kahn will continue to purchase county warrants and gold dust, and illumine our city with his benignant countenance.[81]

Many members of this community extended their business investments and opened branch stores. Documents record the migration of merchants from town to town throughout the entire period in search of a suitable location. In remote Mariposa County, many merchants had two or more stores in different locations. When a partnership was dissolved, one member of the firm might set out on his own in charge of one of the branches, or both partners might move away and sell the business to a third party.[82]

Even in the 1870s, long after the rush of individual miners to California, Jewish merchants came to try their luck in the small towns of the Mother Lode and nearby regions. Many of them traveled from town to town before finding a suitable location for a business. In Amador County, the Coblentz family was so numerous (at various times, the names Gustave, David, Felix, Lambert, and Samuel appeared on the county naturalization records)[83] that different members of the family appeared at varying times as principals of the general merchandise and clothing firms that bore the family name in Fiddletown, Plymouth, Sutter Creek, and El Dorado from 1868 to 1880.[84] The merchant Isaac (or Ira) Kahn, after his arrival in California in the late 1870s, engaged in merchandising in Lundy, Bodie, Bridgeport, Amador City, and Plymouth[85] (the last place in partnership with Lazard Coblentz and Alexander Rosenwald)[86] before finally settling in San Francisco in 1898.

There were also examples of branch merchandising in Nevada County in this period. Two, in particular, reflected the growing importance of the Nevada state trade and the entry of Jewish merchants there. On June 19, 1874, a partnership was formed between drygoods merchants in Virginia City and Grass Valley, and on July 23 of the same year a similar business was formed by clothing merchants in Reno and Grass Valley.[87] Three brothers who maintained a widespread branch business were Hyman Wolf Hyman of Portland, Henry Wolf Hyman of San Francisco, and Michael S. Hyman of Honolulu, who established a branch of their clothing, boot, and hat business in Nevada City in 1874 under the name Hyman Brothers.[88]

Merchandise destined for sale in the Mother Lode country came by ship from all over the world to this isolated area. Adequate facilities were needed in every town to store and sell these goods. The merchants invested much of their capital in combination warehouse-store buildings that also sometimes served as their residences. At first, stores, like many structures, were made of tent material. However, as soon as a merchant was able, he commissioned the building of a fireproof and theft-resistant store of native brick, adobe, or stone, with huge iron doors. If a brick building was large enough, it could also serve as a warehouse for one's newly received goods or for rental space. When merchants commissioned the construction of brick buildings, their enterprise was noted in the local newspaper. In Nevada City, in 1854, the editor announced:

> Fire Proof Buildings.—Simon [Rosenthal] & Bro. next door to Mulford's building, will commence a fireproof brick, the first of next week. It will be 18 feet front and fifty feet back, two stories high.[89]

In Sonora, too, large store buildings of brick were erected by the merchants. Following a fire there in 1856, an editor noted the improvements that were changing the face of the town.

> ... North corner of Linoberg Street, Mr. E[manuel] Linoberg is putting up a stone and brick store-house, 52 feet deep by the same width, which will be divided into three stores; the whole having iron doors and shutters, and fire-proof roof. The stores are understood to be offered for, at large rents. Thus on either side of Linoberg Street, brick fire-proof blocks take place of the wooden houses destroyed.[90]

Another reason the Jewish merchants in the Mother Lode constructed brick buildings was that they were likely to obtain a more favorable premium in their fire insurance than if they housed their large inventories in wooden buildings. And many of these merchants were farsighted enough to carry adequate insurance on their buildings and goods.[91] Moreover, a merchant with a store built of brick could convince a San Francisco wholesaler that he could maintain on credit a larger stock than the one he had been receiving in his former wooden establishment.[92] In Columbia seven of the nine brick buildings completed before the spring of 1856 were built by Jewish merchants, and the other two were soon rented by Jewish merchants.[93]

Rudolf Glanz claims that the brick buildings of the Jews "were used as counter-argument against those anti-Semitic propagandists who charged that the Jews did not plan to stay in the region but rather planned to leave for the East with their acquired treasures."[94] Actually, there were only a few occurrences of anti-Semitism in the mining country during this period.[95]

Some foolhardy merchants believed they would save money in the long run by remaining in wooden buildings.[96] Such merchants were courting disaster, however. Nevada City was completely destroyed by fire in eighty minutes on July 19, 1856. The fire progressed so quickly that the population could only look on helplessly. It is interesting that some of the heaviest sufferers among the Jewish merchants were occupants of brick buildings. In such fires the heat was so intense that even goods inside brick buildings were not safe unless moved to a basement storeroom. The local newspaper had announced, during the previous year, that the merchants H. and M. Hirschman, Simon Rosenthal and Brother, Rosenheim and Brother, J. S. Landecker, C. Josephson, and Sol. Kohlman and Brother, all occupied brick buildings. Yet the losses sustained by this *minyan* of clothing and tobacco merchants totaled $106,000. The total loss to the thirty-eight Jewish merchants involved was $207,000.[97]

The same edition of the newspaper that reported the above losses also told about new stocks of goods already received by the merchants A. Block and Company, Jacobs and Lewis, D. Shirpser, Rosenheim and Brothers, H. and M. Hirschman, Lewis and Rosenbaum, Rosenthal and Brother, Cody and Gatzert, Mayers and Coe, and Stiefel and Cohn.[98] One merchant was particularly singled out for his actions after the great conflagration.

> Nil Desperandum.—On the morning after the fire might be seen our friend General [D. W.] Wulff, beneath a seven by nine American flag nailed to the charred stump of the old flag staff in front of Frisbie's, with two half boxes of well kiln dried cigars, ready to wait on customers, and declaring though cleaned out he was not subdued. Such is the spirit that triumphs over difficulties, and ultimately prevails.[99]

The Nevada City merchants were able to reopen their businesses almost immediately, thanks to the prompt aid rendered by their wholesalers in San Francisco. The newspaper praised the wholesale houses for their generosity.

> The liberality of San Francisco to our people since the late fire is the praise of every one here. Every merchant needing assistance in money or goods, has had it promptly rendered by the citizens of that noble city. . . . Our business men went there depressed and almost helpless, to return elated and with bright prospects ahead. . . . Our merchants found that their credit was not in the slightest impaired by their losses—that the dealers at San Francisco could appreciate the difference between misfortune and rascality. All honor and thanks to the merchants of San Francisco, for their generous confidence in our people in the late distress.[100]

The handiwork of the early brick-makers is still very much in evidence in the Mother Lode. Today, the visitor to the region may see several brick buildings once owned or occupied by Jews.[101]

Jewish participation in the mercantile profession during the gold rush was an important feature of life in this region of early California. While not exclusively merchants, most Jews did engage in merchandising in urban areas. That they did so accounts in large measure for the continued existence of several cities and towns in the Mother Lode and Northern Mines. The Jewish merchants, by their business activity and their participation in the day-to-day life of the communities in which they lived, helped make the cities attractive both to the local residents and the country dwellers. They served as distributors of manufactured goods that brought the comforts of civilization to the people of the interior. The Jewish merchants provided a valuable service as economic middlemen between the distributors of San Francisco and the consumers of the Mother Lode.

·5·

JEWS IN THE COMMUNITY

The Jews were part of a heterogeneous group that came to the region of the gold rush from all over the world.[1] Primarily of Central European origin, these merchants found life in the Mother Lode and Northern Mines to be quite different from Europe.[2] Towns that were founded prior to their arrival, the "tent cities" located close to the mines, did not exist for very long. However, cities such as Sonora, Jackson, Placerville, and Nevada City became permanent trading centers because they were county seats and because the Jewish merchants there catered to the needs of families.[3]

The gold rush was a significant event in Jewish history because it placed Jews side by side with a large and diverse group of races, religions, and nationalities. At first, the Jews were strangers who made their homes among strangers, but they became friendly with their Gentile neighbors and were soon important figures in the communities in which they lived. They established themselves in business, and they also remained true to their ancestral faith by forming benevolent societies, establishing separate cemeteries, and conducting worship services.

It has already been shown that the Jewish merchants in the cities and towns of the Mother Lode were among the wealthiest residents. Their personal and real property was so great that their annual contribution to the operations of local government was far greater than their proportion of the total population.[4]

But the Jews did not allow their businesses to be the overriding interest in their lives to the exclusion of anything else. They took active parts in social and political affairs. They quickly mastered the English language and joined with the other groups in local community activities of a social, educational, and cultural nature.[5] They joined nondenominational social-service agencies and aided in dispensing charity through these organizations. Most important, they were stanch supporters of the local public schools.[6] Their children became part of the dominant culture of the city and were prepared to enter easily into the society of a new city when the family moved away.[7]

All of the Jews who came to California at this time were born in Europe. The majority of them had little, if any, intention of returning to Europe permanently. "Jews came here to stay. When they left their old countries, they burned all their bridges behind them; and at every opportunity they brought their families with them."[8] While some of them made trips to the "old country," it was to visit parents or pick a wife and then return to America.[9] Those merchants no longer interested in living in the Mother Lode country usually moved to San Francisco or to the eastern states, where there were better possibilities for business.

The Jews who came to California declared their intention to become American citizens five years after their arrival in the United States, which was as soon as the law allowed. That there were prejudices against specific groups of foreigners in America at that time is clear, but neither the local prejudices against the Chinese, Chileans, Mexicans, and French, nor the Native American (or Know Nothing) Party on the national scene deterred Jews from seeking naturalization. Indeed, the exhortations of anti–Know Nothing newspapers of the period may be credited with speeding up the process of naturalization, since the Know Nothing platform favored extension of the waiting period between declaration and naturalization. A Democratic newspaper in Volcano editorialized in 1856:

> Be Naturalized.
> We would again remind those of our foreign residents having

their first but not their second papers, that the DISTRICT COURT will commence in Jackson on the *Third Monday in October*. It is to this court you must apply, and this will be your only chance before the election. If you would resist the secret political order that proposes to disfranchise each and every one of you for the period of twenty-one years—and afterwards hold you ineligible to even the smallest office—get out your papers while you may, and vote in solid phalanx for the Democracy.[10]

The Jews were naturalized as soon as they had met the residence requirement of five years. In the eight counties of the Mother Lode and Northern Mines, 812 Jewish males became naturalized citizens of the United States prior to 1880.[11] Over 600 Jews registered to vote, 100 of them on the same day as their naturalization ceremony.[12] The act of registration was their way of proving themselves equal to the other groups in the area. The names of these hundreds of Jews, naturalized either in the local county or in San Francisco or in the eastern states, were enrolled in the county registers of voters.[13]

From the very earliest years of the gold rush, the Jews took an interest in local politics and served in various positions of trust. Emanuel Linoberg was one of the first white settlers in Sonora in late 1848 or early 1849 and a member of the first town council in 1849.[14] In 1857, Jacob Kohlman was elected a trustee (councilman) of Nevada City.[15] L. W. Dreyfuss was city treasurer of Nevada City before 1880,[16] and Abraham Goldsmith was treasurer of Nevada County in 1871–72.[17] In 1882–84 and 1890–1906, Herman Goldner was justice of the peace for the first township of Amador County, which included the county seat of Jackson.[18] In Placerville, L. D. Marks was elected a school trustee from the third ward of the city in 1868.[19] In the period 1848–91, no less than twenty-one Jews served as postmaster in such communities as Columbia, Mokelumne Hill, and Jackson and in such smaller towns as Indian Diggings, Jenny Lind, and Gibsonville.[20]

There were several instances of Jewish delegates elected to county Democratic conventions.[21] On frequent occasions, members of the Jewish community were appointed judges of local elections by county boards of supervisors.[22] In 1859, Joel Levy and Philip Schwartz of Columbia filed bonds with the county in the amounts of $14,000 and $10,000, respectively, to serve as collectors of foreign miners' licenses.[23] Because of their wealth, Jews were frequently sought out as sureties for the bonds of newly elected public officials. For example, when George Durham was elected collector of Amador County in 1871, the sureties for his bond were Felix Coblentz, L. I. Marks, Morris Brinn, Gustav Danielwiez (or Danielewicz), D. Myers, I. B. Isaacs, and G. Newman.[24] The names of Jews who served as members of grand, trial, and coroner's juries throughout the period are legion.[25]

In addition to holding public office, the Jews were interested in the social and fraternal organizations that were established in almost every town of the region. The lodges were quite popular, and the Jews joined them for social contacts and business purposes. Only two cities had Jewish lodges, and the Hebrew benevolent societies did not provide the social contacts sought by the gregarious Jewish merchants. The Masonic and Odd Fellows lodges had no religious restrictions, and their members included men of many nationalities and religions.

From the very beginning, Jews took active roles in these organizations, particularly the Masons. Moses Greenebaum of Missouri No. 36 and Solomon Heyman of Illinois No. 9 were among the charter members of the lodge in Grass Valley that was organized in 1851.[26] Shortly thereafter, in 1854, C. Josephson and Sol Kohlman helped to organize and were elected officers of the Royal Arch Masons chapter in Nevada City.[27] All through the region, Jews were entrusted with responsible offices in the Masonic fraternity.[28] In Placerville, the ubiquitous L. W. Fechheimer served as secretary of El Dorado Lodge No. 26, F. and A. M., Sierra Nevada Council No. 40, Royal and Select Masters, and St. James Royal Arch Chapter No. 16. The next year, he was succeeded in all three positions by Henry D. Raphael.[29]

According to an early directory of Nevada County, one Mason showed his devotion to the order by donating a sizable amount of money to it. P. Zacharias, the charter tyler of Manzanita Lodge No. 129, F. and A. M., of Bridgeport, Nevada County, donated $1,500 in real and personal property to the lodge in 1858 for charitable purposes.[30]

Jews were also active in the Independent Order of Odd Fellows. They were officers in all the lodges from Downieville in the north, where A. Cohn was secretary of Sierra Lodge No. 24, to Hornitos in the south, where in 1863 Davis Rosenthal was a trustee. And several Jews were elected treasurer of their lodges.[31]

Other organizations than the Masons and Odd Fellows did not have lodges in every city and town. But wherever they were found, as long as the rituals did not conflict with the Jews' religious beliefs, there were always Jewish names on the membership and officer rolls, from local lodges of the Ancient Order of United Workmen in Sonora to the Independent Order of Good Templars in Nevada City to the Independent Order of Knighthood in Grass Valley to the Sons of Temperance of Springfield and Nevada City.[32] Abraham Seligman served as a floor manager at a dance given by the Placerville Chapter of E Clampus Vitus on Washington's birthday 1856.[33]

A local civic activity close to the hearts of every resident, especially the Jewish merchants, was the volunteer fire department. Since most of the early records of these organizations no longer exist, knowledge concerning their activities must be drawn from newspapers and occasional city and county directories.

In Columbia, there were ten Jews among the 205 members of Columbia Engine Company No. 2 before 1866.[34] Jews also served as officers of the various companies of the "V.F.D." L. Rosenthal, for example, served as president of the Downieville Fire Department.[35] For his long service as captain of the Volunteer Fire Department of San Andreas, Conrad Prag was presented with a set of pocket derringers when he left that city for San Francisco in 1862 or 1863.[36] Jews also served as treasurers in many fire departments in the Mother Lode.[37]

There is a hard-dying tradition among descendants of this

group of pioneers, who left Central Europe when the liberal political revolutions there failed, that the progenitor of the American family fled Europe to escape conscription into the Germany army. Whether or not this was so, many of the Jews in the gold rush were enrolled in local militias. This sort of military service was voluntary, not coercive as in Europe. Perhaps the Jews joined such groups because most of the male population of a city did so, making this one more organization in which a merchant could participate in the interests of his business. Thirty-two of the fifty-nine Jews on the Tuolumne County assessment roll for 1862 were registered on the county military roll. The next year, twenty-three of the fifty-one Jewish taxpayers in the county were eligible for military service.[38] It is unlikely that any of these militias was ever called into active duty.[39]

None of these militiamen is known to have been on active duty during the Civil War. There is no evidence in print that suggests that the key national issues of the day, slavery and the Civil War, had any lasting effect among the Jewish population of the Mother Lode. There were several Democratic newspapers in the region, and in other parts of the state, that printed anti-Lincoln editorials, but slavery and secession from the Union apparently never became a matter of serious concern. Perhaps California was too far removed from the scene of the fighting, or perhaps merchants did not want to antagonize their clientele by taking a position on the subject.

Although, according to Simon Wolf, twenty-eight Jewish residents of California fought in the Civil War, only one, Henry Schiller, a former miner, was known to have been a resident of the gold rush country.[40] One Civil War volunteer whom Simon Wolf missed was Abraham Gradwohl of Mokelumne Hill, who answered Lincoln's call for interpreters and enlisted as a private on August 21, 1863.[41]

No records document Jewish participation in the vigilance committees of the Mother Lode. However, Herman Goldner of Jackson had been a member of the Second Vigilance Committee in San Francisco,[42] and Emanuel Hirschfelder of Downieville, who witnessed the lynching of a Mexican woman there in 1851, was thought to have been a member of the local vigilance committee.[43] In general, the Jews disliked government by mob, and they joined the forces favoring the establishment of local governments and legally constituted law-enforcement bodies. They were among the petitioners for the incorporation of the towns of Sutter Creek, Placerville, and Columbia.[44] Jewish names were frequently found on petitions to the legislature in favor of a Sunday closing law.[45] And Jewish merchants also served on civic committees and signed petitions supporting local improvements.[46]

In private or purely social activities, too, the participation of Jews was noted. Merchants were always called upon to serve on committees organizing Fourth of July celebrations or dances. Whether the occasion was a masquerade ball, an "Odds and Ends" ball, a Grand German ball, or balls for the celebration of Valentine's Day, Washington's birthday, Leap Year, or the dedication of the new hall of the Amador County Labor Association in Sutter Creek, Jews served on committees of arrangement, invitation, and reception and as floor managers.[47] Representatives of the Jews of the community were always included in the list of belles and beaux of the ball in the next edition of the local newspaper.

In these local social and civic events, there seems to have been a complete openness and lack of prejudice on the part of the participants. Many nationalities and religious groups mingled on the dance floor, or cooperated in the activities of a lodge or the maintenance of a volunteer fire department, or added their names to petitions for civic improvements.

Jews were also active in entertainment societies and amateur theatrical performances. One Rosenheim of Nevada City acted, in 1856, as Hamlet's ghost in *The Jury-Room, or, My Stomach in an Awful Predicament*, and in 1861, L. Jacobi and Herman Wolfe were elected officers of the Columbia Terpsichorean Society.[48]

In 1860, a merchant in remote Bear Valley, Leopold Frankl, presided over the School of Inquiry, which once invited a doctor to lecture on the subject, "The Anatomy and Physiology of the Brain."[49]

Even the children distinguished themselves by earning honor-roll status at schools in Placerville, Sutter Creek, Columbia, and Downieville.[50]

Other members of this community distinguished themselves through specialized talents. Emma Levy of Coloma and Robert Jewell and Mrs. Silbermann of Placerville exhibited their handiwork at the seventh annual fair of the El Dorado County Agricultural Society. Jewell displayed a case of home-manufactured cigars.[51] And Martin Steckler of Jackson won the plaudits of the local newspaper for gaining two falls and a draw at a local wrestling match.[52]

In order to insure uniform competition in the conduct of their businesses, the Jewish merchants joined with their Gentile fellow-merchants on at least two occasions to set uniform rates on the purchase of foreign exchange.[53]

In this first decade of California's statehood, her Jewish citizens were welcomed into the social life of each community and, in turn, gave to the community the benefits they had received from their European education. Whether as public officials or lodge officers, individuals with special talents or merchant-taxpayers, parents who sent their children to the local schools, members of nonsectarian benevolent societies, or petitioners for the establishment and maintenance of law and order, the Jews formed, from the beginning, an important segment of the group oriented toward organized society and respect for the legally constituted authority. They won the respect of their fellow citizens and the open admiration of the most literate group in the region, the newspaper editors. The newspapers often reprinted articles from other papers that reported the honesty and trustworthiness of Jews at other times and in other areas. While editors identified anonymous Jews by religion, the term was almost never used derisively. If a local Jew was the subject of an incident, the editor referred to him by his religion without any prejudice. Since this region was almost wholly composed of newcomers of one kind or another, it served an editor's purpose to identify a Jew as a Jew.

Often unidentified local Jews served as subjects of local humorous articles.

> "A Vesel."—A Jew of our acquaintance came in to his neighbor's place of business, yesterday morning, bringing an intolerable smell with him, and, "fast as a little wagon," made the announcement that he had killed a "vesel," in his "schicken house." He said the animal was "black, mit a vite tail, and schtinks like de tuyvel." A wicked wag, next door, persuaded the victor to bring in his trophy, as he wanted to buy the skin. The Jew soon appeared and drew from his pocket a half grown pole cat.[54]

On the few occasions when local Jews battled Gentiles, the newspaper editor was likely to report the event in as much detail and as humorously as he was able.

> Volcano Items.
> The Spring Fights Commenced.—What the boys call the "spring fights," in Volcano, commenced on Sunday last. On the forenoon of that day, a son of Isreal [sic], whose proportions are not gigantic, desired and insisted that a portly Gentile, of robust dimentions [sic], should pay to him, the said son of Israel, a sum of money due for a rig of "store clothse" [sic]. Hard words ensued, whereupon the Gentile seized the Jew by the capillary substance that vegetates upon the summit of the cranium. The Jew seized a hatchet, and cut the Gentile on the hand. So ended the first heat.—In the afternoon, they again met at the store of the Israelite. Big Gentile seized little Jew by the aforesaid capilary [sic] substance; this time, the latter had a "sticker" that horses are bled with, and the Gentile was cut in divers and sundry places, insomuch that blood flowed profusely. The Gentile was cared for by a physician, and the Jew was terribly frightened lest the populace should become excited and hang him and all his friends.—Next morning, however, Justice Munckton discharged the Jew, and the Gentile, this warm weather, is probably all the better for a little loss of blood. During the day, a good many others engaged in pleasant little knock-downs, without suffering any material damage.[55]

That the newspapers occasionally included articles condemning the existence of anti-Semitism at home and abroad, as well as articles praising the extent to which Jews were being treated as equals with the rest of the population, was indicative of the feeling toward the Jews among all the nationalities and religions in the Mother Lode during and after the gold rush.

> The Lord Mayor of London, Solomons, a Jew, gave an entertainment on the 4th of June, at which was the Archbishop of Canterbury, the Primate of all England! And the Metropolitan was supported by no fewer than ten of his Suffragan Bishops, besides a goodly fellowship of the clergy of London.
> The breaking of bread and drinking of wine between Jews and Christians, shows a great change in public sentiment since the days when Jews were butchered in the streets of London like dogs, and the Israelite was the most despised of human kind. But on this occasion the fellowship was full. The Lord Mayor Jew toasted the Archbishop, and eulogized him for "his boundless zeal in promoting the spiritual welfare of those committed to his care"; and the Archbishop drank his wine and eulogized the Jew. At other similar entertainments, dissenters have been invited and treated in the same way. This is the state of religion in the nineteenth century. How unlike what it was in the 5th or 12th![56]

Noting the failure of the *American Flag,* a newspaper first published in Sonora and then in San Francisco, the editor of the Downieville *Sierra Advocate* reprinted a report from another gold rush paper.

> Dead at Last.
> ... We had almost forgotten to say that it undertook to run all the disloyal Irish and Jews out of the State.... It is now thoroughly dead, we are assured—dead beyond the power of resurrection—and the general opinion is that it lived too long. Sorrowers over its death are found only among the poor printers who were swindled out of their wages.—*Grass Valley Union.*[57]

For their part, the Jews are known to have practiced equality and fairness in dealing with their customers. For example, there are no records of the Jews from this period and region harboring anti-Chinese prejudices or driving away potential customers of Chinese ancestry, as many of the native Americans did.[58]

The many references to the participation of the Jews in local social activities and politics serve as evidence that, at least among the native Americans and northern Europeans, there was generally a feeling of good will and an absence of religious bias. In the gold rush, there was room for representatives of every northern and central European nation in every local civic and social function. Only in a few instances were Jews named and singled out because of their religion. Fewer still were those occasions that were the result of anti-Jewish prejudice, and it is important to compare the event with the local reaction as well as with the prevailing attitudes of anti-Semitism that existed in those times.

In many parts of the United States, the influx of masses of Jews from central Europe after 1840 was followed by an increase in anti-Semitism.[59] However, the gold rush to California, shortly after the beginning of this mass migration, involved only a few overt anti-Semitic outbursts. At times, opinions originally held by only a few individuals crystallized into group attitudes. The motivations for these feelings of anti-Semitism were economic, with the writer of them taking a vague stand against all the unnamed Jewish merchants in one region.[60] Another time, the perpetrator of an anti-Semitic act, William W. Stow, Speaker of the Assembly of California,[61] was angered by a particular Jew and extended his dislike to Jews in general. Thus, although certain prejudicial attitudes were present in the early years of American settlement in California, these attitudes and attacks were rebutted in the general press by both Jews and Gentiles.

From the earliest years of the gold rush, many groups sought legislation enforcing temperance and Sunday closing. Such movements probably originated among Protestants; most meetings of these organizations were held in Protestant churches. By 1855, bills were being offered in the California State Senate and Assembly for the suppression of amusements and business activity "on the Christian Sabbath."[62] On March 16 of that year, during debate on a bill to suppress trading on Sunday in certain counties, the Speaker of the Assembly, William W. Stow, "attacked the Jews as undesirable citizens and said that he was in favor of imposing special taxes on them in order to preclude their being in the state."[63]

The press of the state thereupon attacked Stow for his public expressions of prejudice. From the Stockton *San Joaquin Republican* and the *Los Angeles Star* to the *Sacramento Daily Union*, and nationally, from the Philadelphia *Occident* to the Cincinnati *Israelite*, Jewish and Gentile writers joined in the attack on Stow. The *Union* editorialized:

> The remarks of Mr. Stow . . . in reference to the character and conduct of our fellow-citizens of the Jewish persuasion were . . . obnoxious. . . . It will hardly be contended that the opinions and declaration of Mr. Stow are conclusive as to the rights of those professing the Hebrew faith in California.[64]

The basis for Stow's prejudice was said to have been his anger when one Jewish firm in his home county of Santa Cruz refused to sign a petition in favor of Sunday closing.[65] However, had Stow and others heard of the great Jewish support from the gold rush country for a Sunday closing bill, they might have sung a different tune. On the several petitions supporting a Sunday closing law that were presented to the Senate and Assembly, the names of many Jewish merchants appeared. This was especially so in El Dorado County, where T[heodore] Elkus and J. Morris of Coloma, Joseph Levy of Gold Hill, and D. Baum, B[ernhard] Marks, and D. Kohn of Placerville affixed their signatures to petitions that read, in part:

> Society has now assumed an organized and permanent character, and the reasons which have prevailed in closing the doors of business on that day [Sunday] in the Atlantic States as well as in the whole Christian world, operate with equal force and potency here. It is believed by your petitioners that this measure is earnestly desired by a large majority of the people, traders as well

as customers, but that owing to the perverseness of a few whom no considerations but those of self interest can control, and who persist in keeping open doors on the Sabbath, others are restrained from closing theirs who would otherwise most gladly do so.[66]

In addition, Mary Jacobs, P. H. Wolfe, L. Marks, and Simon Mayers of the same county signed the petition protesting gambling and public amusements on Sunday.

Further evidence of active Jewish support for a Sunday closing law came from Nevada County, where in 1858, a prominent merchant, Jacob Kohlman, was appointed to a committee to circulate a petition memorializing the legislature to enact a Sunday closing law, recognizing the "Christian Sabbath as an institution of divine appointment."[67]

In Nevada City, a newspaper editor, who editorialized in favor of the Sunday closing law, named one Jewish merchant in town, Samuel Haas, who he believed had refused to close his store on Sunday. A month later, however, the editor was forced to apologize publicly for singling out Haas. The articles the editor printed merit notice because they indicate the agreement of almost all the merchants in important trading centers like Nevada City to close on Sunday regardless of what day of the week they observed as their Sabbath.

> Closing on the Sabbath.—A paper circulated among the merchants a few days since agreeing to close on the Sabbath, met with a favorable reception from all parties with a single exception. The sole refusal of Cheap John [i.e., Samuel Haas] thus destroys the good purpose of many of our merchants. It were desirable that a general acquiescence in a reform so salutary might be obtained. Of this, for the present there is little hope.[68]

> Closing on the Sabbath.—Error. We were misinformed a few weeks since in stating that the only obstacle to the closing of places of business on the Sabbath in this city, was Cheap John.—That individual informs us he has never made an objection to closing should all other dealers in articles in his line come into the

arrangement. The refusal to close first came from another house, which led Mr. Haas to decline also. We make this correction in justice to the celebrated establishment of Cheap John.[69]

After the Sunday closing law was finally enacted on April 10, 1858,[70] a newspaper in the Northern Mines opposed its wording, and the item soon appeared as an exchange in Nevada City.

> Sunday Law.—Our Legislature has passed a Sunday law. The first section says that "no person or persons shall, on the Christian Sabbath, or Sunday, keep open any store warehouse" &c., &c. The penalties are fines and imprisonment. If the law had said "*Hebrew*" Sabbath instead of "*Christian*" Sabbath, who is there so blind that they would not have seen that it would be a palpable violation of the constitution. Yet, under the constitution, the Hebrew religion is as sacred and as fully protected as the Christian. This Sunday Law which is to take affect on the first of June next, is a mawkish religious absurdity and will be a dead letter on the staute [sic] book. *Shasta Republican.*[71]

What became very evident was that the Jewish merchants favored Sunday closing because they favored closing their stores on any one day of the week that all the merchants, regardless of religion, could agree upon. State law or no, they reasoned that a day of rest was necessary and that day of rest might as well be Sunday. Once again, in support of law and order (and uniform standards of competition), the Jewish merchants stood together with the other storekeepers in town to agree on one fixed day of rest per week.

Another time when the Jews of this region found themselves singled out as Jews was in U. S. Grant's presidential campaign of 1868 and reelection campaign of 1872. This time, the Jews were drawn into the limelight of national politics by local Democratic newspaper editors who were searching for a campaign issue to use against the popular Civil War hero. Since the Jewish merchants of the gold rush towns were regarded as leading citizens, it was natural for newspaper editors to call attention to any wrongs perpetrated against Jews by Grant during the Civil War. Democratic editors apparently reasoned that if sufficient numbers of local Jews were convinced of Grant's unworthiness as a presidential candidate, they might campaign against him.

For alleged trading infractions along Union and Confederate lines during the Civil War, General Grant had issued General Order No. 11 from Holly Spring, Mississippi, December 17, 1862, concerning the military department of Tennessee:

> The Jews, as a class violating every regulation of trade established by the Treasury Department and also department orders, are hereby expelled from the department within twenty-four hours from the receipt of this order.[72]

Though the order was countermanded shortly thereafter by President Lincoln, the Democratic and much of the Jewish press recalled the incident in the campaign of 1868. Grant, at the conclusion of the campaign, also repudiated the order,[73] but by that time, articles and editorials had appeared in hundreds of newspapers castigating him for his anti-Jewish actions. Almost every city in the region of the gold rush had a Democratic paper that made use of the issue. As early as June 6, 1868, the Placerville *Mountain Democrat* campaigned against Grant with a lengthy doggerel.

> From the Chicago Times.
> General Grant's Attack on the Jews.
>
> He called them Jews in utter scorn,
> As though it were a shame
> To trace their name and lineage back
> To a race of glorious fame!
>
> A race of prophets, priests and kings;
> A great and noble host,
> Whose glorious deeds can yet be traced
> Though time itself were lost!

A race for whom the Red Sea waves
Were parted by their God,
And Israel passed thro' its depths
Unharmed and dry shod.

A race for whom the sun stood still,
And parted Jordan's wave;
A race for whom were wonders wrought,
And Jesus died to save.

Yet the bigoted and senseless Grant
Does Jew and rascal class
In the same list, which plainly shows
That Grant must be an ass,

Who heeds not history's teachings,
Who does its lessons slight,
And vilifies a noble race
To glut his senseless spite;

A spite which is as narrow
As the mind which gave it birth;
A spite which in this latter age
Should crushed be to earth.

But narrow minds like his must e'en
Their native meanness show,
And the great race he libeled has
No answer to bestow.

Save to point him to the Bible,
The prophet and the sage,
Which show to him how great have been
The Jews of every age.[74]

From June 6 until the eve of the general election, eleven articles describing Grant's supposed anti-Semitism were printed in the Placerville *Mountain Democrat*. Most of them were taken from exchanges. The same pattern held for the Democratic press in the rest of the Mother Lode. The pro-Seymour papers also kept their readers informed of the latest articles against Grant that appeared in the national Jewish press, as well as decisions by other Jewish communities to oppose Grant en masse.

> Grant and the Jews.—The Cincinnati Israelite, the organ of the Jews of the West, a paper conducted with marked ability, of wide circulation and vast influence, is handling Grant's unjust, tyrannical and insulting order without gloves. But few Jews in the west, not one of them in the Union, who has the least self-respect, can support the man who without provocation insulted them "as a class."[75]
>
> Gen. Grant and the Hebrews.—The Meadville, Penna Hebrew Society, at a regular meeting on the 1st of March, after electing officers, passed the following resolution, which was ordered published in the Cincinnati Israelite, in which journal we find it:
> *Resolved,* That we, the members of the Meadville Hebrew Society, fully indorse and approve of the editorial in the Israelite of February 28, "concerning the infamous order, No. 11, of Gen. Grant while in command of the department of Tennessee," and that we pledge ourselves not to vote for General Grant as President of the United States, should he secure the nomination of either party, and we will use all honorable means to defeat him for that high and distinguished office.[76]

The issue concerning Grant, however, was not entirely humorless. One newspaper passed along a probably apocryphal statement by Grant on the subject:

> Grant's Order Against the Jews.—The Jewish Sentinel, published at St. Louis, has the following showing the animus of General Grant when he issued his order expelling the Jews as a class, from the department of the Tennessee.
> One of the St. Louisians expressed the opinion that Grant had made a mistake in the order, instead of directing against the Jews, as a class, he ought to have directed it against malefactors of all kinds. Mr. Lincoln remarked that he liked Grant, for there was a

great deal of humor in him, and drew forth and read Grant's letter in reply to one he had written to him, directing him to rescind the order. In this letter Grant said:

"Mr. President as you have directed me, I will rescind the order; but I wish you to understand that these people are the descendants of those who crucified the Saviour; and from the specimens I have here the race has not improved."[77]

The Republican press in California, as elsewhere, rarely replied to any of the anti-Jewish charges against Grant. Only in Mokelumne Hill was there any reply to the Democratic press's charges of anti-Semitism. The *Weekly Calaveras Chronicle* printed exchange items that were just as irresponsible as some anti-Grant allegations by the Democrats. Once the *Chronicle* published an exchange from the *Sacramento Record,* which purported to prove that some Jews were indeed guilty of smuggling during the Civil War, that Grant was justified in issuing the order of expulsion, and that Jews who had not done any smuggling approved the order.

> He [Grant] might have court-martialed them, and on conviction shot them; but he showed them leniency, and only ordered them to the rear. It is perfectly natural that those Jews who were actively engaged in illegal traffic should feel aggrieved at Grant's order, as by it they lost a "good thing," but the portion of the Jews who were not engaged in traffic feel as though Grant did exactly right in issuing the order; and when the Democracy think that, by their low appeals to the prejudice of this class of citizens, they will assure their votes, we can assure them that they are much mistaken.[78]

Hundreds of Jews in California were registered to vote in the general election of 1868. Whatever their feelings were concerning the election, it is certain that their political reading material included anti-Grant articles, but there are no records of Jewish merchants or organizations taking out advertisements announcing whom they would support.

The presidential campaign of 1872 was also of special interest because Grant's running-mate, Senator Henry Wilson of

2. Sonora, January 1853. Courtesy of The Bancroft Library, University of California, Berkeley

3. The Volcano Diggings. Courtesy of The Bancroft Library, University of California, Berkeley

4. Present-day Mokelumne Hill. Store-front of L. Mayer & Son on the left.

5. Entrance to W. Y. O. D. ("Work Your Own Diggings") Mine in Grass Valley, owned by Jacob and Joseph Weissbein.

Courtesy of Mrs. Samuel Kahn, Hillsborough, California

6. Levinsky Brothers Store, Jackson, 1857.
Courtesy of The Bancroft Library, University of California, Berkeley

7. A. Wolf & Brothers, Sonora.
Courtesy of The Bancroft Library, University of California, Berkeley

8. Henry Silvester & Co., Grass Valley, 1858.

Courtesy of The Bancroft Library, University of California, Berkeley

9. Fred Auerbach & Bro., Rabbit Creek, 1862.

Courtesy of The Bancroft Library, University of California, Berkeley

10. Block & Furth, North San Juan, 1858.
Courtesy of The Bancroft Library, University of California, Berkeley

11. Aaron Baruh.
Courtesy of Doris Foley, Nevada City

12. Moses Dinkelspiel.

14. Henry Greenberg.

13. Lewis Gerstle.

16. Jacob Schweitzer.

15. Oser Meyer.

17. Sigmund Steinhart.

18. Joseph Weissbein.

19. Anthony Zellerbach.

20. The family of Kaufman and Fanny Mayer Hexter of Mokelumne Hill in San Francisco about 1885 for the wedding of Louis Hexter. Standing, left to right: Amelia (Mrs. Henry Schrag), Lena (Mrs. Edward Weinlander), Abraham (married Lillie Stern), Aaron (married Dr. Grace Feder), Lillie (Mrs. Lehman Strause), Charles (married Etta Joseph). Seated, left to right: Sarah (Mrs. August Weinlander), Kaufman Hexter, Fanny Mayer Hexter, Louis (married Josephine Weil).

Courtesy of the Misses Irma and Ruth Schrag, San Francisco, California

21. Gravestone of Rachel Levinsky in Jackson.

22. Gravestone of Isaac Peiser in Jackson.

23. Gravestone of Herman Landecker in Placerville.

24. Gravestone of Kalonymos ben Natan in Jackson. There was no English on this gravestone.

25. Gravestone of Jacob Reeb in Sonora.

26. Home of Aaron and Rosalie Wolf Baruh, 516 Main Street, Nevada City, built in 1852.

27. Congregation Ryhim Ahoovim, Stockton, now known as Temple Israel. This synagogue building was erected in 1855.

Courtesy of Rabbi Bernard D. Rosenberg, Stockton

28. Big Oak Flat and Yosemite Stage Company of Chinese Camp, operated by Paul and Saul Morris.

Courtesy of Ruth Newport, Sonora

29. A portion of the gravestone of Isaac Lurch, in the Mokelumne Hill Jewish Cemetery. Note the symbolism from the Masonic funeral service in the carving. Lurch died in Lancha Plana December 28, 1859.

30. Gravestone of Charles Brownstein, the only surviving gravestone in the Shasta Jewish Cemetery.

31. Grass Valley Jewish Cemetery, in process of restoration, 1970.

32. The first synagogue building of Congregation B'nai Israel, Sacramento, used for two months in 1852 until destroyed by fire.
Courtesy of The Bancroft Library, University of California, Berkeley

33. Israel Joseph Benjamin II, who travelled extensively through California and the West, 1859-1862.

34. Washington Street, Sonora, looking toward the north, in the early 1860's. The store of A. Mock is visible in the right foreground. To the right of Mock, out of the picture, was the store of Moses Hanauer.

Photograph courtesy of the late Donald I. Segerstrom, Sonora

מנחה חדשה

אדער

מחזור

על כל השנה

נייא איבערזעטצט

פֿאן

פֿירשטענטהאל אונד קונאוי.

צווייטער באנד:

מחזור פֿיר יום כפור.

נײנטע אויסגאבע.

קראטאשין

בשנת ת׳ר׳כ׳ד לפ׳ק.

(MACHSOR).

Druck und Verlag von B. L. Monasch in Krotoschin. 1864.

Zu haben in Breslau bei M. Monasch
Carlsstraße № 27, Fechtschule.
Zur Messe in Frankfurt in der Bude Nicht- und Jüdenstr.-Ecke.

Sonora Hebrew Benevolent Society Sep. 16th 1876

35. Title-page of Yom Kippur prayer book used in Sonora.

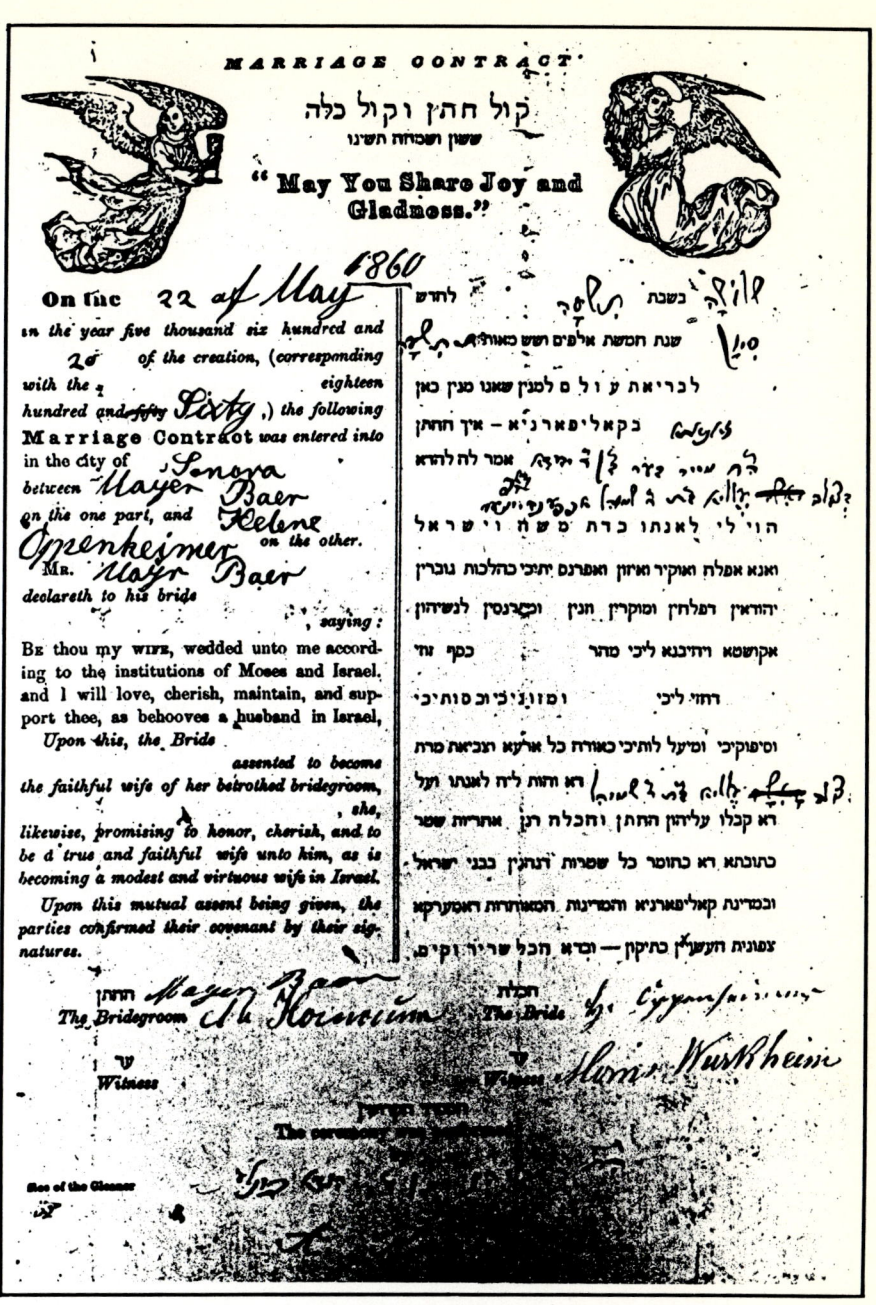

36. Ketubah (marriage contract) printed in San Francisco and used at the marriage of Mayer Baer and Helene Oppenheimer in Sonora in 1860.

Courtesy of the Baer family, Sonora

ELEMENTS OF DISCORD.—That there are elements of discord in the Administration party the quarrels of its leaders and the indignant manifesto of Senator Wade and Representative Davis, prove. The disaffection is wide spread, irrepressible and daily increasing. It promises to result disastrously to the shoddy party and gloriously to the country. The Buffalo Advertiser, a leading Republican organ, thinks political affairs are confused and unsettled, and adds :

"Notwithstanding the fact that the Baltimore Convention has announced its candidate and its platform, it is evident that elements of discord are at work in our midst, which, under the manipulation of disappointed politicians, aided not a little by a recent unfortunate, and we trust misconceived expression of executive policy, is working much mischief in our ranks."

TRUE TO THE LETTER.—Mr. Voorhies declared in Congress that Mr. Lincoln dare not receive propositions for Union and peace, because he knows that his party cannot outlive the war, and that his power and the restoration of the Union are incompatible. Does not this explain why he proposed insulting terms to the peace commissioners? He knew they would not accept them; he offered them because he knew they would be rejected; but he misunderstood the feeling and temper of the people. The masses desire peace ; many of the prominent and influential leaders of his own party are clamorous for peace, and they will place a man in the Presidential chair who will carry out their wishes, in spite of the threats, promises and money of Lincoln and his minions.

The only hope of the country is the election of George B. McClellan.

Books, Stationery, Etc.

PLAZA BOOK STORE,
PLACERVILLE,

Has just received a splendid assortment of

Standard and Miscellaneous Works
STATIONERY, SCHOOL BOOKS,

GIFT BOOKS, ALBUMS, CUTLERY,
TOYS, GOLD PENS, VIOLINS,
GUITARS, ACCORDEONS, MUSIC BOOKS,
ROMAN STRINGS, ETC., ETC.,

Selected expressly for the Country Trade, and selling at greatly reduced rates. Also,

AGENTS

For Sacramento Union, Alta California, Bulletin, Mirror, etc

NEWSPAPERS AND PERIODICALS

Kept constantly on hand, and sold unusually low.

Clothing, Dry Goods, Etc.

OLD ROUND TENT CLOTHING STORE!
ONCE MORE IN FULL BLAST!

The subscriber respectfully informs his friends and the citizens of El Dorado County generally, that he has recommenced business at the old stand, where he has just received and offers for sale a splendid and entirely new stock of

FALL AND WINTER CLOTHING!
BOOTS AND SHOES,
Hats of Every Description,
FURNISHING GOODS,
Rubber Goods, Blankets, Trunks, Etc.,

All of which he will SELL VERY LOW FOR CASH. His old friends are assured that "IT WILL PAY" to give him a call, as he has none but good articles and is determined to sell cheaper than the cheapest. COME AND SEE FOR YOURSELVES.

oct1] L. TANNENWALD.

P. SILBERMANN, H. D. RAPHAEL.

P. SILBERMANN & CO.,
WHOLESALE AND RETAIL DEALERS IN

CLOTHING
AT A. KAHN'S OLD STAND.

THE undersigned having purchased the Clothing Establishment of Mr. AARON KAHN, respectfully invite the attention of their friends and the public generally to their splendid stock of

GENTS' FALL AND WINTER CLOTHING!

Consisting of the best quality of custom-made
Fashionable Dress Coats ;
Black Doeskin Pants ;
Cassimere Business Suits ;
Beaver Suits and Overcoats ;
Blue Flannel Suits ;
Benkert's Boots and Shoes,
Fall Style Silk and Cass. Hats;
Davis and Jones' Shirts ;
Silk, Velvet and Plush Vests;

And a general assortment of

Gents' Furnishing Goods !
Trunks, Valises, Carpet Bags, etc., etc.

Also, a good assortment of YOUTHS' and BOYS'
CLOTHING, BOOTS, SHOES, ETC.,
CONSTANTLY ON HAND.

COLT'S PISTOLS,
Of all sizes, constantly on hand.

☞ Gentlemen desiring the Latest Styles and BEST GOODS to be had, would do well to give us a call before purchasing elsewhere, as we are sure we can suit the taste of the most fastidious
N. B.—New Goods received every Week.
P. SILBERMANN & CO.,
At the old stand of A. Kahn,
sept3] Main st., Placerville.

NEW GOODS!
A. HAAS
HAS JUST RECEIVED A LARGE STOCK OF
NEW DRY GOODS!
Consisting of
DRESS GOODS,

Railroads and Stage Lines.

IMPORTANT
— TO —
SHIPPERS OF FREIGHT.
P. & S. V. R. R.--S. V. R. R.
— AND —
FREEPORT RAILROAD.

GREAT SAVING IN TIME AND EXPENSE.

ON AND AFTER SEPTEMBER 19th, 1864, ordinary Freight will be received at FREEPORT and forwarded to LATROBE without charge for transhipping, drayage or forwarding

Goods shipped by steamers of the California Steam Navigation Company, leaving San Francisco at 4 P. M., daily, can be delivered in Latrobe at 9 o'clock next morning. Freight shipped by sailing vessels will be forwarded with dispatch. No charge on ordinary freight per sailing vessel for levee dues, transhipping, drayage or forwarding.

All Heavy Freights, such as Boilers, Heavy Castings, Steam Engines, etc., will be transhipped at Freeport by powerful derricks directly to the cars, and at Latrobe will also be transhipped by derricks directly to teams. For this class of freight, a charge will be made of cost of labor engaged on derricks only.

Freight Charges of steamers or sailing vessels will be advanced at Freeport and collected at Latrobe without charge.

Mark all Freight " CARE F. R. R., FREEPORT," and send receipts with freight.

PRICES OF FREIGHTING :

FREIGHT, from Freeport to Latrobe, $4 per ton.
DOWN FREIGHTS from Latrobe to Freeport or Sacramento, will be forwarded at the following rates:

Ordinary Freights, per ton..................$3 00
Ores, (shippers to load and unload) per ton.. 2 50
Marble, " " " " 2 50
Lumber, " " " " M.. 8 00
Wood, " " " " car of
6¾ cords 12 00
Hides..................................... 68
Kips...................................... 05
Pelts..................................... 68

Mark Freight, " Care P. & S V. R. R."
J. P. ROBINSON,
F. A. BISHOP,
sept24] Superintendents.

PLACERVILLE AND SACRAMENTO VALLEY RAILROAD.

ON AND AFTER OCTOBER 1st, TRAINS, in connection with the Sacramento Valley and Freeport Railroads, will run as follows:

LEAVE LATROBE at 6¾ and 11 A. M. and 4 P. M.
LEAVE SACRAMENTO at 6½ A. M. and 4 P. M.
LEAVE FREEPORT at 6¾ A. M., 4 P. M. and at Midnight.

ON SUNDAYS, Trains will run as follows:
LEAVE LATROBE for Sacramento only, at 11
A. M. LEAVE SACRAMENTO for Latrobe at 6¾ A. M.
All Trains

---

37. Newspaper advertisements of L. Tannenwald, P. Silbermann, A. Haas, Isaac Barman, Aaron Kahn, from the Placerville *Mountain Democrat*, October 8, 1864.

Courtesy of The Bancroft Library, University of California, Berkeley

W. M. BRADSHAW,

HAS JUST RECEIVED a large invoice of New Goods, consisting, in part, of

STANDARD BOOKS
— ON —
HISTORY, BIOGRAPHY,
ASTRONOMY, GEOLOGY,
BOTANY, RHETORIC, POETRY,
ALBUMS, ETC.

STATIONERY:
LETTER, NOTE, LEGAL,
FOOLSCAP, BILL, BATH,
MOURNING, POSTOFFICE
AND OTHER PAPERS,
Envelopes, Deed and Cash Boxes.

Mathematical Instruments,
RUBBER BANDS,
IVORY HOLDERS,
PORCELAIN SLATES,
TRANSPARENT SLATES.
TABLETS,
CHESSMEN,
CARD CASES,
INDIA INK,
PRINTED NOTES.
BLANK BOOKS,
MEMORANDUMS, ETC.

CUTLERY:
ROGERS' AND WOSTENHOLM'S.

GOLD PENS:
THE FINEST QUALITY.

FANCY GOODS:
LADIES' DESKS,
" TRAVELING COMPANIONS,
VELVET PORTMONNAIES,
PUFF BOXES,
BRUSHES, COMBS,
FANS, PERFUMERY,
TOYS, ETC., ETC.

CIGARS:
Havana and Domestic,
A LARGE STOCK.
☞ Orders Filled at San Francisco Prices.

TOBACCO:
THE FINEST BRANDS.

PIPES:
MEERSCHAUM, GUTTA PERCHA
ETC., ETC., ETC.

W. M. BRADSHAW

GOODS, ETC.,
On the Plaza, Placerville,

RESPECTFULLY informs his friends and the public generally, that having returned to Placerville and located as above, he is again prepared to supply them with every article of

MENS' AND BOYS' WEAR
Cheaper than the Cheapest.
CALL AND SEE!

ISAAC BARMAN.   LEOPOLD BARMAN

BARMAN BRO'S.,
DEALERS IN
GENT'S FINE CLOTHING
— AND —
FURNISHING GOODS,
218 Montgomery St., San Francisco.

THE undersigned take great pleasure in informing their friends and acquaintances that they have opened a Gentlemen's Clothing and Furnishing Store under Platt's Music Hall, Montgomery street, where we will always keep a well selected stock of
Fine Black Frook Coats,
Fine Black Doeskin Pants,
Atkinson's White Shirts,
Davis & Jones' White Shirts,
UNDERWEAR, GLOVES, HOSIERY
NECK TIES, ETC.,
To which we invite their attention when visiting San Francisco, assuring them that our prices shall be as low as those of any other store in the city.
CALL AND SEE FOR YOURSELVES.
BARMAN BRO'S,
(Formerly of the Old Round Tent Clothing Store, Placerville,)
218 Montgomery st., (Under Platt's Music
ap16m6] Hall,) between Pine and Bush.

AARON KAHN,

HAVING sold his Clothing Business to Messrs. P. SILBERMANN and H. D. RAPHAEL, cordially recommends them to his friends as gentlemen every way worthy of their patronage
Being desirous of closing his accounts, he earnestly requests all persons indebted to him or having claims against him to call and settle forthwith.
AARON KAHN.

HIGHEST MARKET PRICE
PAID FOR
County Warrants and Gold Dust.
AARON KAHN,
sept3]   At the Old Stand.

$30 00 REWARD!

STRAYED from the subscriber at Georgetown, in June last, one IRON GRAY FILLY, with black mane and tail, three years old; also, one BROWN ROAN STUD COLT, one year old, and one BROWN ROAN MARE COLT, of same age, the latter having a white spot in the forehead. The above animals followed the Placerville stage to Placerville, whence I have been unable to trace them.
I will pay thirty dollars reward for the delivery of the three animals (or ten dollars each) to me at Georgetown or any place convenient thereto.
☞ The Iron Gray Filly belongs to Mrs. Moore, at Irish Flat.
HENRY LEINTZENGER.
Georgetown, Sept. 21st, 1864.—1m*

Masonic.—Sierra Nevada Council, No. 10, of Royal and Select Masters, holds stated meetings on the evening of the first Tuesday of each month, in Masonic Hall, Placerville.
AARON KAHN, T. I. M.
L. W. FECHHEIMER, Recorder.

Masonic.—St. James Royal Arch Chapter, No 18, holds its regular meetings in Masonic Hall, on the evening of the first Wednesday

---

Will leave Sacramento as follows:
UP TRAIN
Will leave Sacramento at 6¼ A. M., 1 and 5 P. M.
DOWN TRAINS
Leave Folsom at 7 A. M., 12 M., and 5½ P. M.
ON SUNDAY one train only, leaving Sacramento at 6¾ A. M., and Folsom at 12 M.
The 1 and 5 P. M. up trains connect with the cars for Lincoln.

☞ Passengers for Placerville, Coloma, Georgetown, Jackson, Carson City, Virginia City and places east of the mountains, will connect with the stages at Folsom by the 6¼ A. M. up train, and 12 M. down train.

FREIGHT by every up train to Folsom, and by every morning down train to Sacramento.
J. P. ROBINSON, Sup't.
Sacramento, June 10th, 1864.

PIONEER STAGE COMPANY,

— FROM —
PLACERVILLE TO SACRAMENTO!
— VIA —
Diamond Springs, El Dorado, Clarksville and Folsom!
CARRYING THE U. S. MAILS
And Wells, Fargo & Co's Express.

COACHES leave Placerville daily in time to connect with the cars of the Sacramento Valley Railroad to Sacramento. Returning, Leave Folsom on the arrival of the morning train from Sacramento.
Also, leave Placerville daily for Virginia City, via Strawberry, Van Syckle's, Genoa, Carson City, Silver City and Gold Hill.
⁎ None but gentlemanly and experienced drivers are employed.
⁎ Passengers registering their names will be called for in any part of the city.
OFFICES—At the Cary House, and at the Nevada House, Upper Placerville.
LOUIS McLANE & CO.,
Proprietors.
THEO. F. TRACY, Agent.

ESTATE OF H. TONG, DEC'D.

IN THE PROBATE COURT of the County of El Dorado, State of California.
In the matter of the Estate of Hezekiah Tong, deceased.—Order to show cause why Order of Sale of Real Estate should not be made.

It appearing to the Judge of said Court, by the petition this day presented and filed by Sarah Tong and M. Tong, Administrator and Administratrix of the Estate of H. Tong, deceased, praying for an order of sale of real estate, that it is necessary to sell the Tong Toll Road, a portion of the real estate, and certain personal property, to pay the demands against said Estate and the expenses of administration—
It is therefore ordered by the Judge of said Court, that all persons interested in the estate of said deceased, appear before the said Probate Court on the 25th day of October, A D 1864, at 10 o'clock in the forenoon of said day, at the Court Room of said Probate Court, at the Court House in Placerville, County of El Dorado, to show cause why an order should not be granted to the said administrator and administratrix to sell so much of the real estate, and the personal property described in petition.
And that a copy of this order be published at least four successive weeks, in the Mountain Democrat, a newspaper printed and published in said El Dorado County.
Dated, Placerville Sept 26th, 1864.
OGDEN SQUIRES,
Probate Judge.

OFFICE OF THE COUNTY CLERK
of the County of El Dorado.

I, G. J. CARPENTER, County Clerk of the County of El Dorado, State of California, and ex officio Clerk of the Probate Court in and for said County, do hereby certify the foregoing to be a true and correct copy of an order duly made and entered up in the minutes of said Probate Court.

Witness my hand and the seal of said

38. United States Internal Revenue receipt from Anthony Zellerbach, 1863. Bill-heads of S. & H. Levy, Columbia, 1868, and A. Block & Co., Nevada City, 1858.

Courtesy of the California Historical Society, San Francisco

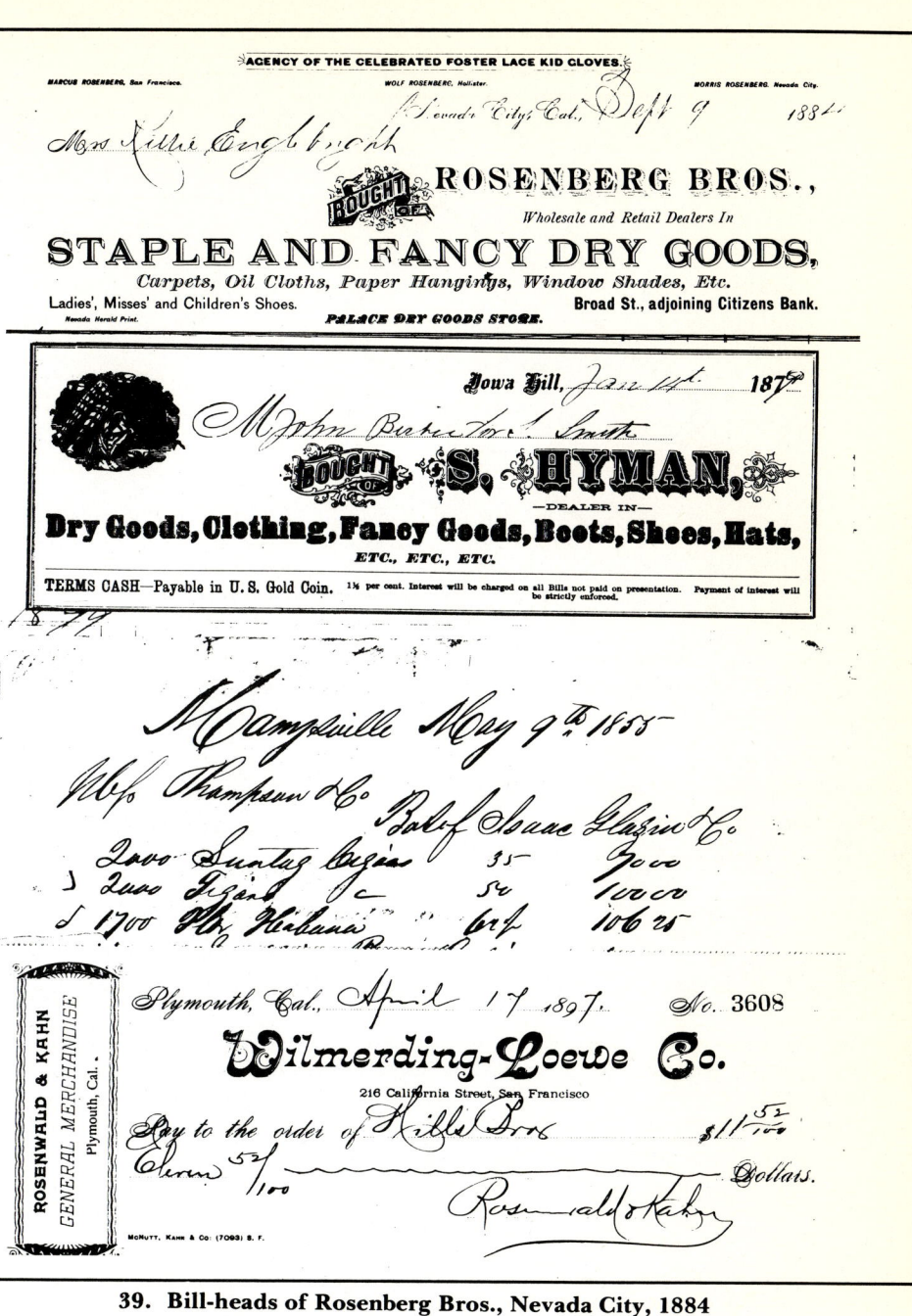

39. Bill-heads of Rosenberg Bros., Nevada City, 1884
    S. Hyman, Iowa Hill, 1879
    Isaac Glazier & Co., Marysville, 1855
    Rosenwald and Kahn, Plymouth, 1897

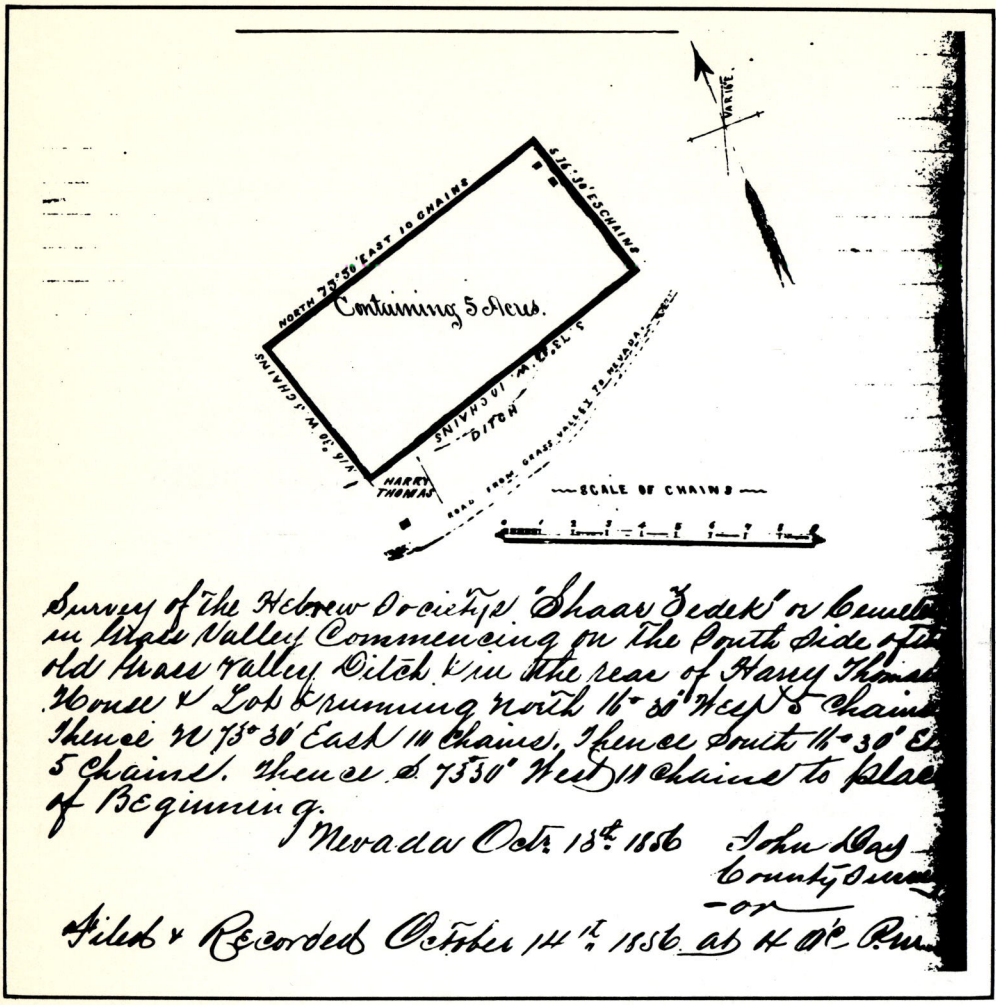

40. Survey of the Hebrew Societys "Shaar Zedek" or Cemetery in Grass Valley, 1856.

Courtesy of the Nevada County Recorder's Office, Nevada City

Massachusetts, had previously made statements against Jews on the floor of the Senate.[79] Once again, the Democratic press revived Grant's Order No. 11 as a campaign issue and coupled it with articles concerning Wilson's initiation into the Know Nothing Party.[80] All this was to no avail, however; Grant carried California and the election.

One phenomenon that was constant in the California gold rush era over the thirty-year period before 1880 was the virtual absence of overt anti-Semitism.[81] Only two documented cases of anti-Semitism are known in the region. Both of them occurred in Columbia. The first instance was in July 1856. All of the details are from the *Placerville American,* which carried an exchange from the *California American.* It was alleged that the Jews of Columbia favored the establishment of vigilance committees. An anonymous letter to the editor of the Columbia *Gazette* by a "Law and Orderite" commented on the Jews who favored such committees: "And the worst of all!—*the worst!*—only see standing before you those circumcised Hebrews, whose forefathers, in a Vigilance Committee form, actually crucified Jesus Christ."

Because the *Gazette* published such a letter, the Jewish merchants in Columbia withdrew all their advertising from the paper. The editor of the *Gazette* thereupon attacked the Jews in the following edition. The attack consisted of

> a volley of editorial abuse very nearly as low and contemptible as that of its correspondent. It speaks of their "dealing in old clothes," carrying packs on their back through the mines, &c., &c., calls them "descendants of the impenitent thief, Judas Iscariot, and other worthies," and applies to them all manner of vile and insulting epithets.[82]

Apparently, the Jews of Columbia found support against their attackers among their brethren in nearby Sonora. The Philadelphia *Occident* reported, in its edition of September 1856: " . . . Mr. [Emanuel] L[inoberg] is a stout defender of Judaism in his neighborhood; and we have received a paper, the *Sonora Herald,* in which Mr. L. bravely rebukes the spirit of illiberality which has found a mouthpiece in another print."[83]

Unfortunately, nothing further is known concerning this incident. It was not mentioned again in the *Gazette* or its contemporary, the *Weekly Columbian.*

The second incident concerned Bernhard Marks, remembered today for the eighteen letters he wrote home to his cousin, Jacob Solis-Cohen, in Philadelphia. Most of the letters were written from Placerville and other El Dorado County towns between August 1853 and September 18, 1857, and in them Marks had much to say about other Jews and Jewish life in the early years of the gold rush.[84] While in Placerville, Marks was the signer of a petition that supported the enactment of a Sunday closing law.[85] Later in life, he became a land developer and speculator and helped establish the Central California Colony, the first irrigation system in Fresno County.[86]

Early in 1860, Marks opened a private school in Columbia that attracted many pupils. This institution was admired by the local press on several occasions.

> A Good School.
> We paid a visit on Tuesday last to the School kept by Mr. and Mrs. Marks, on Broadway, and were much pleased with the system of instruction adopted by those persons. We were agreeably surprised to observe so many children present, 82 in number, who appeared cheerful and happy, and very proficient in their studies. There are but few things that afford us greater pleasure than a visit to a well regulated school.[87]

> School Exhibition.—Mr. Marks, the principal of the largest private seminary, is preparing his pupils for an exhibition to come off at the Theater in a short time. His school is now distinguished for the remarkable proficiency of its scholars, and we confidently expect to see a very superior display of their acquirements.[88]

A year later, Marks was a candidate for a position in the Columbia public school system. An election for the school board took place at the same time, and, according to an exchange of letters in the local press after the election, one slate of candidates was encouraged to run for the sole purpose of defeating Marks's candidacy because he was a Jew. Feelings ran so high in the community that one of the school board candidates, Seymour Hughes, wrote a letter on the subject in which he denied any ill will against Marks.

> I was not a champion for Mr. Marks as reported, and had I been elected I would have done my duty as a citizen and not as a partizan [sic]. In regard to that gentleman's religion I know nothing, nor do I consider it any of my business. A man's religion is an affair between his own consience [sic] and his God, in which no one has any right to meddle or interfere. But since I have been drawn into the matter I have taken the trouble to inform myself concerning his treatment, and have come to the conclusion that he has not had the courtesy shown him that is due to a good citizen and gentleman.[89]

Further correspondence on the subject was even stronger in favor of Marks, but was anonymous. Two days after Hughes's letter appeared in the *Times,* one "V." submitted his thoughts on the subject to the *Courier.*

> The facts connected with the getting up of the opposition ticket, he [Seymour Hughes] treats altogether too gingerly. The ticket was got up *to defeat the appointment of Mr. Marks* as teacher, and for no other purpose whatever, and because *Marks don't* [sic] *attend Church* on *their* hill, and for nothing else. This cannot be denied—it is notorious. Although Mr. Marks is the best teacher ever in Columbia, passed the best examination here, the best before the County Board of Education, and had awarded to him the *highest* grade certificate of qualification, has a family here, owns property here, and has always paid his taxes here, this bigoted clique set him aside, for men who have never paid taxes nor owned property in Columbia,—firstly, for a man so abominably disqualified that they were obliged to turn him out of the school to appease a community grossly outraged, and secondly, for a man brought from another town with qualifications far below, and certificate the same.[90]

Another letter to the *Courier* appeared shortly thereafter over the pseudonym "Nineteen-Hundred."

> What created the wicked, illiberal and unmanly excitement at the late school election?—Simply the fact that the *only* man in the city who, in common honesty could have been appointed Teacher of the Public School, is not a member of their [the newly elected trustees'] church, and does not participate in *their version* of Divine services. It was well known that a very great majority of the families in Columbia, who manifest sufficient interest in the education of their offspring to support private schools when there are no public ones, were strongly in favor of his appointment. It was well known that he was the *only* man of his profession, in this part of the country, who could exhibit a certificate of the proper grade to teach the Columbia School; and it was naturally supposed that if three honest, liberal, unprejudiced men were elected that he would be appointed.
>
> Here commenced the trouble. A few individuals, whose minds and hearts I do not covet, saw an opportunity to exercise their wicked religious hatred. Here was a chance to persecute a man whom they supposed a member of the Jewish church.[91]

Marks chose not to fight. Instead he left Columbia for San Francisco, where he became a grammar school principal.[92] The Sonora and Columbia Hebrew Benevolent Society, a very affluent organization at this time, did not make any public pronouncements in favor of Marks. Perhaps Marks was not a member of the society, since he had married out of the faith in 1859.

Columbia was one of the most important trading centers in the Mother Lode at this time. It boasted a large transient population from all parts of the world. It may have been coincidental that these two manifestations of anti-Semitism occurred in the same city. Whatever the cause, the incidents were soon forgotten. After 1861, no known anti-Semitic acts occurred in Columbia. Many Jewish merchants stayed there and prospered.[93]

There were other minor manifestations of anti-Jewish feeling. One of the most famous of the early California journalists, James Mason Hutchings, wrote *The Miner's Ten Commandments* in 1853, over the name "Forty-Nine." It was published that year in the *Placerville Herald* and the Nevada City *Nevada Journal*. The fourth commandment read:

> Thou shalt not remember what thy friends do at home on the Sabbath day, lest the remembrance may not compare favorably with what thou doest.... For in six days labor only, thou canst not work hard enough to wear out thy body in two years; but if thou workest hard on Sunday also, canst thou do it in six months; and thy son, and thy daughter, thy male friend and thy female friend, thy morals and thy conscience be none the better for it; but reproach thee, shouldst thou ever return with thy worn-out body to thy mother's fireside; and thou strive to justify thyself, because the trader and the blacksmith, the carpenter and the merchant, the tailors, Jews, and buccaneers, defy God and civilization, by keeping not the Sabbath day, and wish not for a day of rest, such as memory, youth and home made hallowed.[94]

As Hutchings later reminisced, he had written *The Miner's Ten Commandments* for a strictly political reason, in support of a Sunday closing law.[95] At the time *The Ten Commandments* were first published, Hutchings may have assumed that because Jews observed a different Sabbath day from Christians, they were necessarily opposed to a closing law, and thus they served as the objects of his derision. That Jewish merchants, too, petitioned for just such a law evidently was not considered very important by Hutchings or may not even have been known by him. However, in 1887, a later edition of the *Commandments* was purged of its anti-Jewish content. The reference to Jews was deleted and in its place was inserted, "the tailor and cheap-john huckster, the gamblers and buccaneers."[96]

In 1855 and 1856, a number of Jewish merchants in a remote section of Tuolumne county were identified as Jews on the county assessment rolls, although the individual responsible as well as the motivation is not known. In 1855, Stamper and Jacobs of Big Oak Flat and Garotte were assessed as "Jews B. O. and Garote [*sic*]," and Isaac Gilbert of Jacksonville was recorded as being a "Jew Merchant."[97] The next year, Stamper and Jacobs and Gilbert as well as J. Kaufman of Shaw's Flat and E. Block of Don Pedros [Bar] were identified by their religion.[98] Why the religion of these five merchants was included on the annual assessment of their property is a mystery. Perhaps the county assessor at that time, or his deputy, disliked them as individuals. This is the likely answer, because a scandal would have been sure to arise had the assessor not liked Jews in general and identified as Jews all sixty-four Jews assessed on the county assessment roll for 1855 or the seventy in 1856. In later years, no other Jews were identified by their religion on the county assessment rolls. Nothing is known of the few merchants so identified, except that they were Jewish and the amounts of property by which their annual assessment was reckoned. And the Jews were the only group identified in these records by their religion.

These few public references to Jews are the only ones known. The comparatively slight anti-Semitism in the period of the gold rush and immediately thereafter indicates that each individual was usually judged on his merits. The same is true today, with the grandchildren and great-grandchildren of the original settlers treating the subject of Jews in the same way as their forebears. Third- and fourth-generation Mother Lode descendants recall with admiration the important role played by the Jewish merchants in their town and the pleasant way in which their families mingled socially with the Jewish families.[99] The absence of overt anti-Semitism in the region of the Mother Lode and Northern Mines thus endures to the present day and is proved further by the continued existence of the six Jewish cemeteries through the twentieth century. Because the Jewish communities disbanded many years ago, the cemeteries became neglected, but the vandalism that occurred therein was the work not of anti-Semites but of common thieves, intent upon stealing gravestones from any convenient cemetery with which to line their patios.

That the Jews were highly regarded in their communities is suggested by the many sites named for early Jewish settlers and their descendants. In Sonora are Linoberg Street, named for Emanuel Linoberg, one of the first settlers, and Toby Street, named after the late city attorney, Tobias M. Wilzinski, a descendant of early Jewish merchants in Sonora and Virginia City, Nevada. Public fountains in Placerville and San Andreas, donated by descendants of merchants, memorialize Max Baer, a city trustee (councilman) in 1918–26, and an early merchant, Arnold Friedberger, and his wife, Lotta, respectively. Also in Placerville may be found Coon Hollow Road, the name being a corruption of the name Kohn, and named for Jacob Kohn,[100] who was buried in the Placerville Jewish cemetery; Goldner Street, which intersects the property of an early merchant and farmer, Julius Goldner; and Simon Drive, named after Albert Simon, a third-generation Jewish resident of Placerville and mayor of that city in 1924–28.

Snows Road, located about nine miles east of Placerville, is named for the family of Samuel Sussman Snow, who farmed in the immediate area,[101] and Marks Avenue in Fresno was named for Bernhard Marks, a gold rush pioneer who settled in Fresno.[102]

The Jews in the newly discovered gold fields of California aided not only in the establishment and maintenance of economic ties to the rest of the world, but also helped bring to this region the comforts of civilization, the establishment of law and order, and those after-hours social activities that worked to fuse the many foreign peoples together into the one American nation. Because of these contributions, the Jews, from the beginning, were part of the everyday life of the gold rush. They welcomed the chance to be of service, and their efforts were appreciated. They were participants as Americans, as Jews, and as merchants. They were like all the other groups, striving for acceptance in the community and participating in civic affairs, in the belief that it was a necessity for a merchant to do so. And the majority of these Jews were but one generation removed from the oppression and civil disabilities of the ghetto; their activities may thus also be partly explained as the fulfillment of their assimilation into American society and the American dream of equal rights and opportunities for all.[103]

·6·

JEWS AND JUDAISM

One of the most important characteristics of the Jewish immigrants to the United States in the middle of the nineteenth century was their mobility. Jews were found all over the United States only a short time after their arrival. "The appearance of a German-Jewish peddler at a frontier point made it easier for civilization to triumph over savagery.... Dozens of communities throughout the United States owe their establishment to the German Jews."[1]

These thousands of post-emancipation pilgrims had two important considerations in mind when they came to America. They would first find an occupation for themselves and, once employed, they would begin to save money for the passage of close relatives to America. They also assumed another task: at the season of the High Holidays, they sought out other Jews and established a Jewish community.[2] These adventurers regarded themselves as members of a religious association and not necessarily as a people under the discipline of their European Jewish communities. They were well aware of the reason that had compelled them to come to California: like everyone else, they wanted to become rich as quickly as possible from the gold economy. Being the most adventurous of their people, and realizing there was no future for them in Europe, they came to the western United States. In all likelihood, they would have gone anywhere else in the world to escape from Europe. The number of new Jewish communities established at this time throughout the world attests to the peripatetic qualities of the Jews.

They were not Orthodox in their religious practices; at best, they had a sentimental feeling about preserving their Judaism and not a day-to-day preoccupation. Once they became accustomed to the cultural shock of the California gold rush, where people of many backgrounds mingled, they chose the path toward complete assimilation with the dominant white, American, and northern European community and kept their Judaic practices in the background. In all probability, they would have done so wherever else in the world they settled. That they chose to come to California made this particular region the beneficiary of a kind of Judaism that was balanced somewhere between a faint appreciation for an Old World past and a present that demanded full political, social, and cultural assimilation in order for one to succeed economically. And in this new American territory, Jews voluntarily sought out their brethren and formed congregations, cemetery and benevolent societies, in part to establish their religious associations and because, as yet, they were neither so well assimilated as to abandon their Jewishness nor consciously disposed toward such an act.[3]

The Jews in the gold rush were accepted as citizens of the towns in which they lived on an equal footing with other northern and central European immigrants of the same period, and, more importantly, with the native-born Americans of the Christian faith. If there was any significant difference between the Jews in the gold rush and those in other parts of the United States, it was that those in the gold rush mingled well from the first with all the various groups and that the "melting pot" of the Mother Lode took on the characteristics of a pressure cooker. The Jews who represented many different nationalities and customs of worship not only became Americans in the process but also formed local religious communities and resolved their ritual differences among themselves amicably. Had they not done so, the result would have been fragmentation and the lack of a *minyan*.

The formation of Jewish communities and the religious services that these immigrants conducted were announced with great fanfare around the world. If Jews had succeeded in practicing their faith through centuries of government-ordained persecutions in the pre-emancipation period, it was obvious that they would worship openly whenever the law allowed. To the Jew, community worship, conducted in a public hall, after previous announcement in the local newspaper to the largely Gentile population, was his way of announcing his emancipation from his fettered past and his attainment of a level of citizenship on a par with the rest of the community. He was commanded to pray three times a day wherever he was. He could pray alone, but worshipping with a *minyan* of friends was of greater personal significance to him. And although the once- or twice-a-year services that were conducted by these immigrants in small towns throughout the West did not follow any strict code of procedure, they still represented the desire to maintain a relationship, if only tangential and sentimental, with the ancestral faith they had left behind them in Europe.

Regardless of a Jew's place of origin or intended destination in the gold rush, his first port of call in California was likely to be San Francisco. This city, a sleepy village since 1776, underwent a phenomenal growth during the years of the gold rush. One had to spend some time in San Francisco before heading for the centers of gold discovery, if only to wait for a suitable means of transportation. From the beginning, some men, such as Levi Strauss and others, were attracted to San Francisco and preferred to remain there and find an occupation. Several firms that would soon supply retail merchants in the mining camps with their goods were thus established.[4] Rabbi Jacob Voorsanger has suggested that two separate divine services were held for Yom Kippur (September 26) 1849.[5] The reason for the two services was not a lack of one large meeting place, but that the migration had brought large numbers of Germans and Poles, whose forms of worship differed. The German *minyan* eventually became Congregation Emanu-El, and those who worshipped according to the Polish *minhag* founded Congregation Sherith Israel.[6] Other organizations were also established. The [First] Hebrew [or Jewish] Benevolent Society was organized in 1849 or January 1850, by the English and Poles,[7] and the Eureka Benevolent Society was organized in September or on October 2, 1850 by the group that founded Congregation Emanu-El. Both organizations had as their purpose the care of the sick and the indigent and the burial of the dead. Thus, the Jew who arrived in San Francisco from the earliest days of the gold rush could feel comfortable in the knowledge that some co-religionists had preceded him to California and had already organized a Jewish community. The fact that a Jewish community could be organized in a region that was unpopulated by Jews only a short time before gave confidence to the Jews who left for the gold fields that Jewish organizations could be established even in remote mountain settlements.

There are scattered secondary reports of early High Holiday services being conducted in the Mother Lode and Northern Mines. *The California Hebrew & English Almanac for the Year 5612* [1851–52] stated, with regard to Marysville and Sonora, "These towns also contain temporary synagoges [sic], to meet the requirements of the communities at the holydays."[8]

The *Miners & Business Men's Directory. For the Year Commencing January 1st 1856* . . . noted the Jewish community in Sonora: "The Israelites have held regular meetings since September, 1851, although as yet they have no synagogue erected."[9]

The federal census for Sonora for 1850, taken May 5–30, 1851, listed twenty-nine males who are believed to have been Jewish (among them being twenty-seven merchants, one tailor, and one miner), so probably High Holiday services were conducted there in the fall of 1851, and perhaps even in the fall of 1850.[10]

A book that historians have learned to use with a great deal of caution, owing to the fact that none of the material contained in it is documented, records a tradition regarding early Jewish services in Columbia, four miles north of Sonora. The author was apparently referring to the year 1854 when she wrote that "the Jewish Synagogue, a two-story building, the upper floor of which was used as a lodge room by the I.O.O.F., was situated on Jackson Street, near the corner of Broadway. This structure was destroyed in the fire of August, 1857."[11]

The earliest known record of a Jewish religious observance in Columbia appeared October 15, 1853: "We noticed that the stores of our Jewish population were closed on Tuesday evening on the occasion of the Feast of Pentecost."[12]

A further indication of services in Columbia is in the minutes of the Columbia Masonic Lodge:

>   1855—September 6, Isaac Levy asked permission to use Hall on occasion of Jewish Festival. Granted.
>   October 4, Levy tendered thanks on behalf of the Hebrew Association for use of Hall.
>   1859—August 4, Jewish fraternity granted use of Hall 28th and 29th instant [sic, i.e., proximo].[13]

The other early mining camp best remembered as the scene of early Jewish services was Coloma, where James Marshall made his famous discovery of gold. The *Asmonean*, an early American Jewish periodical published in New York, referred to this service: "We also learn that there was Synagogue service at Colluma [sic], on the Yuba River, at which all the Hebrews in that section were present."[14] Presumably, the article referred to the High Holidays that had occurred early in September 1850.

The *Jewish Calendar For Fifty Years . . .* by Jacques J. Lyons and Abraham DeSola also mentioned the *minyan* of 1850 at Coloma: "COLLUMA [sic], (California, on the Yuba River.) Organized Congregation, 5610 [sic, i.e., 5611]—1850."[15]

The federal census for 1850, for the town of Coloma and vicinity, which was compiled November 8–15, 1850, just two months following Rosh Hashanah, included only one Jew, Leopold Heilbronn.[16] If a service actually took place, Heilbronn must have sought out at least nine others from neighboring towns and mining camps. Probably he did so, because the news of the service was transmitted to Jewish periodicals three thousand miles away. Because Coloma was the site of Sutter's sawmill, where gold was originally discovered in 1848, it became an important trading center in the early days of the gold rush. Perhaps the remainder of the High Holiday *minyan* of 1850 were merchants on their way from the bay with goods for sale in remote mining camps.

A remarkable fact about the "mining congregations" of this region is the lack of attention given to them in the local newspapers that have been preserved. This is unusual, because the Jews of any given town or mining camp would have wanted to advertise as widely as possible that services were to be held, so that a *minyan* would be guaranteed for the duration of the services. These gatherings were an excellent time for immigrant Jews to meet their fellow merchants from nearby communities, to discuss their mutual problems, perhaps to form partnerships, and, most important, to search out a *landsman* for information on one's birthplace and family. The earliest extant notice concerning High Holiday worship in the gold rush press appeared in the Nevada City *Nevada Journal,* September 17, 1852.

> Notice. The Israelites of Nevada [City], hereby present their sincere thanks to the officers and members of Nevada Lodge No. 13, of F. & A. Masons, for extending to them the free use of their Hall, to conduct their religious ceremonies. By Order of Committee.
> A. Rosenheim, I. Grauman, L. Heilbronn.[17]

The services in Nevada City in 1852 commanded nationwide attention.

> Nevada City, California.—We have before us from one of our subscribers, a letter, which states that on the Rosh-hashana and Yom Kippur last, the Israelites of Nevada City met for worship in the Masonic Hall, which had been gratuitously placed at their command by the fraternity, who had learned that a committee of Israelites had been appointed to obtain a suitable room for a

temporary place of worship. The hall was appropriately furnished, and was crowded with visitors, consisting in part of the first citizens of the place, judges of the courts, &c., who were anxious to witness our ceremonies, and they expressed themselves satisfied with the mode of worship which they witnessed for the first time. Mr. [H.] Leo, a brother of the Rev. Ansel Leo of New York, acted as Hazan, and was assisted by several others.[18]

The Lyons and DeSola calendar also noted this service.

NEVADA CITY, (California.)
First assembly for Worship was on Rosh Shana [sic] 5613–1852 held in the Masonic Hall. Acting Hazan on the occasion Mr. H. Leo. The Number of Israelites in the city in 5613 was Thirty.[19]

The only other early advertisement of High Holiday services came from Placerville. The first service there apparently occurred in 1852.

Holiday.—Our Israelite citizens observed one of their holidays [Yom Kippur] in this place, by closing their places of business, from 5 o'clock, P. M. on Wednesday, to 5 o'clock, P. M. on Thursday; also, by fasting &c.[20]

The absence of advertising for the early worship services may be explained in many ways. There may already have been ten or more adult Jewish males in one town, or on the same street of one town, or even on the same side of one street, so that it was not difficult to arrange for such a meeting. Word of mouth sufficed, especially if time was drawing short and the only Jewish calendar in town was not consulted regularly for the dates of the approaching holidays. Moreover, society in the mines had not yet reached the sophisticated level of formal organization. Congregations and Hebrew benevolent societies would not be formed in most cities until about 1855 or after. In addition, there was not, as yet, any pressing need to organize a Jewish religious society. Most of the merchants were ummarried and in good health. The usual problems of a more settled situation, such as the education of the children or the burial of the dead, were not present here. When Solomon Friedlander died in Sonora, in 1851, his remains were taken to the newly established Jewish cemetery in Stockton, and he is the first person known to be interred there.[21]

The Jewish population of the Mother Lode increased as the tide of Jewish immigration to California continued. Early in 1850, the New York *Asmonean* noted:

> CALIFORNIA.—The cry is still en avant. The Cherokee steamer which left our port on Thursday last took amidst its crowd of passengers a large number of Israelites. We do not recollect in our experience the departure of any vessel when we saw the quay so lined with members of the faith, each hurrying and crowding to join in the heartstirring shout with which many thousand spectators hailed the casting off of the steamer, seeking thereby to cheer the dispirited and incite the hardy on their bold adventure. We endeavored to obtain a list of the departed Hebrews, but found it impossible to make it correct or complete.[22]

The London *Jewish Chronicle* also published articles concerning immigration to California. From articles such as these many Jews in Europe learned that Orthodox Judaism would be practiced in California.

> Departure of Jews for California.—A private letter received per last packet from the United States gives the information that a party of Jews have left New York to settle and form a congregation in California, taking with them a . . . slayer of cattle . . . and a . . . scroll of the law.[23]

Two years later, a ship departed from Europe bound for California that also carried many Orthodox Jewish passengers.

> Jews Leave Havre for San Francisco.
> A ship recently left here for California with many Jews as passengers. They had with them a Chazan, Shochet, Mohel, two Sepherim [sic], all the accoutrements of Judaism.[24]

Jews and Judaism

From the earliest days of settlement in the mining camps and towns of the gold rush, the Jews were an easily identified group. Reference has already been made to the derogatory manner in which some contemporary reporters pictured them. Most of the Jews, recent arrivals in the United States, spoke with a recognizable accent, and the overwhelming majority of them made their living from the various branches of the clothing industry. They were thus known by their religion and occupation to the rest of the community as well as to each other. It was, therefore, not difficult to pass the word that a holiday was approaching and that it ought to be observed with appropriate celebration or solemnity.

The local newspaper editors in the Mother Lode did their part, possibly unconsciously, to preserve the separate identity of their Jewish readers and advertisers and to promote the advancement of Judaism and Jewish learning. Hardly a month went by without at least one or two articles or brief items concerning Jews, past and present, anywhere in the world, in every local newspaper. Usually, these items discussed Judaism in the biblical period, contemporary conditions in Palestine, and the latest accomplishments of the fabulous banking family, the Rothschilds. The number of these items, as well as their accuracy, increased in 1856 and 1857, when the *Voice of Israel,* edited by the Rev. Herman Bien and H. J. Labatt, and Rabbi Julius Eckman's newspaper, the *Weekly Gleaner,* began publishing in San Francisco and were distributed in the Mother Lode country.

Editors had occasional moments of tongue-in-cheek humor. From Nevada City, we learn:

> It it [sic] is stated in an eastern paper that a couple of Mormon apostles set out upon a tour with a Jew upon the plains a short time ago, and that the Jew was afterwards found murdered, with a bloody ax at his side. We understand that the weapon was recognized as the ax of the Apostles.[25]

Perhaps with a view of presenting another side to the

then-current debate concerning a Sunday closing law in California, readers in Nevada City were informed of an interesting occurrence in Boston.

> A Jew Legally Protected.—In the Police Court, Abraham Harris was charged with violating the Sabbath by working at his trade as a tailor.
> He proved, however, that he kept Saturday as the Sabbath, and attended the Jewish Synagogue, and was discharged by the Court.—(Boston Transcript)[26]

On occasion, Jews were referred to as potential converts to Christianity. The Jackson *Weekly Ledger* reprinted a poem, "The Jewish Maiden's Lament," from *The Lady's Book,* which spoke of the unhappiness of a Jewish maiden because she could not join in the joy of the Christian Sabbath. The seventh and final verse stated:

> Thus in wild and bitter anguish
> Bowed the Jewish maiden fair.
> Oh, our Savior pure and holy.
> Listen to the maiden's prayer!
> Guide her to the Christian temple,
> The Messiah waits her there![27]

There is no evidence that articles such as these were ever attacked by local Jews in letters to the editor.

There is only one known instance of a newspaper in the mining region printing attacks on Jews or the Jewish community.[28] On the contrary, items such as the following were likely to appear:

> American Jews.—The *S. F. Sun,* in a very sensible article upon the present condition of Jews, closes with the following paragraph:
> His respect for our laws is shown in the fact that he never violates them. His wealth has gone towards building up and enriching our cities. He cultivates the arts, and goes heart and soul with our active citizens in every useful enterprise. He quarrels but little;

heads a mob—never. You will find him in our courts of Justice, on the Bench, at the Bar, in the Jury box, but seldom ever arraigned for a henious [sic] crimanl [sic] offence. This is the American Jew. Let his good qualities be imitated—his bad ones should be forgotten.[29]

Having noted once before that the Jewish merchants in the gold rush were an easily identified group owing to the fact that their speech was accented, it is worthwhile to recall an editor's indignation when such a Jewish merchant, Simon Rosentorff of Nevada City, was taunted in public for his broken English.[30] Rosentorff accused Francis Barlow in justice's court of stealing $400 from his store while he was away visiting his brother. At the conclusion of the news item that reported the testimony that was presented at the preliminary hearing, the editor wrote:

> We take this opportunity to remark that it is a shame that some of the people who crowd the Court House on such an occasion should insult by jeers or laughter anybody, whether Jew or barbarian, who seeks redress or justice, because his pronunciation of English may be imperfect. Especially is this the case in this city, where many of our best citizens and merchants are Hebrews—men honest, peaceable and liberal, and good citizens in every sense of the term. Such men should be respected, and most especially in the temple of justice, whose doors should never be obstructed.[31]

Thus, Jews were acknowledged in the most important news media of the day both as a recognizable and valued group and as individuals, especially when editors noted the arrival of new stocks of goods at a store.

Following a year or two of gathering to worship on stated occasions, the next need facing these religious communities was the establishment of a place to bury their dead and the organization of a benevolent society to provide for the material needs of the survivors. Buying land for a cemetery before building a synagogue was typical of Jewish communities all over the country at this time. For worship, a bare room or lodge hall sufficed. In Jackson and Placerville, the only two towns of the Mother Lode that had synagogues, the Jewish cemeteries were one and seven years older, respectively, than the synagogue buildings.[32]

The maintenance of a separate, consecrated plot of earth for burial purposes is a Jewish preoccupation dating to the desire of the patriarch Abraham to bury his wife Sarah in a private place. Rabbis later established rules for cemeteries.[33] By 1855, Jewish merchants were moving to the towns of the gold rush as married men. The epidemics that raged at the time were indiscriminate. And it was too expensive to transport corpses to Stockton, San Francisco, or Sacramento for burial.

Usually, a group of men, acting on behalf of the community or as trustees of an organization, purchased land for a cemetery. In some cases, the community never bothered to record the deed transferring title to such land; in other cases, the deed was not recorded until several years after the transaction, following the grant of an entire city from the United States to the municipal government in the early 1870s. It is also extremely difficult to determine when a cemetery in the region of the gold rush was founded, because someone who died in the mountains may have been buried in a family plot in a Jewish cemetery in Sacramento, Stockton, or San Francisco; or vandals may have stolen gravestones, leaving old graves unmarked.

Six Jewish cemeteries in the region of the Mother Lode and Northern Mines are known today. They are in Sonora, Mokelumne Hill, Jackson, Placerville, Grass Valley, and Nevada City.[34] Other cemeteries or separate Jewish sections of cemeteries in other cities in the region, if they ever existed, have not been located. There are, however, graves of individual Jews or Jewish families in general cemeteries, such as the Barlow and Wilzinski families in Sonora and Block in Nevada City.

The Jewish cemeteries of the Mother Lode served larger geographical regions than the cities in which they were located and included burials from towns without such cemeteries. Five members of the Morris family of Chinese Camp, James and his wife, Pauline, two sons, George and Henry, and a granddaughter, Pauline, daughter of Saul and Minnie Morris, were buried in Sonora. David Danielewicz, who was born at Mokelumne Hill and died at Sutter Creek at the age of eleven years, was buried in Jackson. Rachel Haines was also buried in Jackson, in the Goldner family plot, although she died in El Dorado, twenty-four miles to the north. The remains of Isaac Lurch, who died in Lancha Plana, December 28, 1859, were interred in the Jewish cemetery in Mokelumne Hill. The oldest known grave in Placerville is that of the merchant Marcus Abraham, who died October 11, 1856, in Grizzly Flat, about eighteen miles away. In Placerville also is the grave of Ernestein Cahn of Diamond Springs, but there is no other information on the gravestone.

At least two burials in Mother Lode Jewish cemeteries are known where the death occurred out of the state and interment was made in the Mother Lode to maintain a family plot. Bertha Strouse (or Strauss) died in Virginia City, Nevada, December 24, 1875, and was buried in Mokelumne Hill next to two of her sons. Melanie Reeb died in Spokane, Washington, April 13, 1912; her remains were taken to Sonora for burial next to her husband, Moses, who had died June 9, 1891.

The establishment of Jewish cemeteries was the first task of the Jewish organizations in the gold rush country. Until cemeteries were established, the Jewish religious community in any given area was merely a group of merchants engaging in prayer.

No matter how far removed from the Jewish community a man had been during his lifetime, he usually exhibited, during his final illness, an interest in burial in a Jewish cemetery. In addition, the cemetery was the one sign of coercion in the Jewish community. I. J. Benjamin told of two brothers, merchants in Mokelumne Hill, who refused to contribute toward the purchase of land for the cemetery and were later denied permission by the community to bury a son of one of the brothers.[35] Benjamin frequently pointed out that little was being done to preserve Judaism in the towns and cities of the West that he visited. His caustic comments, however, were generally tempered by a report of the Jewish religious activities that took place in these towns.

> In most places in California, if any Israelites live there at all, their first care is to provide themselves with a cemetery. No matter how indifferent and cold in many places our fellow Jews are towards their religion, nevertheless they are never so completely estranged from all religious feeling that it is a matter of total indifference to them where they bury their dead. And so in this town, too [Mokelumne Hill], the Jews have a place provided with an enclosure and set aside as a place of eternal rest.[36]

The coercive aspect of the maintenance of Jewish cemeteries was also noted in Sonora. The only Jewish organization that existed there after the turn of the century was primarily social in nature, but it also maintained the cemetery for future use and charged membership dues.[37]

Shortly after the establishment of the cemeteries, congregations or Hebrew benevolent societies were founded to care for the cemeteries, to dispense charity locally and elsewhere, and, perhaps, to provide social activities.[38] The organizations were known by different names in different cities and fulfilled many more functions than their names indicated. In some cities, the same organization apparently changed its name several times in its history. The first recorded name of a Jewish society in Sonora was the Hebrew Congregation of Sonora. This name was used only once, on a Hebrew marriage contract that was filed for record with the county recorder in 1855.[39] This organization was a congregation without a synagogue as services were always conducted in rented halls or private homes. In 1856, the Sonora Hebrew Benevolent Society was organized.[40] In 1859 or 1860, Jews from Columbia joined the society, and it was known thereafter as the Sonora and Columbia Hebrew Benevolent Society.

The founding of the Hebrew Benevolent Society in Sonora was noted in local newspapers and in the national Jewish press as well. The Philadelphia *Occident* noted in 1856:

Sonora, California.—The Israelites residing in Sonora have formed themselves into a Benevolent Society.... The Columbia Gazette says: "We are glad to learn that the society of our Jewish fellow-citizens is in a flourishing condition. An improved enclosure is in progress of construction around their burial-ground, and other objects of interest to them are receiving attention. Many excellent citizens of our county belong to the ancient faith, from which we ourselves draw so many good precepts. They are a thrifty, peaceable, law-abiding people, always able to take care of themselves, never appealing to others for aid or assistance, and making a dollar where we could not find a dime. Through all the ignorant prejudice that unfortunately still lingers toward them, they are now fast claiming, through their merits as good men, the respect and regard of all enlightened people. We offer our good wishes for the continued success of the Hebrew Benevolent Society in its mission of charity and good will."[41]

There were also Jewish organizations in other cities. From the middle 1850s, there were separate Jewish communities in Grass Valley and Nevada City, which are only four miles apart. The two towns maintained separate Jewish communities through their support of Hebrew benevolent societies and local branches of rival Jewish fraternal organizations, Garizim Lodge No. 43 of the Independent Order of B'nai B'rith in Grass Valley, and North Star Lodge No. 12 of the Ancient Jewish Order Kesher Shel Barzel in Nevada City. One explanation for the presence of two separate organizations in Grass Valley may be that Grass Valley had the largest number of Jewish bachelors of any city in the region. In 1860, Benjamin noted that only twelve of the thirty Jews in town were married.[42] Five years later, nineteen of the thirty-six Jews enumerated in the Grass Valley directory stated that they boarded at restaurants or hotels or with other families.[43] Since their time was their own after business hours, they probably welcomed the presence of two Jewish organizations. At the same time, they sought out the other organizations in town and joined them, too. They may even have constructed a synagogue building at School and Neal Streets, where they owned land since 1861. Many contemporary periodicals referred to a synagogue there.[44]

The Nevada Hebrew Society was founded in Nevada City in August 1854 and was followed in 1868 by the Eureka Social Club. The latter organization was formed "for social and amusement purposes."[45] Its activities consisted largely of dances, which were held several times a year. There were probably some Gentile members in this organization. The San Francisco *Hebrew*'s Nevada City correspondent, "Sinbad," implied this in one of his letters concerning the organization's activities.

> There is probably not another town in California, aside from San Francisco and Sacramento, where the Hebrew element exercises a greater influence than they do in Nevada City. The Eureka Social Club, which has been organized nearly a year and is controlled by Israelites, has had much to do in increasing this influence, and, socially speaking, has done much to harmonize society. The Club gave one masquerade ball last winter, and a subscription dance ball on Thanksgiving evening, both of which were highly successful and the latter particularly surpassed anything of the kind ever before witnessed in this city.[46]

In Jackson and Placerville, the Jewish communities were so affluent that they created synagogue buildings. The only Jewish organization in Jackson was the congregation, which was variously known as Beth Israel and B'nai Israel. No references to a Hebrew benevolent society have been located; the synagogue probably handled matters involving the distribution of charity. On the other hand, a Hebrew benevolent society antedated the congregation in Placerville by seven years and was also the titleholder of the synagogue.[47] When the community decided, in 1903, to sell the land upon which the second synagogue in town stood, Michael Simon acted as surviving trustee of the Hebrew Benevolent Society to negotiate the sale.[48]

In Jackson, the idea of a permanent synagogue, administered by an established congregation, was apparently in the minds of the leaders of the community from the very earliest days. The first High Holiday advertisement in Jackson, in 1856, employed the words synagogue and congregation in the announcement of the services:

> Notice.
> We the Hebrew congregation of Jackson, take this method of notifying our Hebrew brethren, that a Synagogue will be held, in this place on the 30th of September, and on the 1st day of October,—that being their regular New Years day.
> By the order of   JOHN LEVINSKY, Pres't.
> S. Sanders, Sec'y.[49]

The only Jewish organization in Mokelumne Hill was the Hebrew Benevolent Society. This organization was formed in December 1860 at the request of I. J. Benjamin following the establishment of the cemetery there.[50] This society was only short lived, however, as can be seen from a letter in the San Francisco *Hebrew Observer* in 1867 concerning a newly organized Mokelumne Hill Hebrew Benevolent Society: "Such a Society was long needed here, and are all [sic] glad that one has finally come into life."[51]

Only one document has been preserved that describes a small Jewish organization composed of merchants from the neighboring towns of Diamond Springs and El Dorado, located two and four miles from Placerville, respectively. I. J. Benjamin visited these towns in 1860 and found in Diamond Springs six Jewish families, a total of thirty-two individuals, including brothers and sisters of Daniel Levy, a cantor and writer in San Francisco. On November 19, 1865, the Jews of these two communities gathered,

> at the village of El Dorado for the purpose of forming a Cemetery Association at which Meeting was present E[manuel] Berg, M[arks] Lasky, E. Levy, A[braham] Haines, G. Lippman, M. Levy and Nathan Rhine. The Meeting was organized by appointing E. Berg Chairman and Nathan Rhine Secty.
> It was then determined that the Association should be Known and Styled the Shaurey Shomagin [sic].[52]

Apparently, the first Jewish resident of El Dorado to die was Rachel Haines, on April 12, 1868. Her remains were taken to Jackson for interment in the Goldner family plot of the Jewish cemetery in Jackson, because she was a sister of Mrs. Herman Goldner.[53] However, this group eventually established a cemetery on a small hill near present-day Patterson Drive between the two villages. It is generally believed that the bodies buried there were disinterred for reburial in San Francisco sometime before 1900.[54] But the reasons for the founding of the Shaurey Shomagin Cemetery Association are unknown and remain a mystery, especially when the proximity of this community to Placerville is considered. A synagogue and cemetery were located in Placerville for many years before the Jews of Diamond Springs and El Dorado formed their association. Perhaps these merchants desired to maintain the same kind of spirit of independence that occasioned the existence of separate Jewish organizations in Grass Valley and Nevada City, which were only four miles from each other.

One of these benevolent societies became affiliated with a national organization when the Placerville Hebrew Benevolent Society elected Aaron Kahn as its representative to the Board of Delegates of American Israelites in 1865.[55]

An important activity that the Jewish organizations in the gold rush country engaged in was charity. The charitable activities of the congregations and Hebrew benevolent societies in this area were many, and the degree of their benevolence was no less than that of Jewish organizations in other parts of the country. Characteristically, much of the charity given by the Jews of the Mother Lode was made with no fanfare; only a few of these contributions were noted in the local newspapers. That the majority of these contributions were printed in regional and national Jewish newspapers suggests that the Jews of the gold rush subscribed to these papers, were aware of conditions affecting Jews all over the world, and were always ready to aid their brethren in distress. The Jewish merchants were among the wealthiest men in the region, and their great incomes permitted generous contributions. No evidence has been located to suggest that any element of coercion was involved in the collecting of funds for these local and national charities. Contributions to Jewish charities from the Mother Lode were nevertheless great throughout the entire period, 1850–80.

The concept of Jewish philanthropy is a very ancient one. Jews have always maintained local charities wherever they have lived, and they have aided charities in areas far from their homes. Jews in the gold rush country contributed to charity because they considered it a righteous act. They were sensitive about the persecution of Jews all over the world and recalled that they, too, were formerly numbered among the persecuted. And they used a direct form of charity, the total amount of which can never be known, to aid their families in Europe and pay for the passage to America of close relatives.

The Jews of San Francisco knew that other Jews were living nearby and appealed to them for contributions. When Congregation Sherith Israel began a campaign in July 1852 to raise funds for the construction of a synagogue, letters were sent to Jews in Marysville, Stockton, and Sonora, asking them for contributions.[56] Similarly, when "the Israelites of this City," the organization that became Congregation Emanu-El of San Francisco, met March 30, 1851 to plan for the construction of a synagogue building, a report was read from the solicitation committee in Stockton concerning the raising of funds from the interior.[57]

A report of Jewish philanthropy from the mountains in 1860 noted the participation of the Sonora and Columbia Hebrew Benevolent Society.

> ... At a special meeting of the Sonora and Columbia Hebrew Benevolent Society, held at Sonora on the 24th of January, for the purpose of taking into consideration what assistance could be extended to the suffering Israelites now at Gibraltar, the circular letter from the Board of Delegates [of American Israelites] was read and resolutions were adopted that the sum of one hundred dollars be paid from the treasury of the Society for the relief of the Morocco refugees, that special collections be taken up from the

members and others who may be disposed to assist in the charitable cause, and that the amount so collected be sent to the President of the Board of Delegates. Mr. Newstadt, the Presiding officer of the Society, accordingly transmitted the sum of $210.50 to Mr. Hart—this being the first contribution received from California.[58]

Additional contributions from Jewish communities of the region for the Morocco Relief Fund included: Nevada City, $175; Jackson, $62; Sutter Creek, $14; Camptonville, $28; Allighanytown, $25; Hornitos, $20; La Grange, $20; Fiddletown, $15.50; and Auburn, $5.[59]

In 1868, Rabbi Julius Eckman of San Francisco headed the drive for contributions to the Famine Fund, for the benefit of Jews in Eastern Prussia, Poland, and Russia. The San Francisco *Hebrew Observer* reported $227.50 in donations from six contributors in the Mother Lode.[60]

Money for charitable causes was in the treasury of organizations such as Garizim Lodge No. 43 of the Independent Order of B'nai B'rith in Grass Valley (chartered October 6, 1861) and North Star Lodge No. 12 and its women's auxiliary, Sarah Lodge No. 4, of the Ancient Jewish Order Kesher Shel Barzel in Nevada City (chartered May 1873). Garizim Lodge No. 43 was the fourth lodge of B'nai B'rith to be chartered in District Four, the eight western states and British Columbia. The lodge was one of the four charter lodges of District Grand Lodge No. 4, which was established in San Francisco, March 29, 1863. The range in membership of Garizim was forty-three in 1867 and twenty-seven in 1865. The treasury of the lodge stood at $404.29 in 1864 but rose to $2,787.78 in 1877. Throughout the period, Garizim Lodge was active in charitable endeavors. It maintained separate funds for distribution to widows and orphans (in 1874 and 1876, the lodge aided two orphans and eleven widows), to the indigent, to members as sick benefits, to nonmembers as direct donations, and for endowments, burial expenses, and the maintenance of the Grand Lodge. The Grand Lodge noted, in the annual reports for 1893 and 1896, that Garizim was the only lodge in the District to own its own cemetery, valued in 1896 at $1,000.

The generosity of the lodge was noted on a number of occasions both in the local press and in national Jewish periodicals. In 1866, Garizim contributed $100 to the B'nai B'rith Palestine Relief Fund.[61] Four years later, the lodge pledged $1,000 to aid the newly established Pacific Hebrew Orphan Asylum and Home Society in San Francisco.[62] In 1871, Garizim Lodge donated $100 to their brethren in B'nai B'rith in Chicago, sufferers from the great fire. In 1879, Rabbi Aron J. Messing of Congregation Beth Israel of San Francisco came to Grass Valley and asked the lodge for a donation for the construction of a new synagogue and religious school. The lodge donated $25, and several individual members pledged donations as well. Because of a lack of members residing in the immediate area, the lodge was ordered suspended by the Grand Lodge on July 12, 1903.[63]

The lodge of Kesher Shel Barzel in Nevada City was similar to B'nai B'rith in that it was nationwide and dispensed benefits to members and their families as well as charity to distant causes. In 1878, the lodge contributed $25 "for aid for the suffering brethren and co-religionists of the South."[64] Residents of Grass Valley also joined this organization. The lodge conducted elections in 1878,[65] but, owing to the declining population, disbanded shortly thereafter.

The Jewish organizations in the region of the gold rush also came to the aid of visiting Jews and itinerant collectors. I. J. Benjamin indicated in 1860 that he received hospitality and money to continue his world travels from the Jewish communities of Diamond Springs, Nevada City, and Folsom.[66] While in Nevada City, Benjamin noted: "this society is very friendly and helpful to strangers and travelers: I know this from my own experience."[67]

A few years after Benjamin traveled through the gold-rush country, another prominent Jewish visitor came to this famous region. The San Francisco *Hebrew* reprinted an article on his visit in 1868 from the Marysville *Appeal*.

> MARYSVILLE.—Rabbi Nathan Watkin [*sic*, i.e., Notkin], from Jerusalem, visited this city on Tuesday and Wednesday, as accredital [*sic*] Messenger to the Continent of America to gather contributions from the Israelites for the relief of their suffering brethren in the Holy Land. He is accredited from six different Congregations at Jerusalem; also the American Consul-General at that city, and the great English philanthropist, Sir Moses Montefiore. The Marysville Hebrew Benevolent Society, as well as individual members, contributed liberally to the distinguished Rabbi's benevolent object. He paid a visit to his people in Oroville, February 7th, intending to return and go to Grass Valley and Nevada [City], where he will undoubtedly be liberally received.—*Appeal.*[68]

The Nevada City papers informed their readers of Notkin's impending visit, for the above article was reprinted in the *Nevada Weekly Gazette* on February 24 and the *Nevada Daily Gazette* on February 19. But Notkin's journey to the Northern Mines was not very successful. He collected only $10 in Nevada City and $18.50 in Grass Valley.[69] The small contribution might perhaps be explained by the fact that the Jews of these two cities were already supporting several charitable societies.

The congregations and Hebrew benevolent societies usually raised money by direct solicitation among the members. When the Placerville Hebrew Benevolent Society was organized in the fall of 1854, a "commencement fund" of $300 was raised from among the thirty members.[70] The next year, the Nevada (City) Hebrew Society increased its treasury by disciplining two of its members.

> Nevada Hebrew Society.
> Nevada, August 6, 1855.
>
> A regular monthly meeting of this society met at the rooms of Mr. Lachman, in this place, on Monday last. . . .
> The minutes of previous meeting were read and approved. The Committee for procuring a Sefer and Shofar were discharged, after having purchased one and sent bill to the Treasurer.

A motion was made and seconded, that members of the Society shall have the privilege of the front seats of the Synagogue.

On account of disorderly conduct, Mr. Simon Rosenthal was fined $2 50 by the President. For a second offence Mr. R. was fined $2 50. For abusive language to the President Mr. Rosenthal and brother were fined $10 each.—On motion, Mr. Rosenthal and brother were expelled.

On motion, it was ordered that the behavior and expulsion of the Rosenthal's be published in the Nevada papers. . . . On motion, meeting adjourned.[71]

The wealth these organizations possessed enabled them to purchase ritual objects and real property. Benjamin observed that both the Grass Valley and Sonora communities owned Torah scrolls.[72] The Jews of Nevada City also owned a Torah, which was destroyed in the fire of July 19, 1856. Shortly thereafter, they purchased a new Torah and a shofar.[73] The cemeteries in Sonora, Grass Valley, Nevada City, and Marysville had mortuary buildings, where bodies were prepared for burial.[74] When F. Hochstein of Columbia announced his impending departure for New Orleans in 1860, the community presented to him "a magnificent silver goblet" for having conducted their services.[75] There is a tradition that the chandelier that hangs in the Odd Fellows Building in Sonora was a gift of the Jews of that city to the I.O.O.F. as a token of thanks for the use of the building for High Holiday services.[76]

There were ladies' Hebrew benevolent societies in Jackson, Mokelumne Hill, and Placerville[77] and participation by Jews in nonsectarian charities in Nevada City.[78]

The Jews of the Mother Lode were also noted for their acts of charity in local emergencies, particularly following the fires that periodically destroyed whole towns. After one such fire in Drytown, the following notice appeared in a Jackson paper:

Public Meeting.
At a meeting of the citizens of Drytown, convened for the purpose of expressing their thanks for the kindness extended to

the sufferers consequent upon the recent fire in their place . . . the committee made the following report which was unanimously adopted: . . .

Resolved, That we feel truly grateful to Messrs. Levinsky, Harris and Sanders for the bread they brought in our time of need, and will ever remember them as our friends.[79]

In addition to maintaining cemeteries and dispensing charity, the Jewish societies in the gold rush conducted worship services. Services for the High Holidays of Rosh Hashanah and Yom Kippur were held regularly in all the major mining camps and cities of the Mother Lode and Northern Mines until the lack of a *minyan* prevented their continuance. Thus, in Downieville, Yom Kippur was observed at least twice, in 1855 and 1857.[80] In San Andreas, the High Holidays were observed in 1856 and the stores of the merchants were closed. Two years later, the Jews of San Andreas observed Yom Kippur in Jackson at the invitation of the congregation there. Yom Kippur was also observed in San Andreas in 1859 and 1860, but the decline in the population soon ended these services.[81] In Sonora, which had a large and stable population, services were conducted as recently as 1906. Over fifty people from all over the county attended the Yom Kippur services there in 1894.[82]

But even the presence of a synagogue building in some towns did not create added activities in the Jewish community. In Jackson, in spite of the fact that the synagogue was built with funds received in a two-county fund-raising drive,[83] only Rosh Hashanah and Yom Kippur services were held therein and the building was unused the rest of the year. Thus, it becomes evident that day-to-day observance of Judaism was not prevalent in most of these small towns of the West in the nineteenth century. Still, Jews returned to their religious tradition at the time of the High Holidays and, dutifully, they maintained the cemetery and buried their dead. After Benjamin visited Jackson in December 1860, he caustically observed:

There are thirty-five Jews here. They formed a congregation and in 1857 built a synagogue. But it is to be regretted that they have no Scroll of the Torah and must borrow one every year from San Francisco for the high holidays. The synagogue is closed and deserted the rest of the year. Only the passer-by is struck by it as a building of distinction.[84]

A local newspaper noted that High Holiday services for 1866 would be held at the synagogue;[85] however, for unknown reasons, the congregation abandoned the synagogue building in 1869 and thereafter conducted services in the Masonic Hall.[86]

The Jews of Placerville had two successive synagogues. Benjamin rejoiced on hearing the news that the seventy members of the Jewish community there were going to build a synagogue, because it seemed to him the leaders of the Jewish community had been neglecting their religious obligations.

> ... they are planning to build a synagogue very soon; its success as a unifying center is to be most ardently desired. If there is a house of prayer, there must also be a teacher; and the Jewish children of the town will at least have some idea, if only a weak one, of what Jewish character should be and of Jewish religious services, almost completely neglected by their fathers.[87]

The first synagogue, located on Cottage Street, served the Jewish community of Placerville from 1861 to 1878, although High Holiday services were not noted in the newspaper after 1873.[88] Sometime in 1878, Will O. Upton later recalled,

> at 2 o'clock in the afternoon it got almost as dark as night, we of the Intermediate room [of the grammar school located opposite the synagogue on School Hill] saw the Synagogue, a one-story building and basement, suddenly lift up, and, amid the dust that had accumulated for years in its basement, plunge down the hill in a heap. . . . Our teacher, Miss Pringle, dismissed school, after telling the larger pupils to look after the smaller children, who were at the mercy of the hurricane that had demolished the Synagogue.[89]

The trustees of the Hebrew Benevolent Society, Michael Simon, Edward Cohn, and Samuel S. Snow, sold the property on

Cottage Street for $25 and accepted from Henry Louis, a member of the congregation, and his wife, Pauline, a gift of property on the south side of Mill Street, now called Spring Street, for a new synagogue.[90] Will Upton wrote:

> Following this storm [spoken of earlier] a new Synagogue was built on the L. [sic, i.e., Henry] Louis ("Louie") lot, now a part of the Chas. Molinari property. At this time the Rabbi of the Jewish people was L. Louis. . . . Alongside of their residence stood the new Synagogue, which gradually went into disuse with the departure and deaths of the early Jewish families that had contributed to its support. Its last Rabbi was L. Louis, long since dead.[91]

The High Holidays were observed in Grass Valley and Nevada City, too. Other activities during the year in these cities centered around the two fraternal lodges and the social club in Nevada City, spoken of earlier.

With only a few exceptions, the religious services that took place in the Mother Lode were conducted by lay residents of the communities. No ordained rabbis have been discovered residing in the region at the time, but some men were related to rabbis and may have had sufficient training to conduct worship services.[92] Nathan Brinn of Sutter Creek was once identified as "Rev. N. Brinn, (lately of Richmond, Va.)." He conducted services and officiated at funerals in Jackson, but it is not known whether he was ordained.[93]

The newspapers of the region identified many of the laymen of the community who conducted services as rabbis, but it is not likely that they were. Conducting Jewish services or performing rituals does not depend on the presence of an ordained leader. Both Adolph Pinto and A. M. Levy of Sonora were spoken of from time to time in the local newspapers as rabbis of the community.[94]

In later years, the task of conducting all the religious services in Sonora was borne by Mayer Baer, a resident of Sonora since at least December 1851, and, like his predecessors F. Hochstein and Joel Levy, the proprietor of a drygoods store. The Sonora *Union Democrat* noted in 1898:

Yom Kippur. Yom Kippur, the Day of Atonement, resulted in the closing of all the Jewish business places at sundown last Sunday, they remaining so until the following evening. On Monday services were conducted in Washington Hall by M. Baer.[95]

Baer also conducted all the Jewish funerals in Sonora until his death in 1907.[96] During some of the High Holidays, Baer was assisted by John Ferguson, who sounded the shofar. "I do know my father blew the Shofar whether he was supposed to or not, because my brother and I always climbed out of the walnut tree and ran in to hear "Pa" blow the Ramshorn."[97]

Ferguson was the proprietor of the Gold Mountain Water Company, the husband of Rosalie Mock and a convert to Judaism. The Ferguson home in Sonora was thoroughly Jewish. The male children were circumcised, and the family extended hospitality to Rabbi Elias Margolis, of Stockton, who came to Sonora to conduct services on certain occasions.[98]

In Jackson, from 1859 to 1873, High Holiday services were conducted by at least sixteen different men, representing almost all the neighboring towns (Jackson, Sutter Creek, Fiddletown, Volcano, Mokelumne Hill, El Dorado, and Placerville). Only two of the men, B. Berliner and J. Gabriel, were from San Francisco.[99]

It has already been pointed out that many Jews who came to California at this time were Orthodox in their beliefs and practices.[100] Those who came to the Mother Lode were probably forced to make certain concessions in their beliefs and practices, most likely in the observance of the dietary laws and the Sabbath. It must have been more difficult for them to live Jewish lives here than in San Francisco or in some of the eastern cities where Jewish communities were larger and more active.

In addition, the nineteenth century was a period of ferment in Judaism, just as it was in American Protestantism. In contrast to those individuals and communities who attempted to maintain the practice of Orthodoxy, there were men who believed that a reform of Judaism was necessary. From the early part of the century, German Jewish communities experimented with reforms in worship and religious philosophy.

> The tendency developed among the German Reformers to emphasize the progressive nature of Jewish law, the fact that it had, indeed, developed and changed continually in response to different conditions.... One could also find among the German Reformers the position that the law was simply outgrown and that Judaism should base itself on the prophetic and not the legal portions of the Bible.[101]

The Jew of this generation was

> influenced by the French Revolution, by the liberal movements, by Kant, Lessing and Dohm.... He was unable to bridge for long the gulf between the demands of everyday life and those of traditional orthodoxy.[102]

The Hamburg Reform Temple was organized in 1818.[103] Seven years later, there was a short-lived attempt to bring Reform to America, with the founding of the Reformed Society of Israelites in Charleston, South Carolina.[104] As the number of Jews from Germany in the United States increased after mid-century, synagogues were founded as Reform houses of worship.[105]

A number of Jews with Reform beliefs joined the gold rush. By their writings and activity, they led certain communities of the Mother Lode to adopt a Reform ritual. Of course, it is also possible that the geographical isolation of these Jewish communities prevented the perpetuation of certain Orthodox practices. That certain ritual ceremonies were not conducted may indicate the accommodation of a community to its isolation rather than its conscious commitment to Reform Judaism, which, at this time in its development, was doing away with certain ritual practices. So far as is known, there were no organizations or congregations in the gold rush country that were wholly Orthodox or Reform, but individuals of both persuasions were found in the region.

Some residents of the Mother Lode definitely supported Reform Judaism. In 1857, Emanuel Linoberg wrote a letter to the Cincinnati *Israelite* describing Jewish life in Tuolumne County and including his opinion of Reform.

> I fully approve your advocacy of Reform. Orthodoxy suited times past; but reform suits times of progress; be not discouraged; steadily advance, and sound the trumpet of reform constantly; the elevation of our position in society from day to day is caused by the system of religious reform. Orthodoxy would have kept us 500 years back in our position, whereas reform steadily advances our position—socially, morally and religiously—and the will of God will be accomplished.[106]

At the opposite end of the gold rush country, and at the opposite end of the religious spectrum from Linoberg, was the Jewish community of Grass Valley, described thus for Rabbi Julius Eckman by a member of the community, Jacob C. Marks:

> Allow me to inform you that our Society is in a flourishing condition. We were organized Sept. 8th, 1856, and have since that time purchased a Sepher Torah, with the necessary appendages, and also a Shophar.
> We have, too, a fine, well-fenced cemetery, with a substantial building on it, with all the implements required by our rites. May they never be wanted. We kept the last holy-days with great credit to our Hasan, Mr. Pawbroch, who, as a private man, is second to none in this State. We also expect to keep Purim and Pesach, according to our laws, and not according to fashion. As we have the Polish Minhag here, we are of the Orthodox, of course.[107]

Appended to this letter was a caustic comment by Eckman.

> This opinion of our sincere, but mistaken correspondent, is a radical error; it is not what we read, but what we *believe*, that constitutes orthordoxy [sic]. Besides, as neither Moses nor the Prophets have thought proper to give us a "Creed," we have no standard for Orthodoxy or heterodoxy.[108]

In 1860, Isaac Leeser, the leader of the traditional wing of American Judaism at that time, happily reported in his periodical, the *Occident:*

> The Israelites are rapidly increasing all over the state [of

California]. Every where is the feeling for our cause alive. In Sacramento, Stockton, Marysville, Nevada [City], Grass Valley, &c.,—every where, the service was conducted during the festivals without attempt at reform.[109]

From the earliest days of Jewish settlement in the Mother Lode, certain changes in religious custom were noted. These were not necessarily due to a deep belief in the need for a reform of Judaism, but rather because some merchants simply found it inconvenient to close their stores for several days within a three-week period in the autumn. Thus, Sukkoth, the Feast of Tabernacles, which follows Yom Kippur by five days, was ignored in Sonora, while the springtime holiday of Passover was accorded somewhat more importance.

> Jewish Holidays.—As is their custom, from sunset on Tuesday night to sunset on Wednesday night, our Jewish citizens observed as a time of fasting and prayer. The season is called, "The Atonement," and is spent in fasting, humiliation and penitence. Another holiday season commences on Sunday next, but it is not generally observed in this country. It continues a week, and the last two days are set aside, the first praying to the Creator for blessings on the harvest and on all fruits, and the second to giving thanks for his word as expressed in the Book of Moses.[110]

> Feast of the Passover.—In commemoration of the beginning of Passover, the Hebrew fellow citizens closed their places of business last Monday evening. Tuesday was observed by old and young, male and females. Although not so strictly observed, the remainder of the week wore a holiday appearance. The Passover will end next Tuesday evening.[111]

The preparations for the holiday of Passover in the Jewish communities of the Mother Lode were always elaborate. In Sonora, Julius Baer recalled that his parents conducted the Passover Seder at home and that, in anticipation of the holiday, "Dad used to buy 25 to 30 pounds of matzoth."[112]

In Mokelumne Hill, special preparations were also made for Passover, but owing to the remoteness of Mokelumne Hill and the great distance to San Francisco, special holiday foods did not arrive as planned. "My father used to tell me that any celebration of Passover was observed by the time the Matzos arrived in Mokelumne Hill."[113]

However, Aaron Harris, who resided in Yosemite Park in the 1870s and 1880s, wanted to celebrate Passover at the proper time. So that his observance would not be late, as it was in Mokelumne Hill, "the Matzos were always ordered the previous year [from San Francisco] so that they would arrive in time for the Passover."[114]

The trend away from religious observance, whether on account of conviction or simply apathy, noted earlier in other communities, also occurred in Placerville. On the first day of Passover 1854, Bernhard Marks wrote from Placerville to his cousin, Jacob Solis-Cohen, in Philadelphia: "I am reminded that today is the first of . . . Passover and notwithstanding there are over 30 Jews here there is not one among them who keeps the festival. I hope you will all enjoy it as I once used to."[115]

But in Nevada City, which had a greater number of Orthodox Jews, the community placed special significance in commemorating the exodus from Egypt. The Aaron Baruh family maintained separate dishes for Passover and matzo was ordered from San Francisco.[116] So that the entire community would have kosher meat for Passover, the Rev. Samuel M. Laski of San Francisco acted as shokhet and came to Nevada City to slaughter animals in the Orthodox manner.[117]

Traditional Judaism was maintained in the Mother Lode through the perpetuation of certain ceremonies that are not necessarily celebrated during holidays. Weddings and circumcision ceremonies took place many times during the thirty-year period before 1880. However, there is no way of knowing how many male children were not circumcised in religious ceremonies. And the incidence of Jews marrying out of the faith was quite high.[118] When weddings and circumcisions occurred and were celebrated with the proper religious ceremony, they were great events in the Jewish communities. Most of the Jewish weddings in the Mother Lode were conducted by rabbis from

Sacramento or Stockton or they were conducted in San Francisco, even though the presence of a rabbi is not essential. Rabbi Julius Eckman reported in his newspaper, the San Francisco *Weekly Gleaner,* that he had officiated at a wedding in Georgetown that was performed at the town hall, and that the guests were summoned to the wedding by the ringing of the town bell.[119]

A circumcision ceremony that took place in Sutter Creek in 1868 was performed by Rev. Stamper of Sacramento, who was assisted by Henry Louis of Placerville. The ceremony was followed by a banquet that lasted all night.[120]

In 1857, the editor of a newspaper in Nevada City was invited to attend a circumcision, and he printed his impressions of the event in the following edition of the paper.

> Local Affairs.
> Circumcision.—We were induced to witness the rite of circumcision at the house of a Jewish friend, on Wednesday. The officiating priest was the Rev. Mr. Laski of San Francisco. The ceremony consisted of first lighting a couple of candles, putting on of hats by the whole company present, procuring a glass or two of wine, and reading a portion of Hebrew. Second, introduction of the child, nipping in the bud, and a short ceremony of reading. Third, partaking of hospitalities, more reading which was all Hebrew to us, and adjournment. Those curious in such matters are advised to obtain further information by seeing for themselves, or consulting a rare old book a part of which is said to have been written by Moses.[121]

Owing to the many circumcision ceremonies that apparently occurred in the Mother Lode, men trained in the profession of ritual circumcision found it profitable to advertise in the Jewish periodicals of San Francisco, which enjoyed wide circulation in the West. The Rev. A. J. Applebaum, "Late Chasan [*sic*] of the Congregation Sherith Israel," combined his knowledge with an unusual amount of charity.

> I am in possession of the Diploma as Practical Mohel, and will render my services to the poor without charge. . . .

I respectfully inform my co-religionists in the Interior that I am always at their service.[122]

The ceremony of Bar Mitzvah apparently took place only twice in this period, in conjunction with the High Holiday services in Placerville in 1867. Perhaps the communities of the Mother Lode had dispensed with this ceremony and followed the example of Rabbi Isaac Mayer Wise, who introduced Confirmation while in Albany, New York, in 1848.[123] Or it may have been that no one in the towns of this region was qualified or inclined to offer religious instruction. The only people known to have acted as instructors of religious education were Mayer Baer of Sonora[124] and Mrs. Ray Novitzki of Grass Valley. The latter was superintendent of the religious school in that city in 1879.[125]

The extent to which the Jewish communities adopted Reform in their theology and manner of worship is not known for certain. The members of these societies were immigrants who sought out their fellow Jews because they wanted to be part of a religious community. Some were bachelors; others were heads of families. They perpetuated a tradition of worship that crossed over national and Old World community differences. Some were observant and went to great pains to maintain their Orthodoxy; the majority, however, although clinging to their faith, discarded everyday ritual practices. And not a few left the community to marry out of the faith.

Almost everywhere the story was the same. A few merchants in the early days gathered together for prayer on the most important holidays. This informal organization led to a regular society which eventually disbanded near the turn of the century owing to a lack of numbers. Apparently, during the three decades of Jewish communal organization in the Mother Lode, the maintenance and perpetuation of Judaism was not an overriding preoccupation. In general, the only well-publicized religious services of the year occupied a mere two weeks. For the other fifty weeks, the merchants were involved with business and family affairs, organizations such as the Masons, Odd Fellows, and the volunteer fire department, and local politics. These Jews were proud of their faith and perpetuated some of its practices under adverse conditions, but they did not exclude themselves from the everyday affairs of the town in favor of full attention to the congregation, lodge, or Hebrew benevolent society. The practice of Judaism was merely one part of their varied activities.

But some individuals and some communities did perpetuate Orthodox practices. In many instances the degree to which the ritual practices of Judaism were observed depended upon the manner in which these practices were observed during a person's childhood. Several Jewish immigrants to California had come from small towns in Europe, where certain practices may have been performed only with difficulty. Since many Jews who came to America at this time were from Orthodox families, it was only natural for them to want to retain some memories of Orthodox Judaism as their families had observed it. But for the majority, the High Holidays were their only reminder of Judaism. Thus, it is not surprising that some of the gold rush communities regarded themselves as Orthodox, because the only public services conducted during the year followed the Orthodox rite. While the rest of the country and the few rabbis therein were engaged in disputes that led to the several shades of Judaism in the United States today, the Jews of the gold rush avoided such controversy or confined their discussions to an academic consideration of the changes in rites that were being printed in the Jewish newspapers of the period.

Not surprisingly, some Jews maintained both the letter and the spirit of Orthodox Jewish law. In spite of their isolation, the family of Aaron Harris maintained traditional Judaism in Yosemite Park. On the Sabbath, "the hired help took care of lighting the fire."[126]

In Nevada City, S. Rothschild regularly appended to the advertisements of his tobacco business: "Store closed from Friday Evening to Saturday Evening."[127]

Although certain reforms took place in Sonora, several families retained many traditions. In 1872, Rosh Hashanah was observed for one day instead of the traditional two.[128] In later years, the community returned to a two-day observance, although businesses opened on the second day. Several families purchased matzoth for Passover and candles were lighted at the beginning of the Sabbath, before sunset on Friday. However, there being no convenient way of procuring kosher meat, Mayer Baer's family gave up the observance of the dietary laws quite early.[129]

The Jewish community of Jackson and vicinity attempted to retain Orthodoxy by coercion. Congregation B'nai Israel of that city published a constitution, bylaws, and membership list in 1873 that stated the desire of the majority to worship according to the Polish custom. Because the congregation called its cemetery "Giboth Olem" [sic] [Hills of Eternity], probably some of the members of the Jackson congregation were former members of Congregation Sherith Israel in San Francisco, which also followed the Polish custom in its worship and called its cemetery by the same name. Certain rules of the congregation are interesting for the discipline imposed upon the membership.

CONSTITUTION.
Article II, Form of Worship. The religious services in the Synagogue of this Congregation shall be according to Minhag Polen.
Article VII, Duties of the President. Section 5. It shall be his duty to superintend all religious ceremonies in the Synagogue, and to distribute the Mitzvahs. . . .
Article VIII, Duties of the Vice-President. Section 2. It shall be his duty, upon the permit of President for burials, to give proper direction for the funeral and superintend the same personally.
Article XI, Members. Section 2. No Israelite shall be considered qualified for membership who is united in marriage contrary to the laws and ordinances of our religion. . . .
Section 6. Any member who shall marry contrary to the laws and ordinances of our religion, who shall renounce Judaism, shall forfeit his membership.
Section 12. Any member who may refuse to conform to the rules and regulations for order and decorum during Divine Service, after being notified by an officer of the Congregation, shall be liable to a fine, suspension or expulsion. . . .
Section 13. Any member of this Congregation who shall keep, or

> cause to be kept open his usual place of buisness [sic] on . . . Rash Hashanah and . . . Yom Kipur for the purpose of transacting buisness [sic], shall be stricken from the Roll of membership.
> By-Laws of Congregation B'nai Israel.
> Article I. Property. All Sepharim and other property deposited in the Synagogue shall be under the direction and control of the Board of Officers, and no person to whom such Sepher or other property so deposited shall belong, shall be entitled to any exclusive use or right to the same during the performance of Divine Services in the Synagogue.[130]

Perhaps some of the smaller communities maintained elements of coercion in their organizations in order to bind all the Jews of the area to the organization. The leaders may have reasoned that unless a closely governed group held sway, factions would spring up among the members and the group might disband. A merchant in Downieville, A. S. Haxter, complained to the Cincinnati *Israelite* as early as 1855 about those Jews in town who chose not to affiliate with the community.

> There are about 20 of our coreligionists engaged in different kinds of business here, 14 of whom observed the day [Yom Kippur] with becoming solemnity. . . . We . . . passed the day with perfect decorum, and I believe to the satisfaction of all present. If there was anything that annoyed us, it was the unbecoming manner of those who were not disposed to join us in our devotions; they mocked us for upholding the faith of our fathers here in this country.
> Can you imagine anything more despicable? Allow me to remark—, that those who thus adjured or neglected the creed of their ancestors belong to the lowest and most degraded of our nation. . . . They possess all the worst and none of the better qualities that distinguish the character of our race.[131]

One way in which the Jews of the mountain cities were reminded that they were all of one faith was through Jewish newspapers and periodicals. If a person's preference was for traditional Judaism, he subscribed to Isaac Leeser's *Occident and American Jewish Advocate,* published in Philadelphia, or to Rabbi Julius Eckman's San Francisco *Weekly Gleaner.* If he had more liberal religious opinions, he might order the *Israelite* or *Die Deborah*, both of which were published in Cincinnati by Rabbi Isaac Mayer Wise and others. In various years, the Philadelphia *Occident* had subscribers in Sonora, Campo Seco, Downieville, Cosumnes Post Office, and Michigan City.[132] The San Francisco *Weekly Gleaner* had readers in every city, town, and mining camp of the gold rush country and in Victoria, British Columbia, and Panama as well. Occasionally, many Jews in a town subscribed to the *Gleaner* at one time. In one edition, twelve new subscribers were listed from Nevada City. In another edition, it was noted that nine individuals in Mokelumne Hill were receiving the paper.[133]

As the Jewish population declined, along with the rest of the population, the observance and frequency of Jewish religious practices declined also. Where sufficient numbers remained, as in Sonora, the High Holidays were observed with at least a *minyan* through the turn of the century. In other towns, services were discontinued whenever the number of available worshippers fell below ten males. Some individual merchants, however, chose to remain in the mountains the rest of their lives. Owing to the small size of the remaining Jewish community, nonsectarian lodges and fraternal organizations conducted their funeral services.

In Placerville, the synagogue fell into disuse when the community became too small to conduct services. In Jackson, however, the congregation was apparently so successful that it became too large for the synagogue, which it abandoned before 1869 for the Masonic Hall, even though it was filled only two or three days a year. As the Jewish population of Grass Valley diminished, the lot upon which the community intended to build a synagogue was sold.[134] Also alienated were lands and buildings surrounding cemeteries that proved to be in excess of originally projected needs. Such lands in Sonora and Grass Valley were sold, and the mortuary houses, located adjacent to the cemeteries, were demolished. As more and more members of each Jewish community moved away, the upkeep of the cemeteries became too costly or too great a physical burden for the few remaining families, and all six cemeteries fell into disrepair.[135] The lodges and benevolent societies, too, disbanded when, even after attempts were made to invite residents of nearby communities to join, the small membership no longer warranted the continuation of their activities.

The decision of these immigrants to form religious communities, conduct services, establish cemeteries, and distribute charity was entirely voluntary. These merchants and tradesmen desired to be part of a historical tradition that had perpetuated the worship of God for thousands of years. What is significant about the Jews who organized these cemeteries, High Holiday congregations, and benevolent societies is that their decision to organize and maintain these groups also impressed upon them the importance of maintaining Judaism in their homes so that this heritage could be passed on to their children. Accordingly, many such merchants left the gold rush country early because they knew that better advantages for their children, both in general education and Jewish education, existed in San Francisco, as did better business opportunities for themselves. But while they lived in the isolation of the Mother Lode and Northern Mines, they also preserved their Jewishness by continuing some of the practices learned during their childhood and adapting them to the assimilative conditions that existed in the gold rush, the melting pot of many races, nationalities, and religions.

·7·

DECLINE

The rush of individual gold miners was short-lived. It swelled California's population almost overnight, but the forty-niner was seldom the better off for forsaking home, family, and occupation for a vision of sudden wealth. The newcomer was often gullible enough to accept the fantastic claims made by authors of travel guides, who had never visited the areas they described, that gold was lying on the surface waiting to be picked up by anyone who came west. The hard truth was that transportation to and from the Mother Lode and Northern Mines was slow and expensive, obtaining food and shelter was costly and difficult, and the gold itself always seemed to be just out of reach, perhaps a short distance down a creek bed or one more foot beneath the surface.

Within ten years the rush of itinerant miners and prospectors had reached an apex and declined. By the late 1850s the extraction of subsurface gold had become big business. A large influx of capital from the East and from Europe brought scientific timbering, hard quartz mining, stamp mills, and crushing mills to the region.[1] Incorporation papers of many eastern-based mining companies with highly inflated original subscriptions were filed at the county court houses.[2] Some enterprising companies turned to hydraulic mining. They washed whole mountainsides down streams until farmers in the lower valleys took court action to stop these proceedings.

Some easterners, less venturesome than their fortune-seeking brethren, came to California and even to the gold regions and gained wealth not by mining but in the occupations they knew best—farming and cattle raising. Such occupations not only were profitable but also helped to bring food prices down from the stratospheric heights attained earlier in the decade. In 1856, the Tuolumne County assessor reported that 21,888 bushels of wheat and vegetables, 18,853 fruit trees and grapevines, and 11,704 head of livestock were in the county that year.[3] A decade later, more than 250,000 grapevines were listed in the second district of Tuolumne County (Columbia and vicinity) alone, together with great numbers of fruit trees and berry vines.[4]

The rise of agriculture in the region formerly occupied by miners and prospectors was probably a disquieting fact to the Jewish merchants. From an original inclination that eventually became a habit, the Jewish merchant dealt in general merchandise and especially clothing. Those were the goods the transient gold-seeker wanted when he came to town. Despite the decline in the prosperity of individual mining claims in the early 1850s, the Jewish merchant was still able to make a comfortable living from the more settled town population by laying in a line of fine clothing along with the rough ready-to-wear of the miner, and increasing his stock of schoolbooks while decreasing his inventory of small mining tools.

Agriculture helped create a mercantile depression with which the merchants were unable to cope. The family farm tended to be self-sufficient, after the initial capital outlay for necessary items that could not be produced by hand. And, all too often, these items, consisting of agricultural implements and large harvesting machines, were not part of the inventory of a Jewish general merchant or clothing salesman. Food, which a merchant might obtain by barter and then sell, remained on the farm where it was raised and fed the family and the hired help. Farmer's wives and daughters made clothing from bolts of material purchased in bulk, instead of buying one manufactured item at a time, and their purchases from the merchant became less frequent.

Another difficulty for the Jewish merchants was the trend toward specialization among the Gentile merchants in this region. The Jews were not artisans but rather retail sellers who carried many lines of general merchandise and clothing. While it was this experience that eventually carried them into department-store merchandising in large cities, for the moment their future was grim as Gentile merchants opened businesses specializing in one item that they could manufacture and service on the spot or purchase in such quantities as to be able to offer substantial discounts. Instead of a town having only clothing and general variety stores that had met the needs of purchasers for almost two decades, city-dwellers now witnessed the opening of stores devoted solely to cabinet-making, upholstering, trunk-making, boot- and shoe-manufacturing, and the sale of groceries.[5]

The rise of specialized businesses created a competition among the general merchants to rid themselves of their large inventories. Those merchants unable to sell their goods in the face of competition were still charged for them, and the diminishing amount of profits and periods of depressed trading activity that followed hastened the departure of a merchant and his family.

As important as the rise of agriculture and specialized businesses were, probably the most important factor in the decline of trade was the rapid decline in the population of the region. As the miners and prospectors sought riches from other mineral discoveries throughout the West, the merchants were left with a smaller clientele. Whereas in 1852 the population of the eight gold rush counties contained one-half of the population of California, by 1880 their population accounted for only one-tenth of the total population. And the population of the eight counties fell from 123,822 in 1852 to 85,026 in 1880.[6]

The merchants who remained in the West, however, still felt the spirit of adventure, in spite of the hard work required of them to keep their stores open long hours and move large inventories of goods great distances. When new gold discoveries were made all over the West, Jewish traders were just a step behind the first miners and prospectors in search of a new strike. Regardless of the remoteness of a new discovery, the Jews hastened to participate. Having crossed Europe, the Atlantic Ocean, and the Western Hemisphere, the merchants regarded a relocation in the West as an excursion rather than an ordeal. In the 1850s and 1860s, Jewish merchants played prominent roles in the gold rushes to Oroville, Shasta, and Yreka, California; Jacksonville and Baker, Oregon; the Orofino mines in Idaho; the Fraser River and Barkerville, British Columbia; and in the rushes for various minerals associated with the early days of Montana, Nevada, and Colorado.

Some, however, tired of basing their fortunes exclusively on gold and sought security as general merchants in many of the smaller towns in the interior of California, where their businesses might grow together with a newly established town. Abe Haines, after engaging in business in the gold rush towns of Jackson, Buckeye, and El Dorado, established himself in business in the communities of Cottonwood, Madison, Woodland, and Capay, where the economy was not entirely dependent upon gold.[7] The Elias brothers of Columbia found that greater profits were to be made outside the Mother Lode. Edward Elias opened a notions store in Oakdale, and his brother Philip settled in Modesto.[8] Many members of the Coblentz family and Isaac (or Ira) Kahn were found in several towns and cities of California during and after the gold rush.[9] Moses Dinkelspiel had stores in the Mother Lode cities of Campo Seco and Vallecito but removed to Suisun City in 1856 or 1857, where he was in the general merchandise business until his death, May 17, 1897.[10]

A merchant in early California, who sought greater profits in the regions of new mineral discoveries, was Samuel Michelson, the father of Albert Michelson (1852–1931), the first Jew to win a Nobel Prize. The elder Michelson opened a small drygoods store in Murphy's Camp in the summer of 1856, but later moved to Virginia City, Nevada.[11] Albert Michelson received an appointment to the United States Naval Academy, where he graduated in 1873. He was instructor of physics and chemistry at the academy in 1875–79 and thereafter conducted his experimentation with light waves.[12]

Another scion of an early mercantile family from the gold rush region was Julius Kahn. He was born in Kuppenheim, Baden, in 1861 and settled with his family in San Andreas five years later. He tried the acting profession in San Francisco but later became an attorney, served in the state assembly, and represented San Francisco in Congress in 1899–1903 and 1905–25. After his death in the latter year, he was succeeded by his widow, Florence Prag Kahn, who served until 1937.[13] Her father, Conrad Prag, had, like Julius Kahn's father, been a merchant in Calaveras County and had also worked for the N. S. Ransohoff firm in Salt Lake City.[14]

The lure of adventure was still strong in this period, and several wide-open spaces in the American West away from the gold and other mineral regions seemed attractive to Jews as merchants and sutlers. Some, like the Goldwater family, stayed in southern California for a short time before freighting into Arizona. That they settled in Arizona and eventually expanded their general merchandise business exemplified the ambition of many pioneer Jewish merchants to establish a business in an area with little competition, and to engage in a general merchandise business on a relatively large scale, rather than risk their fortune and credit in merchandising a single type of goods.

Others attracted to general merchandising on a large scale in a new locality included Aaron Meier, who had operated a store in Downieville with his brothers, Julius and Emanuel, and who, in 1857, founded the present Meier and Frank Company of Portland,[15] and the Auerbach brothers, whose store at Rabbit Creek (also known as La Porte) was a forerunner of stores in Bodie, California, and Austin, Nevada, and finally the Auerbach Company of Salt Lake City, founded in 1864.[16]

Some Jews entered the occupations of farmer and cattle-raiser, usually as absentee owner. Sol Wangenheim and Louis Rosenberg, of Calaveras County, Emanuel Linoberg of Tuolumne County, and Aaron Harris and Davis Rosenthal of Mariposa County, and others recorded their cattle marks and brands with the county and owned sizable quantities of ranch land, but also maintained their mercantile businesses. They probably did not participate directly in the day-to-day affairs of the ranch and cattle business and may not even have lived on the ranch.[17] No records indicate that Jewish merchants of the gold rush era took part in the formation of the short-lived Jewish agricultural colony in Calaveras County around 1880.[18] If any Jewish merchants actively engaged in agricultural pursuits in this region before 1880, it was not to escape from a depressed mercantile economy, but to try to increase their wealth by diversification.

Another factor that contributed toward the decline in the number of the Jewish merchants and the importance of Jewish merchandising in the area of the gold rush was that many merchants who lived out their lives in the area were not replaced by other Jews. Jewish merchants typically brought over younger relatives to work as clerks in their stores, but fewer Jews came to America in the 1870s from Central and Western Europe than in the 1850s and early 1860s.[19] The few younger relatives who did come to California after 1870 had no incentive to settle in the remote interior when business opportunities appeared in larger cities. In San Francisco, businesses were expanding during the early 1870s. The completion of the transcontinental railroad and the development of San Francisco as a manufacturing city, as well as a trading center, created new positions that established merchants filled with their newly arrived relatives. The custom of sending a younger relative to manage a store in the mountains declined when jobs became more available in San Francisco.

The Jewish immigrants of the 1870s and 1880s came to San Francisco at a time when the social status of the earlier arrivals was undergoing a considerable change. The positions of leadership in the general community that the merchants had held were now in jeopardy as manufacturing displaced trading as the most important economic activity in the city.[20] Newly arrived relatives were needed to fill positions in expanding firms that their families were building so that they could maintain their positions of leadership in the commercial, social, and religious life of the city.

The overwhelming majority of the merchants and their families were gone from the Mother Lode by the late 1890s and the turn of the century. Unfortunately, no accurate census records show how many Jews lived in the Mother Lode region from 1850 to 1890. Benjamin counted 329 in the seventeen towns he visited in November and December 1860.[21] From 1876 to 1878, the Board of Delegates of American Israelites and the Union of American Hebrew Congregations conducted a census that revealed 309 Jews in twelve towns.[22] The latter figure is probably the more accurate of the two. Benjamin visited only a few cities and towns in the gold rush region and did not have the resources of a national organization to help him in his writing. The federal census records and additional information, such as newspaper advertisements and vital statistics, reveal more Jews than Benjamin counted, but it is not possible to determine the exact number of Jews because some of them may have Anglicized their names and because some of the census records are illegible.

While economic considerations primarily influenced the move to larger cities, many families who had maintained ties with the practices of the Jewish faith also looked forward to an environment in which they could more easily practice Judaism and its rituals. Some families who had managed to practice their religion even in these isolated surroundings perceived that among the families based on mixed marriages, the Jewish partner and the children were usually lost to Judaism. The practice of Judaism was much easier in the great Jewish community of San Francisco; this religious factor, as well as the desire of these families to have better public education facilities for their children, contributed to their leaving the interior.

The majority of those who left the mountains went to San Francisco. This was in keeping with the long Jewish urban tradition. Jewish merchants came to the gold rush country to make money. When faced with financial difficulty, they moved to the city. For the most part, it was to the new urban West that these people moved, not to the East or to other small western towns. Some expanded the general merchandise and clothing stores of the Mother Lode region and opened stores in Phoenix, Los Angeles, Stockton, Sacramento, Portland, and Salt Lake City; but the majority of gold rush Jews were soon found in San Francisco. In 1880, the Jewish population of San Francisco was estimated at 16,000.[23]

Harriet Lane Levy reminisced, years later, in regard to her father's generation:

> All the men were united by the place and circumstance of their birth. They had come to America from villages in Germany, and had worked themselves up from small stores in the interior of California to businesses in San Francisco. . . .
> Beginning with Louis Levison, our right-hand neighbor, at 922 O'Farrell Street, down past two solid blocks of houses to the Kauffmans', the heads of the two-story-and-basement wooden houses were as identical in cast as the buildings they owned and occupied—solid merchants who had left villages in Germany and Poland to come as boys to America, sailed around the Horn to California in the early fifties, and started a business in small towns of the interior, in the mining settlements of the Sierras, or in the fertile valleys of the Sacramento and San Joaquin rivers. As soon as they accumulated a little money they came to the city, became wholesale merchants, jobbers, or manufacturers, acquiring prestige and complacency as they rose.[24]

The city of San Francisco was a challenge to their economic talents. With their experience in merchandising in the remote towns of the gold rush, the merchants were prepared to compete in the larger community. Their enterprising spirit was bolstered by the fact that they could count on cooperation from the wholesale houses of the city, which, in some cases, they had dealt with for periods up to thirty years, and which they would now be dealing with on a personal, day-to-day basis. The former mountain merchant who had paid his bills on time was assured of a close relationship with his suppliers, who would aid him getting started once again. In many cases, wholesalers in San Francisco were related by marriage to retailers who formerly lived in the mountains.

The migration to San Francisco from the rural towns and mining camps took place gradually, because the decline of any particular mining camp or town was not necessarily tied to the fortunes of any other such location in the region. Some towns were abandoned in the middle 1850s, while others are still in existence today. A particular location in the early days became a settled community because nearby discoveries of gold portended prosperity. It declined when the gold gave out, when the town was not rebuilt after a fire, or if the general economy was insufficient to maintain the town.

The presence of merchants in a gold rush town was a sign of the continued prosperity of the town. It was only when a town showed sure signs of decline that the merchants left. Fires or bank closures did not lessen the number of merchants. They stayed in the small towns and advertised regularly in the newspapers until unsold inventories, unpaid accounts, and the falling off of profits threatened financial disaster.

In spite of business failures, or general economic depression, few Jewish merchants were insolvent when they left their homes in the mountains. They had usually saved sufficient capital to set up in business in another city, primarily San Francisco. Sholom, Hyman, and Abraham Levy, who operated a store in Columbia, variously called S. and H. Levy and the Three Brothers Store, suffered losses in two fires and twice had their stock seized by the sheriff.[25] Still, they were able to settle themselves comfortably in San Francisco and could twice afford to send Rachel, Sholom Levy's daughter, to Europe.[26]

A family that experienced financial difficulty during its last days in the gold rush country was that of Anthony Zellerbach. According to family recollections, the brothers Marks and Anthony operated a bank in Moore's Flat. Sometime during the Civil War, Marks traveled to Europe, leaving his power of attorney with a nephew who squandered the assets of the bank. As a result, Anthony, his wife, and two children, Jacob and Isadore, were compelled to move to San Francisco.[27]

A more romantic story concerning the move of the Zellerbachs to San Francisco is a reminiscence of the descendants of Charles Hegarty, an Irish Catholic merchant of Moore's Flat. According to the Hegarty family, Anthony Zellerbach and Hegarty were partners in a general store that could support only one family. To solve the predicament, they flipped a coin. The toss was won by Hegarty, and Zellerbach moved to San Francisco.[28]

Arriving penniless in San Francisco in 1868, Anthony Zellerbach traded odd lots of paper and began importing stationery with Adolph Falk in October 1869. As this company grew, it changed its name to A. Zellerbach, Paper Merchant. Later, it was called A. Zellerbach and Sons. In 1907, it became the Zellerbach Paper Company. In 1928, the company merged with the Crown-Willamette Corporation[29] to form the Crown Zellerbach Corporation. The Zellerbach Paper Company, however, remained a separate entity. A grandson of Anthony Zellerbach, James D. Zellerbach, served as United States ambassador to Italy in the Eisenhower administration.[30]

The Fleishhacker family is an example of pioneer Jews from the gold rush country who eventually settled in the city with their profits from the mountains. Aaron Fleishhacker arrived in San Francisco in 1853 but drifted through the Northern Mines of California and the Comstock Lode of Nevada, engaging in mercantile pursuits in Sacramento, Grass Valley, Minnesota, and Forest City, California, and Virginia City and Carson City, Nevada, before returning to San Francisco, where he opened a plant for the manufacturing of paper boxes and the conduct of a wholesale paper business. His sons, Herbert and Mortimer, and his son-in-law, Ludwig Schwabacher, expanded this business and founded the Crown Paper Company. After purchasing the Columbia Paper Company, Crown merged with the Willamette Paper Company and then with the Zellerbach Paper Corporation in 1928.[31]

The sons of Aaron Fleishhacker, Herbert, Sr., and Mortimer, Sr., entered the banking profession. From 1908 Herbert Fleishhacker ran the London Paris National Bank, which became, in 1909, the Anglo and London Paris National Bank of San Francisco. In the latter organization, he was first vice-president and general manager and, from 1911, president. He also headed the Anglo-California Trust Company of San Francisco in 1909 but was succeeded in this capacity by his brother, Mortimer. These two firms consolidated in 1932 as the Anglo California National Bank of San Francisco with Herbert as president and Mortimer as chairman of the board.[32]

The brothers Abraham and Leopold Seligman were merchants in Placerville in the early and middle 1850s. This was probably a branch of the general import firm of J. Seligman and Company, housed in three different locations in San Francisco at various times and managed by the above-named men and two of their brothers, James and Henry. The brothers settled in New York in 1864, where they founded the investment banking firm of J. and W. Seligman and Company.[33]

Another family that had roots in Placerville was the Steinharts. The brothers Sigmund and Frederick Steinhart, merchants in Placerville in 1852, later settled in San Francisco and joined their brother Ignatz in business there. They also engaged in banking and philanthropy. Ignatz Steinhart was co-manager of the Anglo California Bank, Ltd., one of the banks that later merged with the London Paris National Bank in 1909 to form the Anglo and London Paris National Bank of San Francisco, spoken of earlier, which was led by the Fleishhacker family. The Steinhart Aquarium in San Francisco is named for Sigmund and Ignatz Steinhart.[34]

The Levison family was also associated with early-day Placerville. Mark Levison arrived there in 1852, after spending a short time in San Francisco. He later moved to Virginia City, Nevada, where his son, Jacob B., was born in 1862. In 1875, the family settled in San Francisco, and Mark Levison entered the insurance brokerage business. He passed this interest in insurance to his son, who held positions with several firms and joined the Fireman's Fund Insurance Company in 1890. Jacob B. Levison thereafter served as a member of the firm's board of directors, 1906–47, and president, 1917–37.[35]

Isidor Cohen, who came to California in 1863 and was a peddler in El Dorado county, later moved to Sacramento, where he was engaged in a carpet and oil cloth business with his brother, Benjamin. Later, he became a cigar merchant in the same city. He became known for his local philanthropy, especially on behalf of an orphan's home. Isidor Cohen Elementary School in Sacramento, named in his honor, was opened in 1968.[36]

Other merchants continued the migration to the Pacific Northwest begun by Aaron Meier and achieved great reputations for themselves and their children. Bailey Gatzert, a merchant of Nevada City, served as mayor of Seattle. Ben Selling of Portland, whose father, Philip, and uncle, Isaac, were early general merchants in Sonora, became Speaker of the Oregon House of Representatives in 1915 and achieved a national reputation for his philanthropies to Eastern European Jewish immigrants and to the Hebrew Union College Library in Cincinnati, Ohio.[37]

This generation of Jews brought to the United States a love for education, a knowledge of the religious practices of their fathers, and a penchant for hard work, particularly in merchandising. Once settled, the Jewish immigrant in the Golden State, and all over the West, gave to his community the benefits of his education and helped provide the economic stability needed by so many new towns located close to large mining camps or at important railroad or river crossings. The Jew contributed greatly to the economic well-being of the individual purchaser in the early days of California statehood. His honesty was recalled for decades by descendants of his customers.[38]

The Jew made California his permanent home. He displayed a willingness to remain after the glamour of the gold rush wore off. Because he stayed, others were encouraged to stay. Because he changed his inventories and advertisements from time to time, he indicated to the local population that it was still possible to remain and be as comfortable as in the old days, even when a change in some long-standing habits was necessary. Without the Jewish merchant in the gold rush region, the prosperity and permanence of her towns and cities might not have been maintained. The Jews provided sojourners and settlers alike with the necessities and comforts of life, and helped make gold rush existence both meaningful and bearable in those days of '49.[39]

NOTES

NOTES TO CHAPTER 1

1. San Francisco *Californian,* March 15, 1848.
2. James K. Polk, "Fourth Annual Message" [Washington, D.C., December 5, 1848], in *A Compilation of the Messages and Papers of the Presidents* . . . (New York: Bureau of National Literature, Inc., 1897), V, pp. 2485–87.
3. "On October 6, 1848, the *Californian,* pioneer of the Pacific Mail fleet, put to sea from New York to take her place on the line between Panama and the northwest coast." She rounded the Horn and anchored at Panama (City) January 17, 1849. When the next ship, the *Falcon,* left New York December 1, 1848, it stopped at New Orleans. By this time the gold excitement had reached New Orleans and many gold-seekers boarded the *Falcon.* When the *Californian* arrived in San Francisco February 28, 1849, she was deserted by her crew. John Haskell Kemble, *The Panama Route, 1848–1869* (Berkeley and Los Angeles: University of California Press, 1943), pp. 31–36.
4. With the gold rush to California, the American frontier became an island of settlement, with unorganized territories surrounded by the eastern states and the settled possessions of California and Oregon.
5. Ray Allen Billington, *The Far Western Frontier, 1830–1860* (New York and Evanston: Harper and Row, 1956), p. 223.
6. Examples of such books in French and German are found in Carl I. Wheat, *Books of the California Gold Rush* (San Francisco: Colt Press, 1949), n.p., nos. 75, 92, and notes. Contemporary descriptions of the region were also published in Spanish and Hungarian, and several guidebooks were printed in Canada and Great Britain. Ibid., nos. 4, 5, 98, 169, 184, 237.

7. There were, by this time, many Jews of German origin in the United States. By 1725, northern European Jews outnumbered their brethren, the Sephardim, in the English colonies. In 1802, German Jews in Philadelphia founded Congregation Rodeph Shalom. By 1825, enough Jews of German origin lived in New York to form a congregation that worshipped according to Central European traditions rather than by the Spanish and Portuguese ritual of the only other synagogue, Congregation Shearith Israel. From the 1820s, the number of Jewish arrivals in the United States from central Europe increased, and congregations were organized by them in cities in the interior: in Cincinnati in 1824, St. Louis in 1836, and Mobile in 1841. Nationally, B'nai B'rith was founded in New York as a German-speaking organization, Bundes Brüder, in 1843. Jacob Rader Marcus, *Early American Jewry: The Jews of New York, New England and Canada, 1649–1794* (Philadelphia: Jewish Publication Society, 1951), preface, pp. xi–xii; Selma Stern-Taeubler, "Problems of American Jewish and German Jewish Historiography," in *Jews from Germany in the United States*, ed. Eric E. Hirshler (New York: Farrar, Straus and Cudahy, 1955), pp. 11–13; Israel Goldstein, *A Century of Judaism in New York: B'nai Jeshurun 1825–1925, New York's Oldest Ashkenazic Congregation* (New York: Congregation B'nai Jeshurun, 1930), p. 51.

8. Bertram W. Korn, "Jewish 'Forty-Eighters' in America," *Eventful Years and Experiences: Studies in Nineteenth Century American Jewish History* (Cincinnati: American Jewish Archives, 1954), p. 2. Korn discovered only forty Jews who participated in the revolutions of 1848 and later came to America. Five of them immigrated to California. Ibid., p. 6. One of the five, August Helbing, was in business for a short time in the Northern Mines prior to settling permanently in San Francisco. Telephone conversation with August Rothschild, San Francisco, March 9, 1966. The only other individual known to have participated in the European revolutions who also joined the gold rush was Jacob Kohn of Placerville. "My grandfather . . . was born in Buda Pesth, Hungary, where he lived until the ill-fated rebellion wherein Hungary attempted to free herself from Austrian domination. He was forced to flee Hungary with the leader of the rebellion, Louis Kossuth. They arrived in New York but found no interest in their attempt to raise funds for a second rebellion. They then went to St. Louis, a German stronghold at the time, but their efforts were again fruitless. It was at this time . . . [1849] that Kohn joined the Gold Rush, going down the river, across Panama, and up the West Coast."

Letter from Irving Coan, San Francisco, July 26, 1965. For additional information on Jews who participated in the revolutions of 1848 and later settled in America, see A. E. Zucker, ed., *The Forty-Eighters: Political Refugees of the German Revolution of 1848* (New York: Columbia University Press, 1950), pp. 272–357. See also Priscilla Robertson, *Revolutions of 1848: A Social History* (Princeton, N. J.: Princeton University Press, 1952), passim.

9. Marcus Lee Hansen, *The Immigrant in American History,* ed. Arthur M. Schlesinger (Cambridge: Harvard University Press, 1940), pp. 80–81. See also Marcus Lee Hansen. *The Atlantic Migration, 1607–1860: A History of the Continuing Settlement of the United States,* ed. Arthur M. Schlesinger (Cambridge: Harvard University Press, 1940), p. 274.

10. Ibid., p. 277.

11. J. Lamson, *Round Cape Horn: Voyage of the Passenger-Ship James W. Paige, From Maine to California in the Year 1852* (Bangor: Press of O. F. & W. H. Knowles, 1878), pp. 22, 26, 32, 65.

12. John Walton Caughey, *Gold is the Cornerstone* (Berkeley and Los Angeles: University of California Press, 1948), chap. 4; Kemble, op. cit.

13. Octavius Thorndike Howe, *Argonauts of '49: History and Adventures of the Emigrant Companies from Massachusetts 1849–1850* (Cambridge: Harvard University Press, 1923); Kenneth Haney, ed., *From the Journal of Garrett W. Low: Gold Rush by Sea* (Philadelphia: University of Pennsylvania Press, 1941); Lamson, op. cit.

14. Jaquelin Smith Holliday, "The California Gold Rush in Myth and Reality" (Ph.D. diss., Department of History, University of California at Berkeley, 1954), p. 11; Biographical files of members (Society of California Pioneers, San Francisco). For August Helbing's reminiscences of his voyage to California, see Gustav Adolf Danziger, "The Jew in San Francisco the Last Half Century," *Overland Monthly,* April 1895, pp. 385–86.

15. Kemble, op. cit., p. 56. Some Jews, however, made the overland journey, such as Louis Sloss, who later became prominent with the Alaska Commercial Company. See Frank V. McDonald, comp. and ed., *Notes Preparatory to a Biography of Richard Hayes McDonald of San Francisco, California* (Cambridge [England?]: University Press, 1881), pp. 63–75, and appendix, pp. 26, 102, for a description of Sloss's journey in 1849.

16. Adolph Knopf, *The Mother Lode System of California* (Washington: Government Printing Office, 1929), p. 1.

17. Edmund Kinyon, *The Northern Mines* (Grass Valley–Nevada City: Union Publishing Co., 1949), introduction, n.p. This definition would tend to include Marysville and Oroville in the region of the Northern Mines. Jews came to both cities quite early in the gold rush period. The Jewish cemetery in Marysville, located in the southeast corner of the Marysville Cemetery, on the north edge of town, off Highway 70, contains the grave of Arthur Katzenstein, who died in November 1853. The Marysville *Daily Evening Herald* of October 3, 1853, p. 2, contained a news item concerning the dedication of a synagogue there, located on the upper floor of a new brick building on the east side of "C" Street, between First and Second. A B'nai B'rith lodge was established later on. The Jews of Oroville recorded the deed to their cemetery, located at Feather River Boulevard and Mitchell Avenue, April 5, 1859. There are gravestones there dating to the early 1860s. Book E, Deeds, Butte county (Butte County Recorder's Office, Oroville), pp. 260–61.

18. Rodman W. Paul, *California Gold: The Beginning of Mining in the Far West* (Cambridge: Harvard University Press, 1947), pp. 91–93.

19. *Governor's Message; and Report of the Secretary of State on the Census of 1852, of the State of California* (Vallejo[?]: G. K. Fitch and Co., and V. E. Geiger and Co., 1853), p. 57. There were seven counties in the region of the Mother Lode and Northern Mines in 1852, instead of the present-day eight. The state legislature had not yet created Amador County from part of Calaveras County. In addition, the territory covered by the seven counties was greater than their present boundaries, extending from the California-Nevada border southeast of Lake Tahoe to the crest of the Coast Range near San Jose and including present-day Fresno County.

20. The author has concluded, after a close study of federal census records and local vital statistics, that there were no native Americans among the first generation of adult Jews in the California gold rush.

21. Benjamin counted these 962 from reports concerning five Jewish benevolent societies then in existence in San Francisco. Perhaps, however, some of these men were members of more than one such society. Benjamin also counted 400 members in three congregations. [I. J.] Benjamin, *Three Years in America: 1859–1862,* trans. Charles Reznikoff (Philadelphia: Jewish Publication Society of America, 1956), I, 199–210, 225–28.

Benjamin's observations of Jewish life in the gold rush region of

California provide a somewhat sympathetic description of Jews, in contradistinction to accounts by J. D. Borthwick, Hinton R. Helper, and others, infra, and a valuable chronicle of the state of Jewish communal life in that area in 1860. Benjamin helped to organize several Hebrew benevolent societies, as will be noted. It must be borne in mind that he traveled through the Mother Lode with extreme haste; some of his observations, therefore, may not be entirely true. His journey into the interior began November 6, 1860 and was made with Rabbi Henry A. Henry of Congregation Sherith Israel. San Francisco *Weekly Gleaner,* November 9, 1860, p. 5.

22. Charles Peters, *The Autobiography of Charles Peters* (Sacramento: La Grave Co., 1915), p. 139.

23. Harriet Lane Levy, *920 O'Farrell Street* (Garden City, N.Y.: Doubleday and Co., Inc., 1947).

24. See Alexander Iser, comp., *The California Hebrew & English Almanac, For the Year 5612, Corresponding with the Years 1851–2* . . . (San Francisco: Albion Job Press, [1851]), n.p., for a listing of the earliest congregations and organizations that were established.

25. Frank Soulé, John H. Gihon, and James Nisbet, *The Annals of San Francisco* . . . (New York: D. Appleton and Co., 1855), p. 214; Oscar Lewis, *San Francisco: Mission to Metropolis* (Berkeley: Howell-North Books, 1966), pp. 50–51.

26. Soulé, op. cit., p. 216.

27. Charles Caldwell Dobie, *San Francisco: A Pageant* (New York and London: D. Appleton-Century Co., Inc., 1933), chap. xii.

28. Herbert Asbury, *The Barbary Coast* . . . (New York: Pocket Books, Inc., 1947), pp. 59–60, 64–65.

29. Such was the voyage in June 1851 of Garrett W. Low, who took one ship from San Francisco to Sacramento and another from Sacramento to Marysville. Haney, op. cit., p. 159.

30. Frederick J. Teggart, *Around the Horn to the Sandwich Islands and California 1845–1850: Being a Personal Record Kept by Chester S. Lyman* (New Haven: Yale University Press, 1925), pp. 261–65.

31. Friedrich Gerstaecker, *California Gold Mines* (Oakland: Biobooks, 1946), pp. 8–16; Edward Gould Buffum, *Six Months in the Gold Mines* (Ann Arbor:University Microfilms, Inc., 1966), pp. 25–36. For information on the early Jews of Sacramento, see Marlene S. Gaines, "The Early Sacramento Jewish Community," *Western States Jewish Historical Quarterly,* III (January 1971), 65–85.

32. Charles Shinn said: "They held meetings, chose officers, decided disputes, meted out a stern and swift punishment to offenders, and managed their local affairs with entire success." Charles Howard Shinn, *Mining Camps: A Study in American Frontier Governments* (New York: Charles Scribner's Sons, 1855), p. 135.

33. Caughey, op. cit., pp. 179–83.

34. Shinn, op. cit., p. 110.

35. William Perkins, *Three Years in California: William Perkins' Journal of Life at Sonora, 1849–1852,* intro. and annot. Dale L. Morgan and James R. Scobie (Berkeley and Los Angeles: University of California Press, 1964), pp. 101, 105. See also Gerstaecker, op. cit., p. 91, for a description of Stoutenburgh, constructed, for the most part, of tents. Gerstaecker pointed out how important it was for the town, regardless of its size or hoped-for permanence, to be located close to the mines.

36. For example, S. H. Friendly, a merchant in Eugene, Oregon, in the 1880s, also handled most of the wheat and hops raised in Lane County. And there were Jewish slave-owners and slave-traders in the Old South. A. G. Walling, *Illustrated History of Lane County, Oregon* (Portland: A. G. Walling, 1884), p. 502; Bertram W. Korn, "Jews and Negro Slavery in the Old South, 1789–1865," *Publication of the American Jewish Historical Society,* L (March 1961), 151–201.

37. Floyd S. Fierman, "Peddlers and Merchants on the Southwest Frontier: 1850–1880," *Password,* VIII (1963), 2.

38. See n. 23.

NOTES TO CHAPTER 2

1. See chap. 4. See also John Higham, "American Anti-Semitism Historically Considered," in Charles Herbert Stember et al., *Jews in the Mind of America* (New York and London: Basic Books, Inc., 1966), p. 244.

2. Hinton Rowan Helper, *The Land of Gold: Reality Versus Fiction* (Baltimore: Henry Taylor, 1855), p. 53; J. D. Borthwick, *Three Years in America* (Edinburgh and London: William Blackwood and Sons, 1857), p. 116; Hubert Howe Bancroft, *Works,* Vol. XXXV: *California Inter Pocula* (San Francisco: The History Co., 1888), p. 373; Charles Peters, *The Autobiography of Charles Peters* (Sacramento: La Grave Co., 1915), pp. 137–39. However, not all of Peters' remarks concerning Jews were unfavorable. See chap. 1.

3. Helper, op. cit.

4. Borthwick, op. cit.

5. Jacob Kohn prospected in and around Placerville shortly after he arrived in El Dorado County in July 1849. "In Memory of Jacob Kohn," Placerville *Mountain Democrat,* November 8, 1902, p. 4. Abraham Abrahamsohn noted in his memoirs that he prospected near Beavertown in 1851. Friedrich Mihm, *Interessante Berichte über die Reisen Abraham Abrahamsohns nach Amerika und besonders zu den Goldminen Kaliforniens und Australiens* (Ilmenau: Carl Friedrich Trommsdorff, 1856), pp. 18–19. See below, p. 15, for a discussion of another prospector, Lewis Gerstle of Murphys. Henry Schiller, who later served in the Civil War from California as a sergeant, was also a miner in the 1850s. Letter from Barry M. Schiller, Northridge, California, February 11, 1971. Marks Zellerbach also prospected. He "worked with a pick and shovel for nearly three years," following his arrival from New Orleans in 1849, and thereafter opened a small store at Orleans Flat. *San Francisco Examiner,* May 22, 1890, p. 6; telephone conversation with Stephen A. Zellerbach, San Francisco, August 10, 1971.

6. Great Register, Tuolumne County (Tuolumne County Archives, Sonora).

7. Mining Locations, El Dorado County, A (El Dorado County Recorder's Office, Placerville).

8. Record, A, Mining Claims (Amador County Recorder's Office, Jackson).

9. Mining Claims, Calaveras County, A–F (Calaveras County Recorder's Office, San Andreas).

10. Mokelumne Hill *Calaveras Chronicle,* December 27, 1851, p. 4.

11. Gerstle Mack, *Lewis and Hannah Gerstle* (New York: Profile Press, 1953), p. 25.

12. Quartz Claims, A (Mariposa County Recorder's Office, Mariposa), p. 66. Emphasis in the original text.

13. *Columbia Citizen,* August 4, 1866, p. 3.

14. Mining Claims, 6, Nevada County (Nevada County Recorder's Office, Nevada City), p. 579. Jennie, Aaron Baruh's daughter, was born May 5, 1872, and was four years old at the time the above mining claim was recorded. She later married Isadore Zellerbach. The correct spelling of the name is Jennie. See chap. 7 for further information on the Zellerbach family.

15. Angels [Camp] *Calaveras Mountaineer,* December 14, 1872, p. 3.

16. "Letter from Maginnis," El Dorado, November 1865, in Placerville *Mountain Democrat,* November 11, 1865, p. 2.

17. Mokelumne Hill *Weekly Calaveras Chronicle,* June 16, 1866, p. 2. When Cohen died in 1892, he was eulogized as "The Merchant Prince of Calaveras." Cohen, a native of Alsace, came to California in 1850 at the age of twenty-one. He was in partnership with L. Dinkelspiel in Vallecito; their merchandise store was located in the first brick building in town. In addition to his merchandise business, Cohen was postmaster, express agent, and an investor in mining and water interests. On a visit to Alsace in 1870, he was drafted into the French army. After returning to California, Cohen had stores in San Andreas and Angels and was later part of the butcher firm of Gradwohl, Cohen and Company in San Francisco. Sonora *Tuolumne Independent,* October 8, 1892, p. 8. See also Robert E. Stewart, Jr., and Mary Frances Stewart, *Adolph Sutro: A Biography* (Berkeley: Howell-North, 1962), for a discussion of Sutro's participation in the mining industry of Nevada by the same means at about the same time.

18. *North San Juan War Club,* August 3, 1872, p. 3.

19. Nevada City *Nevada Journal,* September 3, 1852, p. 2.

20. [Quartz] Record, C (Mariposa County Recorder's Office, Mariposa), p. 44.

21. Register of Persons and Partnership Under Fictitious Names, Nevada County (Nevada County Recorder's Office, Nevada City), p. 36. This registration, in 1874, was made pursuant to a newly enacted state law. The brothers Marks and Anthony Zellerbach were engaged in banking in Moore's Flat from the early 1860s. Anthony Zellerbach Papers (California Historical Society, San Francisco).

22. Articles of Incorporation (Nevada County Recorder's Office, Nevada City), no. E-12.

23. Articles of Incorporation, 1, Mariposa County (Mariposa County Clerk's Office, Mariposa), no. 78.

24. [I.J.] Benjamin, *Three Years in America: 1859–1862,* trans. Charles Reznikoff (Philadelphia: Jewish Publication Society of America, 1956), II, 28.

25. The only roster of individual foreign miners' payments of this tax the writer could locate was a schedule of names returned by the sheriff of Yuba County in 1853. The great majority of the names were Chinese; there were no Jewish names. Receipts for Foreign Miners License, and Schedule of Names . . . (State of California Archives and Central Records Depository, Sacramento). See also Leonard Pitt, "The

Beginnings of Nativism in California," *Pacific Historical Review*, XXX (February 1961), 23 ff.

26. *Sonora Herald*, July 12, 1851, p. 3. See also the discussion concerning Marks Zellerbach in a similar enterprise, above, p. 18.

27. Ibid., August 16, 1851, p. 2.

28. Jackson *Amador Weekly Ledger*, March 27, 1858, p. 3.

29. Nevada City *Nevada Journal*, February 19, 1852, p. 3; May 1, 1852, p. 3; June 19, 1852, p. 3.

30. Placerville *Mountain Democrat*, January 9, 1864, p. 3.

31. Other examples of Jewish stockholders included L. Elkus, M. J. Rosenberg, and L. Strauss, who were delinquent in their assessments to the Blue Ledge Gold and Silver Mining Company; S. Silberstein, who owned two hundred shares in the Placerville Gold and Silver Mining and Tunnel Company; J. Levy, who owned forty shares of the Clinch Gold and Silver Mining Company of Coloma; Louis Levinsky, whose assessment of $50 on ten shares of Butte Basin Mining Company in the Butte City Mining District of Amador County was unpaid; the merchant Morris Brinn, who owed to the Kennedy Mining Company near Jackson the sum of $9.50; and Morris Cohen, a stockholder in the Calaveras Gold Mining Company, located in the Washington Mining District of Calaveras County. Ibid., May 2, 1868, p. 2; July 16, 1864, p. 3; January 23, 1864, p. 3; Jackson *Amador Dispatch*, February 15, 1868, p. 2; June 4, 1870, p. 3; Angels [Camp] *Calaveras Mountaineer*, December 21, 1872, p. 2.

32. Interview with Mrs. David V. Rosen, Oakland, California, March 7, 1966.

33. A more complete discussion of credit merchandising will be found in the following chapter.

34. Rodman W. Paul, *Mining Frontiers of the Far West, 1848–1880* (New York: Holt, Rinehart and Winston, 1963), pp. 4–5.

NOTES TO CHAPTER 3

1. Nevada City *Nevada Journal*, December 23, 1853, p. 1.

2. Interview with Mrs. Robert Guggenheim, San Francisco, August 16, 1966, concerning the migration of the Haines family to California. See also Robert E. Levinson, "Julius Basinski: Pioneer Montana Merchant," *YIVO Annual of Jewish Social Science*, XIV (1969), 219–33.

3. See, for example, Morris Shloss, "Ups and Downs in Old

California," in Jacob Rader Marcus, *Memoirs of American Jews, 1775–1865* (Philadelphia: Jewish Publication Society of America, 1955), II, 263–67.

4. The inclusive years of the extant volumes of the Great Registers, by counties, are Amador (1866–73), Placer (1866–75), Calaveras (1866–77), El Dorado (1866–78), Sierra (1866–79), Tuolumne (1866–87), and Mariposa (1866–88). See also Richardson Wright, *Hawkers and Walkers in Early America* . . . (Philadelphia: J. B. Lippincott Co., 1927), p. 92; Lewis E. Atherton, "The Pioneer Merchant in Mid-America," *University of Missouri Studies*, XIV (April 1, 1939), 35–37.

5. The other peddlers listed in the Great Registers from 1866 were Samuel Davidson of Mokelumne Hill, Calaveras County; Lewis Levy and Alfred Rosenberg of Jackson, Amador County; Jacob Newman of Sutter Creek, Amador County; and Felix Cohn, of Pine, Placer County. Jacob Heyman was a peddler in the area around Grass Valley before he became a merchant in that city. Lawrence Kinnard, "Alvin Hayman, Jr.," *History of the Greater San Francisco Bay Region* (New York and West Palm Beach: Lewis Historical Publishing Co, 1966), III, 40.

6. Nevada City *Nevada Journal*, May 6, 1853, p. 3. Emphasis in the original text. A business directory of advertisers in the *Nevada Journal* included, in 1858, "H. Horwitz, pedlar, with A. Peyser, in Kidd & Knox's brick." Ibid., May 28, 1858, p. 2.

7. Interview with Jeffrey Schweitzer, Jackson, California, January 31, 1966.

8. U.S., Bureau of the Census, *Eighth Census of the United States, 1860*, California, Mariposa County, p. 34. Rosenthal died in a drowning accident and was buried in the Hebrew Cemetery in Stockton. Jackson *Amador Dispatch*, July 4, 1868, p. 2. Only eight peddlers were recorded in the city and regional directories published during this period, two in Placerville in 1862, five in Grass Valley in 1865, and one in Nevada City in 1867. Thomas Fitch and Company, *Directory of the City of Placerville and Towns of Upper Placerville, El Dorado, Georgetown, and Coloma* . . . (Placerville: Placerville Republican Printing Office, 1862), p. 39; William S. Byrne, *Directory of Grass Valley Township for 1865* (San Francisco: Charles F. Robbins and Co., 1865), pp. 26, 48, 51; Edwin F. Bean, comp., *Bean's History and Directory of Nevada County, California* . . . (Nevada [City]: Daily Gazette Book and Job Office, 1867), p. 138.

9. *Sonora Herald*, July 5, 1851, p. 1.

10. *Statutes of California . . . Second Session* (n.p.: Eugene Casserly,

1851), chap. 32, sec. 1–2, pp. 298–99; *Sonora Herald,* August 2, 1851, p. 4.

11. *Statutes of California* . . ., op. cit., chap. 6, sec. 61, p. 143.

12. *Sonora Herald,* August 2, 1851, p. 4. Many other states enacted prohibitive license fees for peddling: New York (1802, 1859), Georgia (1831, 1837, 1851), Virginia (1834–35), Alabama (1836), North Carolina (1837), Connecticut (1841, 1866), Louisiana (1856), and Ohio (1860). Fred Mitchell Jones, "Middlemen in the Domestic Trade of the United States 1800–1860," *Illinois Studies in the Social Sciences,* XXI (1937), 61–63. See also Wright, op. cit., pp. 90–91, for a discussion of legislation against colonial peddlers.

13. Nevada City *Nevada Journal,* November 20, 1857, p. 1.

14. For examples of Jewish peddlers in other regions, see Abraham Kohn, "A Jewish Peddler's Diary," trans. Abram Vossen Goodman, *American Jewish Archives,* III (June 1951), 81–111; Allan Tarshish, "The Economic Life of the American Jew in the Middle Nineteenth Century," *Essays in American Jewish History* (Cincinnati: American Jewish Archives, 1958), pp. 263–70.

15. William Perkins, *Three Years in California: William Perkins' Journal of Life at Sonora, 1849–1852,* intro. and annots. Dale L. Morgan and James R. Scobie (Berkeley and Los Angeles: University of California Press, 1964), p. 308. Perkins's previous notation of Jews' shops is on p. 289.

16. Ibid., p. 314.

17. J. D. Borthwick, *Three Years in California* (Edinburgh and London: William Blackwood and Sons, 1857), pp. 117–18.

18. Charles Elmer Upton, *Pioneers of El Dorado* (Placerville: Nugget Press, 1906), pp. 42–43. Apparently, at some periods of the gold rush, there were several Jewish peddlers. The presence of such men may be accounted for in the transiency of the occupation. Since peddlers moved from place to place, they most likely did not have a permanent residence or did not record their occupation with the county.

19. James H. Carson, "A Jew in the Mines," *Early Recollections of the Mines, And a Description of the Great Tulare Valley;* 2d ed. (Stockton: San Joaquin Republican, 1852), p. 40. Emphasis in the original text. Much has been written in the literature of western America concerning the outrageous prices that prevailed in gold rush towns. When one considers the available means of transportation to the interior during this period, together with the primitive roads, the justification for high

prices becomes apparent. Prices, in general, fell when transportation improved from mule train to steamboat to railroad. See chap. 5 for a discussion of the nonexistence of overt anti-Semitism in the California gold rush, which may also help to answer the charges of these authors that were always leveled against *unnamed* Jews.

20. Nat. P. Brown and John K. Dallison, *Brown and Dallison's Nevada, Grass Valley and Rough and Ready Directory, For the Year Commencing January 1st, 1856* . . . (San Francisco: Town Talk Office, 1856), pp. 47–101.

21. Hugh B. Thompson, *Directory of the City of Nevada and Grass Valley* . . . (San Francisco: Charles F. Robbins, 1861), pp. 21–58; Bean, op. cit., pp. 137–51.

22. Thompson, op. cit., pp. 99–126.

23. Byrne, op. cit., pp. 17–57.

24. Fitch, op. cit., pp. 21–67. At this time, Jews controlled three-fourths of the clothing companies in the United States. Tarshish, op. cit., p. 281.

25. See chap. 7 for a discussion of Jewish farmers in the region of the gold rush.

26. George Cohen, *The Jews in the Making of America* (Boston: Stratford Co., 1924), pp. 120–23.

27. Ibid., p. 70.

28. Barry E. Supple, "A Business Elite: German-Jewish Financiers in Nineteenth-Century New York," *Business History Review,* XXXI (Summer 1957), 152–54, 163–74; Stephen Birmingham, *"Our Crowd": The Great Jewish Families of New York* (New York: Harper and Row, 1967).

29. Gerstle Mack, *Lewis and Hannah Gerstle* (New York: Profile Press, 1953), pp. 116–26.

30. *Statistics of the Jews of the United States* . . . (Philadelphia: Union of American Hebrew Congregations, 1880), pp. 48, 50–53.

31. Louis Lobenstein Livingston, "Memoirs Experiences Observations" (California State Library, Sacramento), p. 7. Emphasis in the original text.

32. Nevada City *Nevada Journal,* December 18, 1857, p. 2.

33. *San Andreas Independent,* November 8, 1856, p. 3. Another variety store that operated in close cooperation with a San Francisco-based firm was N. Cohn and Company, of Mariposa, whose partner at the bay was Griesman and Company, 88 Sacramento Street. J. S. Landecker, of San Francisco, supplied the grocery and provision store of Bailey Gatzert in Nevada City. (Gatzert later moved to Washington,

became mayor of Seattle, and had a steamboat and a marching song named after him.) A. Wolf and Brothers of San Francisco served as the parent firm of H. Wolf, Sonora. The latter sold "French, English and Domestic winter Dry Goods, Embroidery, Fancy Goods, &c." *Mariposa Chronicle,* April 7, 1854, p. 1; Nevada City *Nevada Journal,* September 5, 1856, p. 1; *Sonora Herald,* February 21, 1857, p. 2.

34. *Volcano Weekly Ledger,* October 27, 1855, p. 3. Emphasis in the original text. For additional information about Abraham Klauber, see Laurence M. Klauber, "Abraham Klauber—A Pioneer Merchant (1831–1911)," *Western States Jewish Historical Quarterly,* II (January 1970), 67–90.

35. Examples include Michael Abels (or Abel) of Mokelumne Hill and Albert (or Aron) and Mary Jacobs of Jamestown. Estate of M. Abels, deceased (Calaveras County Recorder's Office, San Andreas), probate box 20; Estate of A. and M. Jacobs, deceased (Tuolumne County Clerk's Office, Sonora), probate box 44.

36. Harriet Lane Levy, *920 O'Farrell Street* (Garden City, N.Y.: Doubleday and Company, Inc., 1947), pp. 155–56.

37. Ibid., pp. 232–33.

38. Rodman W. Paul, *Mining Frontiers of the Far West, 1848–1880* (New York: Holt, Rinehart and Winston, 1963), pp. 48–50.

39. Jacob Rader Marcus, ed., "An Arizona Pioneer: Memoirs of Sam Aaron," *American Jewish Archives,* X (October 1958), 98–99.

40. Robert E. Levinson, "The Jews of Jacksonville, Oregon" (Master's thesis, Department of History, University of Oregon, 1962), pp. 12–13, 19.

41. Julius J. Nodel, *The Ties Between: A Century of Judaism on America's Last Frontier* (Portland: Temple Beth Israel, 1959), pp. 63 ff.

42. David Rome, *The First Two Years: A Record of the Jewish Pioneers on Canada's Pacific Coast, 1858–1860* (Montreal: H. M. Caiserman, 1942), pp. 17, 22, 31, 113–14, 118–19; Nevada City *Nevada Journal,* September 10, 1858, p. 2.

43. Jackson *Amador Weekly Ledger,* June 26, 1858, p. 2.

44. Mack, op. cit., chaps. 4–6.

45. See, for example, Maurice H. Newmark and Marco R. Newmark, eds., *Sixty Years in Southern California, 1853–1913, Containing the Reminiscences of Harris Newmark;* 3d ed. (Boston and New York: Houghton Mifflin Co., 1930), p. 730, where there are thirty index entries under the heading "dependence, in general, of Los Angeles upon . . . [San Francisco]."

46. Their San Francisco store sold, for the most part, wholesale

wines and liquors. Jacob Rader Marcus, ed., "An Arizona Pioneer ...," op. cit., n. 104.

47. Prescott *Weekly Arizona Miner,* September 7, 1877, quoted in Floyd S. Fierman, "Peddlers and Merchants on the Southwest Frontier, 1850–1880," *Password,* VIII (1963), n., p. 11.

48. Interview with Julius Kahn, Jr., San Francisco, November 11, 1965; Leon L. Watters, *The Pioneer Jews of Utah* (New York: American Jewish Historical Society, 1952), p. 126.

49. Ibid., p. 131.

50. Ibid., p. 140. The uncle of the Cohn brothers, Heiman (or Henry) Cohn, preceded them in business in Poker Flat, as well as being in St. Louis, Sierra County. Henry Cohn, *Jugenderinnerungen* (Stettin: M. Bauchwitz, 1914); Fritz Ludwig Cohn, trans. and ed., "St. Louis and Poker Flat in the Fifties and Sixties: From the Jugenderinnerungen of Henry Cohn," *California Historical Society Quarterly,* XIX (December 1940), 280–89.

51. "Frederick H. Auerbach" (Biographical Sketches: Utah, Bancroft Library, n.d.), p. 9. For a description of Jewish merchandising in general in the Trans-Mississippi West of this period, see "Trail Blazers of the Trans-Mississippi West," *American Jewish Archives,* VIII (October 1956), 59–130. On p. 96 are some recollections of an early Arizona merchant, Samuel H. Drachman, concerning the difficulty experienced by local merchants as a result of accepting paper money for their retail sales but incurring debts for merchandise ordered from San Francisco that were payable in gold coin, then worth 15–25 cents more than paper.

52. Henry Louis operated the Orleans Hotel in Placerville; Samuel Suisman (or Susmon) Snow of Diamond Springs and Emanuel Linoberg of Sonora were farmers; Charles Steckler was the proprietor of a saloon in Volcano and later in Jackson; Frederick Katz of Michigan Bluff was a teamster; the brothers Louis Wendelin Dreyfus and Julius Dreyfus (also spelled Dreyfuss or Dreifoss) operated the United States Bakery in Nevada City; Kaufman Hexter was a butcher in Mokelumne Hill; Samuel Haas of Nevada City was an auctioneer; J. M. Levey was a daguerreotypist in Nevada City; Davis and Benjamin Lachman and A. Block, Emanuel Furth, and E. Block, Jr., all of Nevada City, sold hay and barley. Placerville *Mountain Democrat,* May 23, 1868, p. 2; Great Register, El Dorado County (El Dorado County Clerk's Office, Placerville); Reva Clar, "Samuel Sussman Snow: A Pioneer Finds El Dorado," *Western States Jewish Historical Quarterly,* III (October 1970),

3–25; Cincinnati *Israelite,* November 13, 1857, p. 145; *Volcano Weekly Ledger,* December 22, 1855, p. 3; Great Register, 1866, Amador County (Amador County Clerk's Office, Jackson); Great Register, Placer County (Placer County Clerk's Office, Auburn); Nevada City *Nevada Journal,* June 1, 1855, p. 3; Letter from Mrs. Milton Marks, Jr., San Francisco, June 24, 1965; Register of Partnerships, 1, Calaveras County (Calaveras County Recorder's Office, San Andreas); Nevada City *Nevada Journal,* October 2, 1857, p. 2; September 5, 1856, p. 2; March 31, 1855, p. 1; Nevada City *Nevada Democrat,* March 5, 1863, p. 3.

53. *Sonora Herald,* August 20, 1853, supp. p. 1; Sonora *Union Democrat,* October 13, 1855, p. 4.

NOTES TO CHAPTER 4

1. Assessment Roll, 1860, Sheriff's Office (Calaveras County Assessor's Office, San Andreas); *Population of the United States in 1860; Compiled from the Original Returns of the Eighth Census* . . . (Washington: Government Printing Office, 1864), pp. 22–27.

2. Assessment Roll, Tuolumne County, 1860 (Tuolumne County Archives, Sonora); *Population of the United States in 1860* . . . , op. cit. In 1860 Cohen and Levy of Vallecito declared themselves to be owners of two lots and stone stores, valued at $2,100, and personal property, probably their inventory of store goods, worth $25,951.50. Their tax payment of $544.98 was the fifth highest in Calaveras County, lower only than four water-ditch and canal companies. In Tuolumne County, Harris Levy and Company of Columbia declared themselves to be the owners of four pieces of property in Sonora and Columbia; the value of the real estate and improvements was $3,800, and the personal property therein was worth $12,050. Their tax payment in 1860 was $322.85. L. (or Z.) Jalumstein of Sonora declared himself the owner of a brick store and the jewelry therein, the total value of both being $30,825. His assessment for 1860 was $647.32½. Assessment Roll, 1860 . . . (Calaveras County), op. cit.; Assessment Roll, Tuolumne County, 1860, op. cit., pp. 61, 72.

3. " . . . one of every six Americans who went to California was a native of New England." Earl Pomeroy, *The Pacific Slope: A History* . . . (New York: Alfred A. Knopf, 1965), p. 41.

4. Jackson *Weekly Ledger,* May 16, 1857, p. 2. Emphasis in the original text.

5. Nevada City *Nevada Journal*, March 28, 1856, p. 3.
6. Ibid., July 8, 1853, p. 3.
7. See p. 35 for a further discussion of credit merchandising.
8. Jackson *Amador Dispatch*, December 24, 1870, p. 2.
9. Gerald Carson, *The Old Country Store* (New York: Oxford University Press, 1954), p. 77.
10. Records, Judgment in District Court, B (Amador County Clerk's Office, Jackson), pp. 255–66.
11. Nevada City *Nevada Journal*, December 28, 1855, p. 2.
12. Ibid., October 5, 1855, p. 4.
13. John W. Caughey, *California: A Remarkable State's Life History* (3d ed.; Englewood Cliffs, N.J.: Prentice-Hall, Inc., 1970), p. 403; Le Roy R. Hafen, W. Eugene Hollon, and Carl Coke Rister, *Western America* . . . (3d ed., Englewood Cliffs, N.J.: Prentice-Hall, 1970), p. 525; Estate of Charles Steckler, deceased (Amador County Clerk's Office, Jackson), probate box 33.
14. Downieville *Sierra Age*, June 24, 1871, p. 1.
15. Downieville *Sierra Citizen*, November 19, 1859, p. 3. Marysville was a convenient wholesale shopping town for the merchants of the Northern Mines because it was located near the head of navigation of the Sacramento River. Marysville had a Jewish community dating from the early 1850s that eventually included a B'nai B'rith lodge and a cemetery.
16. Nevada City *Nevada Journal*, November 18, 1853, p. 2.
17. Ibid., March 21, 1856, p. 3.
18. Ibid., October 2, 1857, p. 2.
19. Brands, 1, Tuolumne County (Tuolumne County Recorder's Office, Sonora), p. 1.
20. Sonora *Union Democrat*, July 28, 1866, p. 1.
21. Columbia *Weekly Columbian*, March 7, 1857, p. 2. Today, the journey from Stockton to Columbia, via State Highway 4, is a mere ninety minutes by automobile.
22. Nevada City *Nevada Journal*, November 27, 1857, p. 2.
23. Oscar Osburn Winther, *Express and Stagecoach Days in California from the Gold Rush to the Civil War* (Stanford: Stanford University Press, 1936), pp. 10–13; Rodman W. Paul, *California Gold: The Beginning of Mining in the Far West* (Cambridge: Harvard University Press, 1947), p. 71.
24. Placerville *Mountain Democrat*, October 8, 1864, p. 3; Winther, op. cit., pp. 15–16, 168–69.

25. *Columbia Weekly Times,* August 8, 1861, p. 3.

26. *Columbia Citizen,* December 1, 1866, p. 2.

27. Ibid., June 29, 1867, p. 3.

28. *Volcano Weekly Ledger,* November 3, 1855, p. 3; Nevada City *Nevada Journal,* August 8, 1856, p. 2; September 18, 1851, p. 4; *Mariposa Chronicle,* January 20, 1854, p. 3. Kohlman's store was called the New Orleans Wholesale and Retail Clothing Depot. The name of the store is most likely based upon Kohlman's former residence. See *The Israelites of Louisiana* (New Orleans: W. E. Myers, 1904), p. 39. Kohlman's wife died December 27, 1858 and was buried in the Nevada City Hebrew Cemetery. The epitaph on her gravestone states that she was formerly of New Orleans.

29. San Andreas *Calaveras Weekly Times,* June 6, 1863, p. 1.

30. *Sonora Herald,* June 11, 1853, p. 1.

31. See pp. 42-44 for a discussion of the problems concerning transporting goods to the mountains.

32. Nevada City *Nevada Journal,* September 30, 1853, p. 2.

33. Jackson *Amador Dispatch,* December 17, 1864, p. 3. Emphasis in the original text.

34. Placerville *Mountain Democrat,* October 8, 1864, p. 3.

35. Sonora *Union Democrat,* October 24, 1863, p. 1. Emphasis in the original text.

36. Nevada City *Nevada Journal,* October 10, 1856, p. 3; Jackson *Amador Dispatch,* May 28, 1870, p. 2.

37. Ibid., March 13, 1869, p. 2.

38. Estate of Marcus Abraham, deceased (El Dorado County Clerk's Office, Placerville), inventory, probate box 2.

39. Estate of Elias Levi, deceased (Amador County Clerk's Office, Jackson), inventory and appraisement, old probate index 182.

40. Estate of M. Abels, deceased (Calaveras County Recorder's Office, San Andreas), inventory and appraisement, probate box 20.

41. Nevada City *Nevada Journal,* March 20, 1852, p. 3.

42. *San Andreas Independent,* October 11, 1856, p. 3.

43. *Grass Valley Telegraph,* July 6, 1854, p. 2; July 27, 1854, p. 2.

44. Sonora *Union Democrat,* June 6, 1868, p. 3. Emphasis in the original text.

45. Columbia *Weekly Columbian,* June 28, 1856, p. 3.

46. *San Andreas Independent,* January 10, 1857, p. 3. Other merchants who sold tobacco products and books and stationery from the same establishment were M. Seeligsohn of Sonora, I. S. Rosenbaum

and Company of San Andreas, and S. Harris, who operated one such store in Placerville and another in Austin, Nevada. Sonora *Union Democrat,* April 7, 1855, p. 3; *San Andreas Independent,* October 4, 1856, p. 3; Placerville *Mountain Democrat,* October 8, 1864, p. 3.

47. Nevada City *Nevada Journal,* December 7, 1855, p. 3; May 23, 1856, p. 3.

48. Ibid., December 11, 1857, p. 2. It is noteworthy that these merchants continued to sell and circulate their books in Nevada City in spite of competition from the Nevada Library Association, one of the earliest public libraries in California, which opened in December 1857. Ibid., January 1, 1858, p. 2.

49. *Mariposa Chronicle,* April 7, 1854, p. 3.

50. Nevada City *Nevada Journal,* August 15, 1856, p. 3.

51. Downieville *Sierra Democrat,* February 27, 1864, p. 3. Early-day jewelers in Sonora included Jacob and Lisette Zuckerman and Zelko Jalumstein. Separate Property of Wife and Sole Trader (Tuolumne County Recorder's Office, Sonora), VIII, pp. 13–14; 1855 Assessment Roll, Tuolumne County (Tuolumne County Archives, Sonora), p. 24; Assessment Roll, Tuolumne County, 1860 (Tuolumne County Archives, Sonora), p. 72.

52. Jackson *Amador Dispatch,* August 22, 1868, p. 2. A short time later, the newspaper carried the following article concerning the Brumls' new endeavor: "Punch.—Mr. Bruml is making a new style of 'punch' at his saloon in this place which is said to be far superior to the celebrated Squarza punch, and is two-to-one better than a 'punch in the snoot.'" Ibid., November 14, 1868, p. 2.

53. Separate Property of Wife and Sole Trader (Tuolumne County).

54. 1855 Assessment Roll, Tuolumne County, op. cit., p. 17.

55. Separate Property of Wife and Sole Trader (Tuolumne County), op. cit., pp. 14–15.

56. Sonora *Union Democrat,* March 15, 1856, p. 3. Other members of the Goldwater family (Joseph and S[am?]) lived near Sonora. They operated a cigar store in Shaw's Flat in 1856. [1856] Assessment Roll, Tuolumne County (Tuolumne County Archives, Sonora), p. 35.

57. *Los Angeles Star,* January 14, 1860, quoted in Max Vorspan, "History of the Jews in Los Angeles, 1850–1900" (D.H.L. diss., Jewish Theological Seminary of America [University of Judaism], 1961), p. 54. See also *Los Angeles Star,* December 17, 1859, p. 2.

58. Bankrupts in this region and period included Emanuel Scharff,

of Yuba County, who advertised his insolvency in Nevada City; Abraham Haines of El Dorado; David Newbauer of Placerville; and Moses Reeb of Sonora. Nevada City *Nevada Journal,* July 20, 1855, p. 3; Placerville *Mountain Democrat,* March 2, 1867, p. 2; June 30, 1866, p. 4; Sonora *Union Democrat,* April 17, 1869, p. 4.

59. Downieville *Sierra Citizen,* February 18, 1860, p. 2.

60. Nevada City *Nevada Journal,* August 14, 1857, p. 3.

61. Sonora *Union Democrat,* March 20, 1869, p. 2.

62. About 1919, the bank was reorganized by Max Mierson, the second son of Augustus, and it was eventually purchased by the Bank of America. Interviews with Augustus Mierson, San Francisco, March 9, 1966, and Alfred A. Baer, San Francisco, August 31, 1966; Branch Historical Directory (Bank of America Archives, San Francisco).

63. Register of Persons and Partnership Under Fictitious Names, Nevada County (Nevada County Recorder's Office, Nevada City), p. 92.

64. One of the large mines they owned was the "W.Y.O.D." ("Work Your Own Diggings") Mine.

65. Interview with Julian W. Weston, San Francisco, March 9, 1966.

66. Articles of Incorporation (Nevada County Recorder's Office, Nevada City), nos. W-20, W-21.

67. Julian W. Weston, a son of Jacob Weissbein, did not know the latter three men and how they came to be associated with the firm. Neither did Alvin Hayman, Jr., a grandson of Jacob Heyman. Interview with Alvin Hayman, Jr., San Francisco, August 16, 1966.

68. Some correspondence of Marks and Company may be found in the Anthony Zellerbach Papers (California Historical Society, San Francisco).

69. Block and Furth advertised thus in 1863: " . . . Drafts to New York. We are prepared to furnish exchange, at the best rates. . . . Legal Tender Bills. Always on Hand and For Sale by A. Block & Co." The principals of the firm at this time were A. Block, S. Furth, and E. Block, Jr. Nevada City *Nevada Democrat,* March 5, 1863, p. 3. There is a receipt in the National Hotel Museum, Nevada City: "Block and Furth, bankers, North San Juan, 1867." In addition to serving as a banker, Daniel Furth, another member of the firm, was Wells Fargo agent for North San Juan. Index to People (Wells Fargo Bank History Room, San Francisco); telephone conversation with Victor L. Furth, Walnut Creek, California, September 8, 1966.

70. *Columbia Citizen,* October 30, 1852, p. 3. In the early part of this

century, Saul Morris, who was descended from pioneer merchants in Chinese Camp, was president and a director of the First National Bank of Sonora. This bank was later purchased by the Bank of America. *Tuolumne County, California, Opportunities and Possibilities* (Sonora: Union Democrat, 1909), pp. 83–105. The iron doors to the Morris family general store in Chinese Camp are on display in the Wells Fargo Bank History Room, San Francisco. For an account of the Morris family in Chinese Camp, see Irene D. Paden and Margaret E. Schlichtmann, *The Big Oak Flat Road: An Account of Freighting from Stockton to Yosemite Valley* (San Francisco: Lawton Kennedy, 1955).

71. Banks in California Outside San Francisco (Wells Fargo Bank History Room, San Francisco), Files B-6, B-6.1.

72. Placerville *Mountain Democrat,* September 3, 1864, p. 2.

73. Charles Peters, *The Autobiography of Charles Peters* (Sacramento: La Grave Co., 1915), pp. 14, 137–39.

74. Ibid., pp. 139–40.

75. Sonora *Union Democrat,* October 24, 1863, p. 3.

76. Ibid., June 6, 1868, p. 3.

77. Baer's Store, Sonora, Records.

78. They included Henry Greenberg, who later moved to San Francisco; Isaac and Leopold Barman; Philip and Charles Silbermann; L. Tannenwald, who later moved to Cincinnati; and Michael Simon. Martin A. Meyer, "Henry Greenberg," *Western Jewry: An Account of the Achievements of the Jews and Judaism in California Including Eulogies and Biographies* (San Francisco: Emanu-El, 1916), pp. 97–98; Placerville *Mountain Democrat,* April 16, 1864, p. 2; April 9, 1864, p. 3; October 8, 1864, p. 3; October 1, 1864, p. 2; letter from Estelle Simon, San Francisco, August 24, 1966.

79. *Mariposa Star,* January 24, 1860, p. 3.

80. Jackson *Amador Weekly Ledger,* April 17, 1858, p. 3.

81. Placerville *Mountain Democrat,* September 3, 1864, p. 2.

82. Cohen, Samuels and Company had a drygoods and clothing establishment in Mariposa and Agua Fria, and sold out in a short time to Liebman and Company. J. M. Posner and Company sold drygoods in Mariposa and Carson Creek but sold out in 1854, "with a view of returning to the Atlantic States." When L. Frankl, Mayer S. Aschheim, and Julius Salomonson dissolved their partnership in Mariposa and Carson Creek, it was announced that Frankl would continue the business in Mariposa and "receive all the debts due the late firm." Frankl later moved to southern California, where he founded San

Simeon and sold seven leagues of land to Senator George Hearst for $85,000. *Mariposa Democrat,* August 5, 1856, p. 3; *Mariposa Star,* June 5, 1860, p. 2; *Mariposa Chronicle,* January 20, 1854, p. 1; April 7, 1854, p. 3; Yda Addis Storke, *A Memorial and Biographical History of the Counties of Santa Barbara, San Luis Obispo and Ventura, California* (Chicago: Lewis Publishing Co., 1891), p. 277.

83. Uncertified Index to Naturalizations (Amador County Clerk's Office, Jackson).

84. Jackson *Amador Dispatch,* February 22, 1868, p. 2; **Register of Partnerships**, 1, Amador County (Amador County Clerk's Office, Jackson); *McKenney's District Directory for 1879–80, of Sacramento, City and County, Amador, Eldorado* [sic], *Placer and Yolo Counties* (Sacramento and San Francisco: L. M. McKenney, 1879), pp. 374, 382, 401. The name of another Coblentz, A., appears, ibid., p. 401, as a partner of the store in the city of El Dorado, but he was not related to the aforementioned family. Letter from Zach B. Coblentz, M.D., San Francisco, February 10, 1968.

85. Interview with Edgar M. Kahn, San Francisco, December 21, 1965.

86. Register of Partnerships, 1, Amador County, op. cit.

87. The partners in Virginia City and Grass Valley were Jacob Morris and David Nathan. The partners in Reno who opened a branch in Grass Valley were Nathan Nathan and Morris Nathan. Register of Persons and Partnership Under Fictitious Names, Nevada County, op. cit., nos. 44, 135.

88. Ibid., no. 40. It has been necessary to restrict the discussion of branch merchandising in this region to the 1870s, for the most part, because the state law requiring businesses to file their assumed names was not enacted until 1873.

89. Nevada City *Nevada Journal,* July 7, 1854, p. 2.

90. *Columbia Gazette, and the Southern Mines Advertiser,* March 26, 1856, p. 2.

91. The earliest available official reference to fire insurance rates in this general area, published in 1886, reveals that a class B building, constructed entirely of brick, stone, and iron, could be insured for from 20 to 80 percent less than a class C building of partial frame construction. (A class C building was designated as having at least one wooden wall, a shingle roof, or a frame structure on the roof.) It was also more expensive to insure clothing and other combustible goods inside a class C building than a class B building. The rates were

uniformly 20 percent higher for goods in buildings that were not all brick, stone, or iron. *Book of Rates. No. 3. For the Use and Guidance of Fire Underwriters on the Pacific Coast* (San Francisco: Pacific Insurance Union, 1886), pp. 5, 11–15.

92. Interview with Richard B. Masters, C.P.C.U., Executive Manager, Insurance Educational Association, San Francisco, March 8, 1966.

93. Interview with Barbara Eastman, Oakland, California, July 19, 1966.

94. Rudolf Glanz, *The Jews of California From the Discovery of Gold Until 1880* (New York: Waldon Press, Inc., 1960), p. 50.

95. See chap. 5.

96. For example, Grauman and Josephson, proprietors of the Kentucky Store, a men's clothing establishment in Nevada City, thus advertised early in 1856: "We intend to sell 25 per cent cheaper than those who occupy Brick buildings, and *whatever we say, we do!*" Nevada City *Nevada Journal,* January 4, 1856, p. 2. Emphasis in the original text.

97. Ibid., August 8, 1856, pp. 1–2, 4. This was the first edition of the paper published after the fire.

98. Ibid., p. 3.

99. Ibid., p. 4.

100. Ibid. Like so many other cities and towns, Nevada City was visited by fire on more than one occasion. On May 24, 1858, the town was destroyed again. However, the conflagration of 1856 had taught the merchants some valuable lessons. Before the second fire, more brick buildings were erected, and those already built were improved. Since the flames spread more slowly in the second fire, the merchants had time to store their merchandise in fireproof cellars. This time, the loss was only $200,450. The total lost by the twenty-four Jewish merchants involved was $26,550. Ibid., May 28, 1858, p. 1.

The tragedy of fire occurred at least once in every major town, and in the smaller towns one fire was sufficient to drive all the residents to new surroundings, leaving the townsite desolate. Local newspapers, or those in nearby towns, printed what they considered an accurate estimate of the losses incurred, and the Jewish merchants were always at or near the head of the roster of sufferers. For example, in Sonora, November 2, 1853, Philip Selling lost $8,000; in Grass Valley, September 13, 1855, J. Cohn lost $7,000; in small Chinese Camp, on June 8, 1856, Wolf and Company's loss of $6,000 was the second highest in town; in larger Placerville, Mark Levison suffered $3,500 in damages July 6, 1856. The great fire in Columbia, August 25, 1857, which destroyed an estimated $582,190 worth of property, was the occasion of a $17,000 loss to S. Levy and Brother, the sixth greatest loss that day. In Forest City, April 11, 1858, the total losses of fifteen Jewish merchants, $26,500, were nearly one-fourth of the total $112,250 loss. In the last-named fire, Fleishhacker and Company lost $2,500 worth of goods in their store there. *Columbia Gazette,* November 5, 1853, p. 2; Nevada City *Nevada Journal,* September 21, 1855, p. 2; *Volcano Weekly Ledger,* June 14, 1856, p. 2; July 12, 1856, p. 2; *Columbia Gazette,* September 1, 1857, p. 1; Nevada City *Nevada Journal,* April 16, 1858, p. 1.

101. Such buildings include the stores of the Levy families in Columbia, Moses Dinkelspiel in Vallecito, Rosenblum in Chinese Camp, Rosenberg in Jenny Lind, Michael Gilbert in Big Oak Flat, and the brothers Aaron, Julius, and Emanuel Meier in Downieville. The Gilbert building is now the left-hand portion of the Big Oak Flat I.O.O.F. Hall. Gilbert was Wells Fargo agent for Big Oak Flat in 1859 and a charter member of Yo Semite Lodge No. 97, I.O.O.F. The Gilbert store and the I.O.O.F. Hall, which share a common wall, were the only buildings in Big Oak Flat to survive the fire of 1863. Interview with Jerome Salomon, San Francisco, November 10, 1965. There is a plaque in front of the Thompson Building in Murphy's indicating that it was occupied as a store by Oser Meyer and Friedlander in the late 1850s or early 1860s. Henry O. Meyer, "A Brief Account of the Family of Oser Meyer and Bertha Michelson Meyer and its Relationship to the Michelsons" (South San Francisco: n.p., n.d.), n.p. The book by Raymond Early, *Columbia* (San Francisco: Fearon Publishers, 1957), contains, on pp. 18 and 70, early maps of Columbia giving the location of the buildings of Jewish merchants.

NOTES TO CHAPTER 5

1. Rodman W. Paul, *Mining Frontiers of the Far West, 1848–1880* (New York: Holt, Rinehart and Winston, 1963), p.15.
2. Rodman W. Paul, *California Gold: The Beginning of Mining in the Far West* (Cambridge: Harvard University Press, 1947), pp. 27–28. Jewish merchants were also found in the other gold rushes that rimmed the Pacific Ocean during the century and in the small trading

posts and new cities of the American Middle West and Southwest. Philip Ross May, *The West Coast* [of New Zealand] *Gold Rushes* (Christchurch, N.Z.: Pegasus Press, 1962), pp. 316–17; William J. Parish, *The Charles Ilfeld Company: A Study of the Rise and Decline of Mercantile Capitalism in New Mexico* (Cambridge: Harvard University Press, 1961), pp. 6–7.

Regarding the countries of origin of California's early Jews, see Norton B. Stern and William M. Kramer, "The Major Role of Polish Jews in the Pioneer West," *Western States Jewish Historical Quarterly*, VIII (July 1976), 326–44.

3. See chap. 3, pp.57-60, concerning the large number of brick buildings in the towns of the Mother Lode that were built by Jews.

4. See chap. 3, p. 38, for a discussion of the property taxes paid by Jews.

5. Lewis Atherton, *Main Street on the Middle Border* (Bloomington: Indiana University Press, 1954), chap. 6. See also Lewis E. Atherton, "The Pioneer Merchant in Mid-America," *University of Missouri Studies*, XIV (April 1, 1939), 26–30, for a study of the involvement of merchants in general in community life in the Middle West.

6. Timothy Smith, "New Approaches to the History of Immigration in Twentieth Century America," *American Historical Review*, LXXI (July 1966), 1272–73.

7. The absence of ethnic neighborhoods in the cities of this area, outside of the "Chinatowns," aided in the rapid acculturation of Jews but was also a factor in the occurrence of marriages out of the faith. Ibid., p. 1268.

8. C. Bezalel Sherman, *The Jew Within American Society: A Study in Ethnic Individuality* (Detroit: Wayne State University Press, 1961), p. 60.

9. Three merchants who found wives in Europe while visiting their parents were Henry Cohn of St. Louis and Poker Flat, Aaron Meier of Downieville, and Sol Wangenheim of Jenny Lind. Cohn, however, remained in Europe. Fritz Ludwig Cohn, trans. and ed., "St. Louis and Poker Flat in the Fifties and Sixties," *California Historical Society Quarterly*, XIX (December 1940), 289, taken from Henry Cohn, *Jugenderinnerungen* (Stettin: M. Bauchwitz, 1914); Joseph Gaston, "Aaron Meier," *Portland, Oregon, Its History and Builders* . . . (Chicago and Portland: S. J. Clarke Publishing Co., 1911), II, 234; biographical information of Sol Wangenheim, supplied by Mrs. George Heyneman, San Diego, California, July 13, 1966.

10. *Volcano Weekly Ledger*, September 27, 1856, p. 2. Emphasis in the original text. See also ibid., August 30, 1856, p. 3.

11. Uncertified Indices to Naturalization (County Clerks' Offices).

12. Each county maintained its copy of the Great Register of voters, which was begun July 5, 1866. There was no official book of registered voters before 1866.

13. The Great Register . . . (County Clerks' Offices).

14. J. Heckendorn and W. A. Wilson, *Miners & Business Men's Directory. For the Year Commencing January 1st, 1856* . . . (Columbia: Clipper Office, 1856), pp. 37-38.

15. Nevada City *Nevada Journal*, May 8, 1857, p. 2.

16. H. L. Wells, *History of Nevada County, California* . . . (Oakland: Thompson and West, 1880), p. 217.

17. Ibid., p. 139; letter from Arthur A. Goldsmith, Portland, Oregon, June 15, 1965; Nevada City *Weekly National Gazette*, May 18, 1872, p. 2.

18. Mrs. J. L. Sargent, ed., *Amador County History* (Jackson: Amador County Federation of Women's Clubs, 1927), p. 30.

19. Placerville *Mountain Democrat*, April 25, 1868, p. 2. The same position was held in Jackson by Samuel Levey. Jackson *Amador Dispatch*, December 19, 1868, p. 2.

20. Columbia: Edward Elias (1875-77) and Louis Levy (1877-81); Mokelumne Hill: Lewis M. Hellman (1857-59), Max Hellman (1865-66), and Samuel L. Davidson (1887-88); Jackson: Herman Goldner (1885-89); Indian Diggings: Jacob Wolf (1853-54); Jenny Lind: Louis Rosenberg (1864-67); Gibsonville: Nathan Scheeline (1858-60), Alexander Scheeline (1869-70), and Moritz Newhouse (1870). Records of the Post Office Department, [Microfilm] Record Group 28, Records of Appointments of Postmasters, State of California, 1848-1930 (Washington: General Services Administration, National Archives and Records Service, 1953).

21. Emanuel Linoberg in Tuolumne County (*Columbia Gazette*, June 23, 1855, p. 2); P. B. Openheim in Nevada County (Nevada City *Nevada Journal*, July 16, 1858, p. 1); J. Klipstine, Michael Borowsky, Moses Hyneman, Henry D. Raphael, and P. Cobletz [*sic*, i.e., Coblentz] in El Dorado County (Placerville *Mountain Democrat*, September 10, 1864, p. 3; August 25, 1865, p. 2; May 2, 1868, p. 2); and Samuel Levy in Amador County (Jackson *Amador Dispatch*, June 26, 1869, p. 2). In Fiddletown, M. Raphael was a member of the executive committee of Fiddletown Democratic Club No. 4, and in Mariposa, Joseph Blumenthal served as secretary of the Mariposa Democratic Club. *Volcano Weekly Ledger*, September 6, 1856, p. 3; *Mariposa Democrat*, August 5, 1856, p. 3.

22. Such positions were held by Emanuel Linoberg of Sonora (*Columbia Gazette,* September 1, 1857, p. 2); J. Fleishman of Greenwood Valley (Placerville *Mountain Democrat,* April 6, 1867, p. 2); and Samuel Levy of Jackson and Aaron (or Aron) Weil of Amador City (Jackson *Amador Dispatch,* August 19, 1871, p. 3).

23. Sonora *Union Democrat,* October 8, 1859, p. 2.

24. Jackson *Amador Dispatch,* July 15, 1871, p. 2.

25. On the grand jury level were, for example, Charles Fridenberg and Moses Cohen of Tuolumne County (Columbia *Weekly Columbian,* June 6, 1857, p. 3) and Marks Lasky of El Dorado County (Placerville *Mountain Democrat,* January 9, 1864, p. 2). In El Dorado County, Henry Louis, Henry D. Raphael, Augustus Mierson, and Michael Borowsky served as trial jurors in the District Court at the same time (Placerville *Mountain Democrat,* February 16, 1867, p. 2). B. Isaacs and Aron Weil held the same position in Amador County (Jackson *Amador Dispatch,* March 14, 1868, p. 2; September 23, 1871, p. 2). Members of coroner's juries included Ben Strauss in Calaveras County (*San Andreas Independent,* October 4, 1856, p. 2) and Samuel Levy and M. Bruml in Amador County (Jackson *Amador Dispatch,* February 29, 1868, p. 3).

26. Nevada City *Nevada Journal,* December 27, 1851, p. 2.

27. Ibid., November 3, 1854, p. 2.

28. D. W. Lubeck was elected treasurer of Eureka Lodge No. 16, Free and Accepted Masons of Auburn, and Arnold Friedberger was elected to the same position in Calaveras Lodge at San Andreas. Bernard Isaacs served as worshipful master (i.e., the presiding officer) of Ione Lodge No. 80, F. and A.M., and Jews were elected and reelected to positions in the Grass Valley, Sutter Creek, Diamond Springs, Coloma, and Georgetown lodges. In Jackson, Mark Levinsky rose from junior warden to senior warden of Amador Lodge No. 65, F. and A.M., and also served as principal sojourner of Sutter Chapter No. 11, Royal Arch Masons. Placerville *Mountain Democrat,* December 5, 1868, p. 3; Angels [Camp] *Calaveras Mountaineer,* January 1, 1873, p. 3; Jackson *Amador Dispatch,* December 30, 1871, p. 2; Nevada City *Nevada Journal,* January 1, 1852, p. 2; Jackson *Amador Dispatch,* December 30, 1871, p. 2; Placerville *Mountain Democrat,* December 30, 1865, p. 2; December 21, 1867, p. 2; December 17, 1864, p. 2; Jackson *Amador Dispatch,* December 14, 1867, p. 2; January 1, 1870, p. 2; December 11, 1869, p. 2.

29. Placerville *Mountain Democrat,* January 2, 1864, p. 3; January 21, 1865, p. 2. In addition, Jewish members of lodges were occasionally

appointed to special committees to draft resolutions of condolence on the occasion of the death of a fellow member or to aid in the planning of a lodge ball. Jackson *Amador Weekly Ledger,* March 27, 1858, p. 3; Jackson *Amador Dispatch,* May 16, 1868, p. 2; Placerville *Mountain Democrat,* May 25, 1867, p. 2; Sonora *Union Democrat,* June 12, 1869, p. 2.

30. Edwin F. Bean, comp., *Bean's History and Directory of Nevada County, California* ... (Nevada [City]: Daily Gazette Book and Job Office, 1867), p. 338.

31. Louis Lippman of Tuolumne Lodge No. 21 of Columbia, S. Harris of Zeta Encampment No. 5 of Placerville, Daniel Schwartz of Momento Lodge No. 37 of Georgetown, Raphael Levy of Diamond Springs Lodge No. 9, and Morris Brinn of Sutter Creek Lodge No. 31. *Columbia Gazette,* July 14, 1855, p. 2; Placerville *Mountain Democrat,* January 13, 1866, p. 2; February 1, 1868, p. 2; ibid.; Jackson *Amador Dispatch,* January 6, 1872, p. 2.

32. In the last-named organization, Richard Cohn and L. Landecker served as officers in Nevada City and M. Wolf in Springfield. Nevada City *Nevada Journal,* December 16, 1853, p. 2; June 30, 1854, p. 2; *Columbia Gazette,* October 14, 1854, p. 2.

33. Abraham Seligman and his brother, Leopold, merchants in that city, and owners of the "Seligman Block," left Placerville shortly thereafter for New York to aid in the founding of the investment firm of J. and W. Seligman and Company in 1864. Albert Shumate, *A Note on ECV in the Gold Fields* (San Francisco: Lawton Kennedy, n.d.), n.p.; Ross L. Muir and Carl J. White, *Over the Long Term . . . the Story of J. & W. Seligman & Company* (New York: J. & W. Seligman & Co., 1964). E Clampus Vitus, "a sort of parody of the solemn and mysterious fraternal orders then so popular in the States." *Credo Quia Absurdum: Being a Compilation of Historic Documents and Trivia Pertinent to a full Understanding of the Meaning and Purpose of the Ancient and Honorable Order of E Clampus Vitus* (Placerville: n.p., 1949), introduction, n.p.

34. Membership Roster, [Columbia] Engine Co. No. 2 (Columbia State Park Museum).

35. Downieville *Sierra Advocate,* December 8, 1866, p. 2. In Placerville, Henry Louis was a long-time foreman and L. Landecker a second assistant and trustee, successively. Placerville *Mountain Democrat,* March 28, 1868, p. 2; May 11, 1867, p. 2. In Columbia, the office of first assistant was held by Albert Jacobi and L. Levy. *Columbia Citizen,* December 8, 1866, p. 3; February 9, 1867, p. 3.

36. Interview with Julius Kahn, Jr., San Francisco, November 11, 1965.

37. In Placerville, Aaron Kahn was treasurer of the fire department in 1862, and four years later, C. Silberman held the position of financial secretary. In Grass Valley, Henry Silvester was charter treasurer of Protection Hose Co. No. 1 in 1861, and in 1867, the same office was occupied in Tiger Hook and Ladder Co. No. 1 by L. Zacharias. D. Furth was charter treasurer of Hydraulic Hose Co. No. 1 of Bridgeport Township, which was established October 13, 1862, and Jacob Weis served Columbia Engine Co. No. 2 in that capacity in 1865. Thomas Fitch and Company, *Directory of the City of Placerville and Towns of Upper Placerville, El Dorado, Georgetown, and Coloma* . . . (Placerville: Placerville Republican Printing Office, 1862), p. 17; Placerville *Weekly Recorder*, August 15, 1866, p. 3; William S. Byrne, *Directory of Grass Valley Township for 1865* (San Francisco: Charles F. Robbins and Co., 1865), p. 68; Bean, op. cit., pp. 197, 338; Membership Roster, [Columbia] Engine Co. No. 2, op. cit.

38. Assessment Roll . . . Tuolumne County [1862 and 1863] (Tuolumne County Archives, Sonora).

39. Harris Levy of Columbia was aide-de-camp with the rank of captain in the Second Brigade, Third Division, California State Militia. His fellow townsman, Herman Wolf, served a few years later as orderly sergeant of the Tuolumne National Guard. In Nevada City, a Volunteer Rifle Company was organized by Sol. Kohlman, J. Jacobs, Simon Mayers, Aaron Baruh, and others on January 26, 1858. Later that same year, S. Lewis, Aaron Baruh, and J. M. Levy (or Levey) participated in a target shooting competition, and A. Rosenheim and J. M. Levy served on committees for a military and civic ball sponsored by the Nevada Rifles. Columbia *Weekly Columbian,* May 30, 1857, p. 2; *Columbia Citizen,* September 1, 1866, p. 2; Nevada City *Nevada Journal,* January 29, 1858, p. 2; April 16, 1858, p. 2; June 18, 1858, p. 2.

40. Simon Wolf, *The American Jew as Patriot, Soldier and Citizen* (Philadelphia: Levytype Co., 1895), pp. 125–26; letter from Barry M. Schiller, Northridge, California, February 11, 1971. Schiller enlisted as a private January 7, 1863 and was discharged November 8, 1865 as a sergeant in Company A, Second Cavalry Regiment. For additional information concerning these twenty-eight California Jews in the Civil War, see Sylvan Morris Dubow, "Problems in Jewish Military Service Research," *Western States Jewish Historical Quarterly,* II (January 1970), 101–5, and pt. II of the same article in ibid., IV (April 1972), 146–48.

41. Muster Roll, Capt. Hopkins Company ... 3rd Brigade, 1st Division (Secretary of State's Office, Sacramento). According to family tradition, Gradwohl's brigade saw a great deal of service: in the gold fields of California and around Los Angeles, where they discouraged some secessionist sentiment in those locations; in several western states and territories against the Indians; and in West Texas, where they encountered Confederate troops. Telephone conversation with Arthur Gradwohl, San Francisco, February 7, 1968; interview with ibid., March 8, 1966; letter from ibid., July 29, 1971.

42. Interview with Roy Gottheimer, San Francisco, July 13, 1966.

43. Interview with Erwin M. Hirschfelder, San Francisco, July 14, 1966; interview with Lester Bernheim and Miss Hortense Bernheim, Los Angeles, conducted by Norton B. Stern, August 13, 1966.

44. Those in favor of incorporating Columbia in 1854 included Isaac Levy, N. Levy, A. Friedman, A. Lewisson, and S. Friedman. In the matter of the petition of the citizens of Columbia for incorporation, Articles of Incorporation (Tuolumne County Clerk's Office, Sonora), no. 23. See also Record, County Court Records, A (Amador County Clerk's Office, Jackson); Minutes of Judgment Book, B, County Court (El Dorado County District Attorney's Office, Placerville), September term, 1852, pp. 58–60.

45. Petitions supporting the Sabbath Observance Law (State of California, Archives and Central Records Depository, Sacramento). See below for further discussion on this subject.

46. When a petition was circulated among the citizens of Mokelumne Hill, September 20, 1851, that recommended Charles A. Leake for county judge in case a vacancy should occur in that office, the result was ten Jewish petitioners of the total 106. Following the disastrous fire of June 18, 1852 in Sonora, Emanuel Linoberg was appointed to a committee to advise the city council on the laying of new streets. Calaveras County, Records (T. W. Norris Collection, Bancroft Library); *Sonora Herald,* June 19, 1852, pp. 2–3.

47. Jackson *Amador Dispatch,* June 4, 1870, p. 2; May 20, 1871, p. 2; February 10, 1872, p. 2; *Columbia Citizen,* September 1, 1866, p. 3; Jackson *Amador Dispatch,* March 25, 1865, p. 3; Placerville *Mountain Democrat,* February 2, 1867, p. 2; Jackson *Amador Dispatch,* March 9, 1872, p. 2; January 7, 1871, p. 2.

48. *Columbia Weekly Times,* June 6, 1861, p. 2; Nevada City *Nevada Journal,* February 22, 1856, p. 2.

49. *Mariposa Star,* January 24, 1860, p. 3.

50. Placerville: Flora, Jacob, and Sarah Nachman, Nathan and Sarah Kohn, Samuel Cohn, S. Lewis, Henry Wulff, and Henry M. Wolfe; Sutter Creek: Isaac Marks, Lena Weldman, and Ida Herman; Columbia: David Levy; Downieville: Fannie Hirschfelder. Placerville *Mountain Democrat,* April 18, 1868, p. 2; April 25, 1868, p. 2; June 13, 1868, p. 2; November 7, 1868, p. 3; Jackson *Amador Dispatch,* March 27, 1869, p. 2; Sutter Creek *Semi-Weekly Independent,* April 4, 1874, p. 3; Columbia *Weekly Columbian,* April 4, 1857, p. 2; Downieville *Sierra Advocate,* February 2, 1867, p. 3.

51. Placerville *Mountain Democrat,* September 16, 1865, p. 2.

52. Jackson *Amador Weekly Ledger,* May 15, 1858, p. 2.

53. Nevada City *Nevada Journal,* February 16, 1855, p. 2; May 13, 1859, p. 3.

54. Ibid., October 22, 1858, p. 2.

55. Jackson *Weekly Ledger,* April 25, 1857, p. 2.

56. Ibid., August 29, 1856, p. 1.

57. Downieville *Sierra Advocate,* January 5, 1867, p. 2.

58. Alexander McLeod, *Pigtails and Gold Dust: A Panorama of Chinese Life in Early California* (Caldwell, Idaho: Caxton Printers, Ltd., 1947), p. 45. See also ibid., pp. 45–46, for an unauthenticated confrontation between a Jewish merchant and a Chinese customer.

59. John Higham, "American Anti-Semitism Historically Reconsidered," in Charles Herbert Stember and others, *Jews in the Mind of America* (New York and London: Basic Books, Inc., 1966), p. 244.

60. John Higham, "Social Discrimination Against Jews in America, 1830–1930," *Publication of the American Jewish Historical Society,* XLVII (September 1957), 3–7.

61. [Jacob Rader Marcus], "Anti-Jewish Sentiment in California, 1855," *American Jewish Archives,* XII (April 1960), 15.

62. *Statutes of California, Passed at the Sixth Session of the Legislature* . . . (Sacramento: B. B. Redding, State Printer, 1855), chap. XLVI, pp. 50–51.

63. [Marcus], op. cit.: *Sacramento Daily Union,* March 17, 1855, p. 3. The writings of the Rev. William Ingraham Kip, Episcopal bishop of California, also included statements blaming Jewish merchants for keeping their stores open on Sunday and making the enactment of a Sunday closing law difficult. William Ingraham Kip, *The Early Days of my Episcopate* (New York: Thomas Whittaker, 1892), p. 145. See also "Sabbath Movements in the Mountains," San Francisco *Pacific,* September 10, 1852, p. 2, in which there is an unsupported allegation

that Jews were the only merchants in Grass Valley who kept their stores open on Sunday.

64. *Sacramento Daily Union,* March 19, 1855, p. 2. See also *Los Angeles Star,* January 10, 1857, quoted in Justin G. Turner, "The First Decade of Los Angeles Jewry: A Pioneer History (1850–1860)," *American Jewish Historical Quarterly,* LIV (December 1964), 135–36; Stockton *San Joaquin Republican,* March 18, 1855, p. 2; March 20, 1855, p. 2; March 21, 1855, p. 2; March 22, 1855, p. 2; Cincinnati *Israelite,* May 11, 1855, pp. 345–46.

65. [Marcus], op. cit.; *Sacramento Daily Union,* March 17, 1855, p. 3.

66. Petitions for enactment of a Sabbath law (State of California, Archives and Central Records Depository, Sacramento).

67. Nevada City *Nevada Journal,* January 29, 1858, p. 3.

68. Ibid., September 4, 1857, p. 2.

69. Ibid., October 2, 1857, p. 2.

70. Turner, op. cit., pp. 135, 164.

71. Nevada City *Nevada Journal,* April 30, 1858, p. 3. Emphasis in the original text.

72. Bertram W. Korn, *American Jewry and the Civil War* (Cleveland and New York: World Publishing Co., and Philadelphia: Jewish Publication Society of America, 1961), p. 122.

73. Joakim Isaacs, "Candidate Grant and the Jews," *American Jewish Archives,* XVII (April 1965), 3 ff.

74. Placerville *Mountain Democrat,* June 6, 1868, p. 4.

75. Ibid., August 8, 1868, p. 2.

76. Jackson *Amador Dispatch,* June 20, 1868, p. 2.

77. Ibid., October 24, 1868, p. 1.

78. Mokelumne Hill *Weekly Calaveras Chronicle,* September 12, 1868, p. 1.

79. Korn, op. cit., pp. 168, 173.

80. Sonora *Union Democrat,* August 31, 1872, p. 1.

81. This was not so for the rest of the country. The increase in the Jewish population created many anti-Semitic feelings, which manifested themselves in Grant's Order No. 11 and in negative opinions on the appointment of Jewish chaplains for the Union in the Civil War. Korn, op. cit., pp. 122, 56–97.

82. *Placerville American,* July 19, 1856, p. 3. Emphasis in the original text.

83. Philadelphia *Occident,* September 1856, p. 311.

84. J[acob] Solis-Cohen, Jr., "A California Pioneer: The Letters of

Bernhard Marks to Jacob Solis-Cohen (1853–1857)," *Publication of the American Jewish Historical Society,* XLIV (September 1954), 12 ff.

85. See above, page 72.

86. *History of Fresno County, California* . . . (San Francisco: Wallace W. Elliott and Co., 1881), pp. 111–14, 219–21. For additional information on Marks's later career, see Irena Penzik Narell, "Bernhard Marks: Retailer, Miner, Educator and Land Developer," *Western States Jewish Historical Quarterly,* VIII (October 1975), 26–38.

87. *Columbia Times,* March 15, 1860, p. 2.

88. Columbia *Tuolumne Courier,* May 5, 1860, p. 2.

89. *Columbia Times,* April 11, 1861, p. 2.

90. Columbia *Tuolumne Courier,* April 13, 1861, p. 2. Emphasis in the original text.

91. Ibid., May 4, 1861, p. 2. Emphasis in the original text.

92. Ibid., June 15, 1861, p. 2.

93. Letter from Barbara Eastman, Oakland, California, November 16, 1966.

94. Nevada City *Nevada Journal,* October 14, 1853, p. 1.

95. James Mason Hutchings, *The Miner's Ten Commandments* (San Francisco: J. M. Hutchings, 1887), n.p. The publication of the commandments served the movement for a Sunday closing law very well; 97,000 copies of the tract, with its anti-Jewish sentiment, were sold in a little over one year.

96. Ibid., n.p. Perhaps Hutchings's new partner in the publishing business, a Mr. Rosenfield, who joined the firm in the late 1850s, was responsible for Hutchings changing his mind about Jews. An early work published by Hutchings and Rosenfield was *Scenes of Wonder and Curiosity in California* (San Francisco, 1860).

97. 1855, Assessment Roll, Tuolumne County (Tuolumne County Archives, Sonora), pp. 54, 71.

98. [1856] Assessment Roll, Tuolumne County (Tuolumne County Archives, Sonora), pp. 36, 54, 71, 74.

99. While the author's research was somewhat hampered by people's insistence that Judaism is a nationality, thereby making difficult the determination of a particular Jew's country of origin, such misidentification was not made out of malice.

100. "In Memory of Jacob Kohn," Placerville *Mountain Democrat,* November 8, 1902, p. 4.

101. Reva Clar, "Samuel Sussman Snow: A Pioneer Finds El

Dorado," *Western States Jewish Historical Quarterly*, III (October 1970), 3–25.
102. Narell, op. cit.
103. Sherman, op. cit., p. 70.

NOTES TO CHAPTER 6

1. C. Bezalel Sherman, *The Jew Within American Society: A Study in Ethnic Individuality* (Detroit: Wayne State University Press, 1961), p. 63.
2. "Trail Blazers of the Trans-Mississippi West," *American Jewish Archives*, VIII (October 1956), 59–130. Several European publishers prepared pocket-sized prayer books for the Jewish immigrants so that they could always carry one with them.
3. Sherman, op. cit., p. 72.
4. See chaps. 3 and 4.
5. Jacob Voorsanger, *The Chronicles of Emanu-El: Being an Account of the Rise and Progress of the Congregation Emanu-El Which Was Founded in July, 1850* . . . (San Francisco: George Spaulding and Co., 1900), note, p. 16. The large number of Jews permitted separate services to be held in San Francisco. In the mountains, the relatively few Jews present overcame their national prejudices and conducted one service.
6. [I. J.] Benjamin, *Three Years in America, 1859–1862*, trans. Charles Reznikoff (Philadelphia: Jewish Publication Society of America, 1956), I, 199, 204; Edgar M. Kahn, "The Saga of the First Fifty Years of Congregation Emanu-El, San Francisco," *Western States Jewish Historical Quarterly*, III (April 1971), 129–47. References to the first Jewish religious services in San Francisco, for Yom Kippur 1849, are contained in letters from one of the officiants, Lewis Lewis, to Alexander Badt, January 25, 1904, in which Lewis recalled: "In 1849 the first Jewish divine service was held in a house in which we built, at the end of Kearny street which the Commercial Hotel now stands . . ."; and from M. Schloss to the "Honorable Board of Trustees Congregation Sherith Israel," August 3, 1904, who said, in part: "I truely beleave [*sic*] that I am the only survivor of the fiften 15 man which Names I have in my possession of over a halfe a Century who worshipt the first Day of Atonement . . . in 1849 in a Tent on Jackson St near Pacific. . . . from thence and from that time only originated the first burial Ground, the First Hebrew Benevolent Society, and Congregation Shereth Israel."

Interview with Adolph Rosenberg, Archivist, Congregation Sherith Israel, San Francisco, November 17, 1976, and Congregation Sherith Israel Archives. See also William M. Kramer and Norton B. Stern, "A Search for the First Synagogue in the Golden West," *Western States Jewish Historical Quarterly,* VII (October 1974), 3–20.

7. Alexander Iser, comp., *The California Hebrew & English Almanac, For the Year 5612, Corresponding with the Years 1851–2* . . . (San Francisco: Albion Job Press, [1851], n.p.; [I. J.] Benjamin, op. cit., I, 227.

8. Iser, op. cit., n.p. See also Gustav Adolf Danziger, "The Jew in San Francisco the Last Half Century," *Overland Monthly*, April 1895, p. 386. These two sources gave different dates for the founding of the Eureka Benevolent Society.

9. J. Heckendorn and W. A. Wilson, *Miners & Business Men's Directory. For the Year Commencing January 1st, 1856* . . . (Columbia: Clipper Office, 1856), p. 45. Writing in 1902, Rabbi Jacob Voorsanger was not sure whether High Holiday services were conducted in Sonora as early as 1851, but he did state, without noting his reference, that a Hebrew Benevolent Society was organized there in 1852. Rabbi Rudolf I. Coffee added to tradition and noted, thirty-eight years after Voorsanger, "Sonora had a Hebrew Benevolent Society and a cemetery in 1851." Jacob Voorsanger, "California," *Jewish Encyclopedia*, ed. Isidore Singer, III (1902), 511; Rudolf I. Coffee, "California," *Universal Jewish Encyclopedia*, ed. Isaac Landman, II (1940), 643. Voorsanger also preserved the traditions of, "Jesu Maria: A mining camp in Amador County, where services were held by Jewish miners in 1853," and of "Fiddletown: Organization in 1857 of a Jewish society." Voorsanger, "California," op. cit. No primary materials have been located verifying the existence of Jewish societies in these two towns, but the latter may have been a reference to a letter to the editor of the New York *Asmonean* from Fiddletown that reported on the founding of the Jewish community of Jackson. New York *Asmonean*, January 30, 1857, p. 124.

10. Edward Levi was the tailor; the miner was L. Jacobs. Eleven gave their birthplace as Germany; eight were from Prussia; seven were from Poland; two from Russia; and one, A. Lyons, from France. M. Hanover [Hanauer?] was the only one enumerated as the head of a family. The ages of these twenty-nine men ranged from eighteen to sixty-six years. Fourteen were twenty-five years old or less. U.S., Bureau of the Census, *Seventh Census of the United States, 1850,* California, Tuolumne County, pp. 299–362. This followed the census of 1850 for the

population of California as a whole: "... over half of all Californians in 1850 were in their twenties." Earl Pomeroy, *The Pacific Slope: A History* ... (New York: Alfred A. Knopf, 1965), pp. 40–41. Since Alexander Iser's *California Hebrew & English Almanac For the Year 5612* was for the Hebrew calendar year commencing September 27, 1851, the general information contained therein, that Sonora already had a temporary synagogue, was most likely based upon a High Holiday service conducted there the previous year, in the early part of September 1850. Iser, op. cit., n. p.

11. Edna Bryan Buckbee, *The Saga of Old Tuolumne* (New York: Press of the Pioneers, Inc., 1935), p. 99. The I.O.O.F. building in Columbia was completed just prior to the fire of 1854 and was saved. But there are no records that it was either built as a synagogue or used at any time for services.

12. *Columbia Gazette*, October 15, 1853, p. 2. Actually the date was Yom Kippur eve. It is possible that separate services were held in Sonora and Columbia that year.

13. Minutes, Columbia Lodge No. 28, F. & A. M., in the possession of Tuolumne Lodge No. 8, F. & A. M., Sonora, books I and 2A, n.p. See also Columbia *Tuolumne Courier*, September 11, 1858, p. 2, for an article describing Rosh Hashanah services at the Columbia Masonic Hall.

14. New York *Asmonean*, November 15, 1850, p. 28. Coloma is actually on the American River. Rudolf Coffee also noted that a congregation was formed there in 1850. Coffee, op. cit.

15. Jacques J. Lyons and Abraham DeSola, *A Jewish Calendar for Fifty Years* ... (Montreal: John Lovell, 1854), p. 153.

16. U.S., Bureau of the Census, *Seventh Census of the United States, 1850*, California, El Dorado County, pp. 789–803.

17. Nevada City *Nevada Journal*, September 17, 1852, p. 3. This notice was repeated in the *Nevada Journal* editions of September 24 (p. 3) and October 1 (p. 3). L. Heilbronn was probably the same as Leopold Heilbronn, a resident of Coloma enumerated in the census of 1850.

18. Philadelphia *Occident*, May 1853, p. 124. Leo later moved to Shasta and was a co-founder of the Hebrew Benevolent Society there. Cincinnati *Die Deborah*, December 12, 1856, p. 134. The Shasta Hebrew Benevolent Society was organized in 1857. The community established a cemetery, one-half mile west of town. Only one grave remains, that of Charles Brownstein, who died December 14, 1864, at the age of eight months. The gravesite has been designated as a historical

landmark by the California State Division of Highways. San Francisco *Weekly Gleaner*, March 6, 1857, p. 67; Beth Shuford, "Report on Cemeteries and Lone Graves," *Covered Wagon* (1965), 40–42; interview with Myron Putzel, Oakland, December 15, 1968.

19. Lyons, op. cit., p. 159.

20. Placerville *El Dorado News*, September 25, 1852, p. 1.

21. The date of Friedlander's death varies. The New York *Herald* stated it was October 4. New York *Herald*, November 30, 1851, quoted in "Excerpts from the Scrap Books of Rev. J. J. Lyons," *Publications of the American Jewish Historical Society*, XXVII (1920), 509. Friedlander's gravestone in the Temple Israel Cemetery presents the problem of a variance in the dates as written in Hebrew and English. The English date is October 16 and the equivalent of the Hebrew date is September 29. See Mrs. David ("Bea") Schwartz, "Oldest Jewish Cemetery in the West—Stockton, California," *Western States Jewish Historical Quarterly*, I (January 1969), 66–74. The earliest known grave in a Jewish cemetery in the Mother Lode is that of Hartwig Caro, who died August 17, 1853 and was buried at the Jewish cemetery in Sonora.

22. "Names of Jews Leaving New York for California," New York *Asmonean*, January 25, 1850, p. 109. The article concluded with a list of twenty-eight known Jewish passengers. See also London *Jewish Chronicle*, February 22, 1850, pp. 159–60.

23. Ibid., March 8, 1850, p. 174.

24. Leipzig *Allgemeine Zeitung des Judenthums*, August 16, 1852, p.402. See also Philadelphia *Occident*, November 1852, p. 416.

25. Nevada City *Nevada Journal*, March 19, 1858, p. 3.

26. Ibid., November 26, 1852, p. 1.

27. Jackson *Weekly Ledger*, April 25, 1857, p. 1.

28. *Placerville American*, July 19, 1856, p. 3. See above, pp. 79-80.

29. *Columbia Gazette*, October 6, 1855, p. 1.

30. Nevada City *Nevada Journal*, December 3, 1852, p. 2. Two weeks later, the merchant was identified as "Mr. Rosenbaum." Ibid., December 17, 1852, p. 2.

31. Ibid. There is only one recorded instance of Jewish participation in the journalistic profession from this period. M. Blumenthal of Grass Valley was the first publisher of *The Union*, which began publication October 28, 1864. Edmund G. Kinyon, "E. G. Kinyon Tells History of The Union," Grass Valley *Union*, January 9, 1965, sec. 2, p. 3.

32. In Stockton the cemetery antedated the synagogue by four

years. In Victoria, B.C., the cemetery was established in 1861 and the synagogue was completed in 1863. Hebrew Cemetery No. 1 of Galveston, Texas, was dedicated in 1852, while Congregation B'nai Israel was not organized in that city until 1868. George H. Tinkham, *A History of San Joaquin County with Biographical Sketches* . . . (Los Angeles: Historic Record Co., 1923), p. 159; David Rome, *The First Two Years: A Record of the Jewish Pioneers on Canada's Pacific Coast, 1858–1860* (Montreal: H. M. Caiserman, 1942), pp. 18, 33; A. Stanley Dreyfus, *Hebrew Cemetery No. 1 of Galveston* (Galveston: Congregation B'nai Israel [?], 1965), pp. 3, 9.

33. Solomon Ganzfried, *Kitzur Shulchan Aruch*, trans. Hyman E. Goldin (New York: Hebrew Publishing Co., 1927), chap. 199, pp. 103–15.

34. Sonora: Yaney Avenue and Oak Street, west of the Tuolumne County Court House. Mokelumne Hill: behind the Protestant Cemetery, at the foot of the historic route of Highway 49. Jackson: behind the cemeteries that begin at Church Street, near Stasal Avenue. Placerville: along Myrtle Avenue, above Highway 50. Grass Valley: near Wilson Street and Blossom Lane. Nevada City: behind the Lew Wanamake farm on Lower Grass Valley Road, near Walwrath Avenue.

35. I. J. Benjamin, op. cit., II, 95.

36. Ibid.

37. Records of the Hebrew Cemetery, Sonora (Western Jewish History Center, Berkeley); interview with Julius E. Baer, Sonora, California, September 14, 1963. The initiation fee was $2 and the monthly dues 25 cents.

38. See below, p. 102, for a discussion of a social club in Nevada City with a large Jewish membership.

39. Marriages (Tuolumne County Recorder's Office, Sonora), vols. 1–4, pp. 38–40. The wedding took place at the residence of Emanuel Linoberg. Robert E. Levinson, "Ketubot From Early California," in *Michael: On the History of the Jews in the Diaspora*, ed. by Lloyd P. Gartner, bk. 11 of *Publications of the Diaspora Research Institute*, ed. by Shlomo Simonsohn (Tel-Aviv: Diaspora Research Institute and Haim Rosenberg School of Jewish Studies of Tel-Aviv University, 1975), III, pp. 34–41.

40. The officers were H. Wolf, president; M. Goldwater, vice-president; M. Seeligsohn, secretary; J. Joseph, treasurer; and E. Gumpert, M. Hanauer, and M. Cohen, trustees. Stockton *Daily San Joaquin Republican*, January 13, 1856, p. 2.

41. Philadelphia *Occident*, April 1856, pp. 45–46. The Hebrew Benevolent Society, reestablished and incorporated October 5, 1961, maintained the Sonora Hebrew Cemetery until it was deeded to the Commission for the Preservation of Pioneer Jewish Cemeteries and Landmarks in January 1969. The Jewish Friendship Club was established in Sonora in the autumn of 1976.

42. I. J. Benjamin, op. cit., II, p. 47. In the summer of 1876, David A. D'Ancona of San Francisco, the President of District Grand Lodge No. 4 of B'nai B'rith, toured California and Nevada and visited, among other cities, Marysville and Grass Valley, both of which had active B'nai B'rith lodges at the time. In Grass Valley, he noted: "The Jewish population of Grass Valley is small, there being no more than twelve families. The only bond of union among them is Garizim Lodge No. 43, I. O. B. B." David A. D'Ancona, *A California-Nevada Travel Diary of 1876: The Delightful Account of a Ben B'rith*, ed. William M. Kramer (Santa Monica: Norton B. Stern, 1975), pp. 57–59, 64–67.

43. William S. Byrne, *Directory of Grass Valley Township for 1865* (San Francisco: Charles F. Robbins and Co., 1865), pp. 17–57.

44. San Francisco *Daily Alta California*, December 9, 1856, p. 1; *Volcano Weekly Ledger*, December 13, 1856, p. 2; San Francisco *Weekly Gleaner*, August 30, 1861, pp. 2, 7; Harold F. Reinhart, *Temple B'nai Israel and the Sacramento Jewish Community* (Sacramento: News Publishing Co., 1927), p. 12. For references to a "Jewish community" or "congregation" in Grass Valley, see Martin A. Meyer, *Western Jewry: An Account of the Achievements of the Jews and Judaism in California Including Eulogies and Biographies* (San Francisco: Emanu-El, 1916), p. 16; London *Jewish Chronicle*, June 6, 1862, p. 5; Cincinnati *Israelite*, March 15, 1861, p. 293; Deeds, 10, Nevada County (Nevada County Recorder's Office, Nevada City), pp. 184–85.

45. San Francisco *Hebrew*, February 20, 1868, p. 4.

46. Ibid., December 10, 1868, p. 4. "Sinbad" also noted a Jewish wedding in Nevada City, conducted by "the Rev. S. Rosenthal, of Grass Valley."

47. The synagogue in Placerville was called, "Bench Berith [sic], i.e., [B'nai B'rith] Children of the Covenent [sic]," San Francisco *Weekly Gleaner*, September 29, 1858, p. 4.

48. Deeds, 62, El Dorado County (El Dorado County Recorder's Office, Placerville), pp. 18–20.

49. *Volcano Weekly Ledger*, September 20, 1856, p. 3. This advertisement was repeated September 27, p. 3. Of all the gold rush cities,

Jackson was the most consistent advertiser of High Holidays well in advance of their occurrence so that co-religionists from small nearby towns could plan to attend. See Mrs. J. L. Sargent, ed., *Amador County History* (Jackson: Amador County Federation of Women's Clubs, 1927), p. 105, for a brief history of the Jackson synagogue.

50. I. J. Benjamin, op. cit., II, 95. The earliest known burial in the Mokelumne Hill Jewish Cemetery was of Isaac Lurch, who died December 28, 1859 in Lancha Plana.

51. San Francisco *Hebrew Observer*, February 15, 1867, p. 4.

52. I. J. Benjamin, op. cit., II, 26; Records, A (El Dorado County Recorder's Office, Placerville), p. 76. *Shaurey Shomagin* [sic], i.e., Shaareh Shomayim, Gates of Heaven.

53. Interview with Roy Gottheimer, San Francisco, July 13, 1966.

54. Interview with Oscar Jones, Diamond Springs, January 21, 1966.

55. Philadelphia *Occident*, August 1865, p. 237.

56. [Congregation Sherith Israel] Minutes, from April [13] 1851 [to October 19, 1856], San Francisco, p. 39.

57. [Congregation Emanu-El] Minutes, March 30, 1851, San Francisco, p. 1.

58. New York *Jewish Messenger*, March 2, 1860, p. 77; London *Jewish Chronicle*, March 30, 1860, p. 6.

59. San Francisco *Weekly Gleaner*, February 24, 1860, p. 4.

60. The contributions included $30 from Garizim Lodge No. 43, B'nai B'rith, Grass Valley; from E. Abramson, Secretary, Sonora and Columbia Hebrew Benevolent Society, $50; from H. Harris, by the Jews of Jackson and Sutter Creek, $45; from J. Greenwald of the Nevada [City] Hebrew Benevolent Society, $50; from the congregation in Jackson, $50; from A. A. Sanders, Grass Valley, $2.50. San Francisco *Hebrew Observer*, June 19, 1868, p. 4; June 26, 1868, p. 4; July 17, 1868, p. 4; May 28, 1869, p. 4. Another example of charity to an overseas cause came from Mokelumne Hill in 1870, when thirteen Jewish residents contributed $61 to the German Sanitary Commission (also called the German Sanitary Verein), apparently for use in the Franco-Prussian War. Mokelumne Hill *Weekly Calaveras Chronicle*, September 3, 1870, p. 3. Jewish merchants in this region were also among the earliest contributors to Hebrew Union College, established in Cincinnati, Ohio, in 1875. "The First Fund-Raisers for the Hebrew Union College in the Far West," *Western States Jewish Historical Quarterly*, VIII (October 1975), 55–58.

61. *Proceedings of District Grand Lodge No. 4, Independent Order of B'nai B'rith* (1863, 1865, 1867, 1874, 1876–77, 1893, 1896). A contribution of $35.90 for the same project was received from Miriam Lodge No. 56, Marysville. Cincinnati *Israelite*, February 16, 1866, p. 261. The Placerville Hebrew Benevolent Society contributed $55 to the Palestine Fund. Philadelphia *Occident*, January 1866, pp. 471–72.

62. Nevada City *Weekly National Gazette*, May 7, 1870, p. 3.

63. *Proceedings of District Grand Lodge, No. 4, of the Independent Order of B'nai B'rith ... January, 1872* (San Francisco: M. Weiss, 1872), p. 52; ibid., *1880* (San Francisco: Joseph Winterburn and Company, 1880), pp. 30–39. Messing served as rabbi of Congregations Sherith Israel (1870–73) and Beth Israel (1877–90) of San Francisco. His memoirs state that he traveled to Grass Valley, Nevada City, and Marysville, among many other cities, and performed rabbinical duties there. Aron J. Messing, *A Farewell Gift To His Friends from Aron J. Messing, Rabbi of Congregation "Beth Israel." July 1890–5650* (San Francisco: Francis, Valentine and Co., Printers, 1890), p. 25.

64. *Proceedings of the M[ost] W[orthy] Grand Lodge, Ancient Jewish Order Kesher Shel Barzel* (San Francisco: Winterburn and Co., 1874), pp. 145–47; San Francisco *Jewish Progress*, September 13, 1878, p. 6.

65. Ibid., July 5, 1878, p. 2.

66. I. J. Benjamin, op. cit., II, 26, 36, 55.

67. Ibid., II, 36. Another prominent Jewish visitor to Nevada City about this time was I. N. Choynski, the associate editor of the San Francisco *Weekly Gleaner*, who was feted with a supper by the community. Nevada City *Nevada Journal*, December 2, 1859, p. 1.

68. San Francisco *Hebrew*, February 21, 1868, p. 4.

69. Nevada City *Nevada Weekly Gazette*, February 24, 1868, p. 1; Nevada City *Nevada Daily Gazette*, February 19, 1868, p. 1. That he actually arrived in Nevada City was recorded by the *Nevada Daily Transcript*, which listed his arrival and overnight stay at the National Exchange Hotel in Nevada City February 18. The newspaper stated that he was from "Jerusalem, Egypt." Nevada City *Nevada Daily Transcript*, February 19, 1868, p. 2. See also Salo W. Baron and Jeannette M. Baron, "Palestinian Messengers in America, 1849–79: A Record of Four Journeys," *Jewish Social Studies*, V (July 1943), 239–40, 274, 281.

70. Philadelphia *Occident*, December 1854, p. 472.

71. Nevada City *Nevada Journal*, August 10, 1855, p. 3.

72. I. J. Benjamin, op. cit., II, 47, 77. In Sonora, for religious ser-

vices at times of the year other than the High Holidays, such as Passover or a *yahrzeit* observance, the community gathered for worship at the residence of Abraham Barlow, where, it is believed, the Torah scroll was kept when it was not in use. (Interview with Issic and Israel Drabkin, Sonora, February 21, 1966.) However, Rene I. Hibbard, a daughter of Abraham Barlow, did not recall that the Torah was kept in her father's house. (Letter from Rene I. Hibbard, Lakeport, California, September 14, 1971.) When asked what became of the Sonora Torah, ninety-six-year-old Julius E. Baer could not remember. (Interview with Julius E. Baer, Sonora, April 30, 1972.) Rabbi Bernard D. Rosenberg of Temple Israel, Stockton (formerly Congregation Ryhim Ahoovim), a long-time student of the Jewish history of his community (the closest nineteenth-century Jewish community to Sonora) did not know if either of the two Torahs acquired by his congregation in the nineteenth century (which, incidentally, are almost identical in appearance) was ever used in Sonora. Nor did he know from whom or when the Stockton Torahs were acquired. (Telephone conversation with Rabbi Dr. Bernard D. Rosenberg, Stockton, June 30, 1972.)

A fire that occurred the same month the Shaar Zedek Hebrew Society of Grass Valley was organized in 1855 destroyed the Torah and other property belonging to the society that had been purchased only a few days before. (Cincinnati *Israelite*, March 15, 1861, p. 293.) Apparently, the community purchased a new Torah sometime prior to Benjamin's visit in 1860.

The Israelite erred in identifying Nevada City as the location of the Shaar Zedek Hebrew Society. The Torah used by the Grass Valley community was donated to Congregation Emanu-El of San Francisco in 1906 after the great earthquake and fire of that year destroyed the synagogue of Emanu-El, then located at the present site of the 450 Sutter Street building. William Kaye, "Tale of a Scroll," *The Scroll*, 1975, p. 47.

73. San Francisco *Weekly Gleaner. As a Voice to Israel,* April 3, 1857, p. 92.

74. Sonora: I. J. Benjamin, op. cit., II, 77; Grass Valley: New York *Asmonean,* January 2, 1857, p. 92; Nevada City: San Francisco *Weekly Gleaner. As a Voice to Israel,* April 3, 1857, p. 92; Marysville: I. J. Benjamin, op. cit., II, 25.

75. Sonora *Union Democrat*, September 29, 1860. The "magnificent silver goblet" turned up 114 years later in a New York auction

catalogue and was purchased by Max Eis of Oakland for display in the Western Jewish History Center of the Judah L. Magnes Memorial Museum, Berkeley. "Voorsanger Archive Room To Be Dedicated At Magnes," San Francisco *Jewish Bulletin*, November 1, 1974, p. 7.

76. Interview with Israel Drabkin, Sonora, February 21, 1966.

77. I. J. Benjamin, op. cit., II, 96; San Francisco *Weekly Gleaner*, April 11, 1862, p. 2; Placerville *Weekly Mountain Democrat*, October 26, 1861, p. 2.

78. Edwin F. Bean, comp., *Bean's History and Directory of Nevada County, California* ... (Nevada [City]: Daily Gazette Book and Job Office, 1867), pp. 103–4; Articles of Incorporation (Nevada County Clerk's Office, Nevada City), no. N-11.

79. Jackson *Weekly Ledger*, June 20, 1857, p. 2. Emphasis in the original text.

80. Cincinnati *Israelite*, November 16, 1855, p. 155; Downieville *Sierra Democrat*, October 3, 1857, p. 2.

81. *San Andreas Independent*, October 4, 1856, p. 2; San Francisco *Weekly Gleaner*, September 29, 1858, p. 4; *San Andreas Independent*, October 1, 1859, p. 2; September 29, 1860, p. 2. And in those small towns of the region without Jewish cemeteries, bodies were sometimes taken to Stockton. Perhaps freight moved easier from the mountains to Stockton at certain times, rather than from one mountain town to another. The remains of Joseph Rosenthal of Hornitos were interred in Stockton as were those of Jacob Abrams of San Andreas. Jackson *Amador Dispatch*, July 4, 1868, p. 2; *San Andreas Independent*, September 19, 1857, p. 3.

82. Sonora *Union Democrat*, October 13, 1894, p. 3.

83. New York *Asmonean*, January 30, 1857, p. 124.

84. I. J. Benjamin, op. cit., II, 96. The synagogue building still stood in 1902. Jacob Voorsanger noted, "Jackson: Congregation organized for the autumn holidays of 1856. At a meeting held April 18, 1857, it was decided to build a synagogue, the first erected in the mining districts. This synagogue still exists, but, owing to the migration of the members of the congregation, is subverted to secular purposes." Voorsanger, "California," op. cit.

85. Jackson *Amador Weekly Ledger*, September 8, 1866, p. 2.

86. Ibid., September 25, 1869, p. 2. The synagogue served as a schoolhouse until 1888. After that, it was moved to a nearby lot, where it was used as a private dwelling. The building was razed in 1948. In June 1976, the Commission for the Preservation of Pioneer Jewish

Cemeteries and Landmarks dedicated California Registered Historical Landmark No. 865 on the original site.

87. I. J. Benjamin, op. cit., II, 28.

88. In an article regarding the High Holidays of 1871, the editor noted: "In this connection we would mention that our Hebrew people have recently been making quite extensive repairs on their synagogue." Placerville *Mountain Democrat*, September 16, 1871, p. 3.

89. Will O. Upton, *Churches of El Dorado County: Their History Covering a Period of Ninety Years from 1850 to 1940* (Placerville: Old Hangtown Press, 1940), p. 43.

90. Deeds, V, El Dorado County (El Dorado County Recorder's Office, Placerville), pp. 457–58, 36–38.

91. Upton, op. cit.

92. In Columbia, the brothers Edward and Philip Elias were the sons of a rabbi. George H. Tinkham, "Solomon Philip Elias," *History of Stanislaus County, California* . . . (Los Angeles: Historic Record Co., 1921), p. 340. An early spiritual leader of the Jewish community in Mokelumne Hill was Marx Gradwohl, whose father, Lazare Gradwohl, was cantor of the synagogue at Thann, Haut-Rhine. Whenever High Holiday services were held in Mokelumne Hill, the several Gradwohl brothers would come to Mokelumne Hill, some from as far away as Grass Valley, to worship together as a family. Letters from Arthur Gradwohl, San Francisco, August 16, 1965 and August 9, 1971, and interview, March 8, 1966. See pages 167–68 for a discussion of H. Leo, who conducted services in Nevada City and who was a brother of the Rev. Ansel Leo of New York.

93. San Francisco *Hebrew Observer*, October 14, 1870, p. 4; interview with Roy Gottheimer, op. cit.

94. Pinto was probably the same person as an early member of Congregation Sherith Israel in San Francisco. His signature is appended to the original constitution of the congregation, but it is not known if he was a charter member. [Congregation Sherith Israel] Minutes, op. cit., p. 24. During his residency in Sonora, Pinto officiated at the marriage of Mayer Baer and Helena (or Helene) Oppenheimer, May 22, 1860. The Baer family still has the *ketubah* from this wedding ceremony, the marriage contract executed by Pinto on a form printed at the office of the *Weekly Gleaner,* an early San Francisco Jewish newspaper. Baer Family Papers, Sonora. This particular *ketubah* is one of only three copies known to be still extant. The presence of several lacunae in the *ketubah* probably indicates that Pinto could not read

Aramaic and did not know what to insert. Interview with Rabbi Dr. Max Vorspan, Los Angeles, March 17, 1966. Another wedding ceremony performed by Pinto in Sonora followed a civil ceremony. "Married in Sonora on the 13th, by C. L. Street, and afterwards by Rabbe [sic] Pinto, Mr. M[athias] Meyer to Miss Jeanette Selling, all of Sonora." Sonora *Union Democrat,* July 19, 1862, p. 2. Jeanette Selling was a sister of Ben Selling, a prominent philanthropist and politician in Oregon in the early twentieth century. Letter from Arthur H. Myer, Berkeley, California, June 14, 1965. See chap. 7 regarding Ben Selling. See Edgar M. Kahn, "Pioneer Jewish San Francisco Stock Brokers," *Western States Jewish Historical Quarterly,* I (January 1969), 64, for additional information on Matthias Meyer. "Rabbi A. M. Levy" was listed as the officiant at the marriage of Julius Jacobs to Rose Kaufman in Shaw's Flat in 1864. Sonora *Union Democrat,* March 19, 1864, p. 2, quoted in Jack Benjamin Goldmann, "A History of Pioneer Jews in California, 1849–1870" (Master's thesis, University of California at Berkeley, 1940), p. 60. Other laymen in Mother Lode communities exhibited a knowledge of Biblical lore and Hebrew. In reply to a query by one Elder Grant on immortality and the nature of the soul, Julius Goldner of Placerville submitted a full three-column letter to the editor, complete with Biblical quotations in transliterated Hebrew. Placerville *El Dorado County Republican,* September 26, 1872, pp. 1–2.

95. Sonora *Union Democrat,* October 1, 1898, p. 3. For a service conducted by Hochstein, see ibid., September 29, 1860. Joel Levy of Columbia conducted the High Holiday services in Sonora in 1867. Ibid., September 28, 1867, p. 2.

96. Interview with Julius E. Baer, Sonora, September 14, 1963.

97. Letter from John A. Ferguson, San Francisco, June 30, 1965.

98. Ibid., June 30 and July 19, 1965. The Fergusons were married in Stockton, February 10, 1873. The service was conducted by the Rev. H. Loewenthal of that city. Sonora *Union Democrat,* February 15, 1873, p. 2. It is assumed that Ferguson was instructed in Judaism by the Rev. Mr. Loewenthal. Rabbi Margolis was ordained by Hebrew Union College in Cincinnati in 1901 and was rabbi of the congregation in Stockton in 1902. Letter from Rabbi Sidney L. Regner, Executive Vice President, Central Conference of American Rabbis, New York, February 7, 1968. Apparently, Margolis was of a more traditional orientation than the other members of the Central Conference of American Rabbis, for he left that organization, joined the conservative Rabbinical Assembly, and became the first rabbi to serve as president of

the Rabbinical Assembly who was not ordained by the conservative Jewish Theological Seminary of America. Letter from Rabbi Wolfe Kelman, Executive Vice-President, The Rabbinical Assembly, New York, June 25, 1971. For additional information on Loewenthal's rabbinical career, in California, the Middle West, and the Deep South, see Stephen D. Kinsey, "They Called It Home: The Development of the Jewish Community of San Jose, California, 1850–1900" (Master's thesis, Department of History, California State University, San Jose, 1973), pp. 13–16; Bertram Wallace Korn, "An American Jewish Religious Leader in 1860 Voices his Frustration," in *Michael: On the History of the Jews in the Diaspora*, ed. by Lloyd P. Gartner, bk. 11 of *Publications of the Diaspora Research Institute,* ed. by Shlomo Simonsohn (Tel-Aviv: Diaspora Research Institute and Haim Rosenberg School of Jewish Studies of Tel-Aviv University, 1975), III, pp. 42–47.

99. San Francisco *Weekly Gleaner,* October 19, 1859, p. 5; September 25, 1861, p. 7; October 21, 1864, p. 4; San Francisco *Hebrew,* October 20, 1865, p. 4; San Francisco *Hebrew Observer,* October 14, 1867, p. 4; Jackson *Amador Dispatch,* October 3, 1868, p. 2; Jackson *Amador Ledger,* September 25, 1869, p. 2; San Francisco *Hebrew Observer,* October 14, 1870, p. 4; Jackson *Amador Dispatch,* October 15, 1870, p. 2; Jackson *Amador Weekly Ledger,* October 4, 1873, p. 2. Perhaps there was such diversity so as to recognize the many towns the members of the congregation came from, and to allow all the different national customs and forms of prayers to be observed. The year after Berliner conducted High Holiday services in Jackson, he was invited to Placerville for the same occasion. Placerville *Mountain Democrat,* September 23, 1865, p. 2.

100. In San Francisco in 1851, there were at least two kosher boarding houses, one kosher butcher shop, and one baker of matzoth. Iser, op. cit. In 1859, advertisements from six kosher butcher shops appeared in the *Gleaner.* San Francisco *Weekly Gleaner,* December 30, 1859. See also Leipzig *Allgemeine Zeitung des Judenthums,* August 16, 1852, p. 402, for an article concerning Orthodox Jewish emigres to California.

101. Nathan Glazer, *American Judaism* (Chicago: University of Chicago Press, 1957), p. 31.

102. Eric E. Hirshler, *Jews From Germany in the United States* (New York: Farrar, Straus and Cudahy, 1955), p. 47.

103. Ibid.

104. Charles Reznikoff and Uriah Z. Engelman, *The Jews of*

Charleston: A History of an American Jewish Community (Philadelphia: Jewish Publication Society of America, 1950), pp. 127–28.

105. Har Sinai, Baltimore, 1842; Emanuel, New York, 1845; Sinai, Chicago, 1858. Glazer, op. cit., p. 3.

106. Cincinnati *Israelite*, November 13, 1857, p. 145.

107. San Francisco *Weekly Gleaner*, February 13, 1857, p. 36. In a later edition of the *Gleaner*, the name Pawbroch was corrected to Jacobson. Ibid., February 27, 1857, p. 54.

108. Ibid., February 13, 1857, p. 36. Emphasis in the original text.

109. Philadelphia *Occident*, November 15, 1860, p. 208.

110. *Sonora Herald*, September 12, 1867, p. 3.

111. Sonora *Union Democrat*, April 11, 1868, p. 2, quoted in Goldmann, op. cit., p. 56.

112. Interview with Julius E. Baer, Sonora, September 14, 1963.

113. Letter from Mrs. J. Aaron Levy, Sumter, South Carolina, July 16, 1965.

114. Letter from Hazel L. Wise, San Francisco, August 10, 1965.

115. J[acob] Solis-Cohen, Jr., "A California Pioneer: The Letters of Bernhard Marks to Jacob Solis-Cohen (1853–1857)," *Publication of the American Jewish Historical Society*, XLIV (September 1954), 31.

116. Aaron Baruh, whose marriage to Rosalie Wolf, October 22, 1861, was recorded with the county in the form of the traditional Hebrew marriage contract, fastened a mezuzah to every doorpost in his house. The Baruh family and others in town observed the dietary laws. The mezuzoth in the Baruh home, 516 Main Street, Nevada City, are still visible. The home, which was built in 1852, is maintained by descendants of the family. Marriage Certificates, 1, Nevada County (Nevada County Recorder's Office, Nevada City), pp. 93–94; Robert E. Levinson, "Ketubot From Early California," op. cit.; interview with Stephen A. Zellerbach, April 22, 1966. In 1975, the Baruh home was designated a historic landmark by Hydraulic Parlor No. 56, Native Sons of the Golden West. Nevada City *Independent*, April 16, 1975, p. 2.

117. San Francisco *Weekly Gleaner*, April 9, 1858, p. 5. The Jews of Nevada City conducted High Holiday services regularly, but in 1876, the Yom Kippur services were interrupted when the cantor, M. Rosenberg, was summoned to appear in court shortly before the Kol Nidre service and forced to serve on a jury all the next day. Magdeburg *Israelitische Wochenschrift*, 1876, p. 475.

118. For example, of seventeen marriages contracted in Tuolumne County from April 18, 1853 to September 16, 1891, in which one of the

partners was known to be Jewish, eight were contracted with Gentiles. 1 [and 2], Index, Marriage Certificates, Men, Tuolumne County; Marriage Licenses, Tuolumne County (Tuolumne County Recorder's Office, Sonora).

119. Rabbi Eckman, an Ashkenazic Jew, reported: "We then chanted (using the Portuguese mode) the Hebrew formulas of the marriage ceremony." Eckman also noted that the bride's family observed the dietary laws. San Francisco *Weekly Gleaner,* February 11, 1859, p. 2.

120. San Francisco *Hebrew,* January 10, 1868, p. 4.

121. Nevada City *Nevada Journal,* December 11, 1857, p. 2.

122. San Francisco *Hebrew,* November 5, 1869, p. 8. Moses Hyman of Sacramento advertised as a mohel in the *Weekly Gleaner.* It is presumed that his proximity to the Mother Lode resulted in invitations to perform circumcisions. San Francisco *Weekly Gleaner,* January 8, 1858, p. 409. A report of a circumcision conducted in Grass Valley appeared in ibid., August 10, 1861, pp. 2, 7; such a ceremony performed on a son of Kaufman Hexter of Mokelumne Hill was reported to the *Gleaner,* April 11, 1862, p. 2.

123. Placerville *Mountain Democrat,* October 5, 1867, p. 2; James G. Heller, *Isaac M. Wise: His Life, Work and Thought* (New York: Union of American Hebrew Congregations, 1965), pp. 157–58. Confirmation of both boys and girls was introduced at Congregation Beth Israel, Portland, Oregon, in 1872. Julius J. Nodel, *The Ties Between: A Century of Judaism on America's Last Frontier* (Portland: Temple Beth Israel, 1959), picture facing p. 37. Also in 1872, Rabbi Aron J. Messing conducted the first Confirmation ceremony at Congregation Sherith Israel, San Francisco, for a class of twenty-two students. Messing, op. cit., p. 22. The first Confirmation in San Jose occurred in 1874 under the direction of Rabbi Myer S. Levy. Kinsey, op. cit., pp. 18–19.

124. Interview with Julius E. Baer, Sonora, conducted by Norton B. Stern, July 24, 1967, p. 1.

125. Cincinnati *American Israelite,* January 31, 1879, p. 5.

126. Letter from Hazel L. Wise, op. cit.

127. Nevada City *Nevada Democrat,* March 5, 1863, p. 1; Nevada City *Nevada Daily Gazette,* September 27, 1865, p. 2.

128. Sonora *Union Democrat,* September 28, 1872, p. 3.

129. Interview with Julius E. Baer, Sonora, September 14, 1963.

130. *Constitution and By-Laws of Congregation B'nai Israel Located at Jackson Amador County California* (San Francisco: M. Weiss, 1873), pp. 3,

6, 9–10, 13. The names of eighteen members were included in the pamphlet, only four of whom lived in Jackson at that time. Of the others, eight lived in Sutter Creek, three were from Ione, and two from Amador City. The residence of Samuel Levy was not known. For a comparison of the regulations of this congregation with those of Congregation Sherith Israel in San Francisco, see Michael M. Zarchin, *Glimpses of Jewish Life in San Francisco,* 2d ed. (Oakland: Judah L. Magnes Memorial Museum, 1964), pp. 104–6.

131. Cincinnati *Israelite,* November 16, 1855, p. 155.

132. Philadelphia *Occident,* October 1855, p. 2A; May 1856, p. 2A; November 1856, p. 2A; April 7, 1859, p. 1A; August 23, 1860, p. 1A. See also Rudolf Glanz, "Where the Jewish Press Was Distributed in Pre-Civil War America," *Western States Jewish Historical Quarterly,* V (October 1972), 1–14.

133. San Francisco *Weekly Gleaner,* January 14, 1859, p. 5; November 11, 1859, p. 4; November 25, 1859, p. 4; July 6, 1860, p. 4.

134. See above, n. 44, for references to a synagogue that may have been built in Grass Valley on the lot referred to in the text.

135. In 1962, the Commission for the Preservation of Pioneer Jewish Cemeteries and Landmarks of the Judah L. Magnes Memorial Museum of Berkeley, California, was founded for the purpose of securing legal title to the six cemeteries and restoring them. See chap. 7 for a discussion of Jews leaving the Mother Lode after the end of the gold rush.

NOTES TO CHAPTER 7

1. Ray Allen Billington, *The Far Western Frontier, 1830–1860* (New York and Evanston: Harper and Row, 1956), pp. 241–42; Rodman W. Paul, *California Gold: The Beginning of Mining in the Far West* (Cambridge: Harvard University Press, 1947), chaps. 9 and 10.

2. Articles of Incorporation (County Clerks' Offices).

3. Columbia *Weekly Columbian,* January 17, 1857, p. 1.

4. *Columbia Citizen,* April 27, 1867, p. 2. See also Earl Pomeroy, *The Pacific Slope: A History* . . . (New York: Alfred A. Knopf, 1965), pp. 48–49, and Paul, op. cit., p. 173.

5. Sonora *Union Democrat,* January 9, 1869, p. 3.

6. Paul, op. cit., pp. 242–43; *The Seventh Census of the United States: 1850* (Washington: Robert Armstrong, 1853), p. 982; House of

Representatives, *Compendium of the Tenth Census* (Washington: Government Printing Office, 1883), pt. I, 16–17.

7. Interview with Mrs. Robert Guggenheim, San Francisco, August 16, 1966.

8. Columbia *Tuolumne Independent,* July 2, 1892, p. 5; George H. Tinkham, "Solomon Philip Elias," *History of Stanislaus County, California* . . . (Los Angeles: Historic Record Co., 1921), pp. 340–41. Sol P. Elias, a son of Philip Elias, served as mayor of Modesto, California, in the 1920s.

9. See chap. 4.

10. Martin A. Meyer, "Moses Dinkelspiel," *Western Jewry: An Account of the Achievements of the Jews and Judaism in California Including Eulogies and Biographies* (San Francisco: Emanu-El, 1916), p. 87; interview with John Walton Dinkelspiel, San Francisco, March 9, 1966.

11. Bernard Jaffe, *Michelson and the Speed of Light* (Garden City, New York: Doubleday and Co., Inc., 1960), pp. 37–38. Samuel Michelson was a brother of Mrs. B. H. Levy of San Francisco ("Mother" in *920 O'Farrell Street* by Harriet Lane Levy [Garden City, N.Y.: Doubleday and Co., Inc., 1947]) and of Bertha Meyer, whose husband, Oser Meyer, was an early merchant in Murphy's. Interview with Ruth Elkus, San Francisco, May 13, 1966; Henry O. Meyer, "A Brief Account of the Family of Oser Meyer and Bertha Michelson Meyer and its Relationship to the Michelsons" (South San Francisco: n.p., n.d.), n.p. In 1975, Matuca chapter and grand council, E Clampus Vitus, dedicated a historical marker in front of the Michelson family home in Murphy's, where Albert Michelson lived in 1856–67. Hildred Cooper, "Clampers dedicate Michelson home in Murphys," Angels Camp *Calaveras Californian,* May 29, 1975, p. 1.

12. H. Barrett Learned, "Michelson, Albert Abraham," *Dictionary of American Biography,* 1964 ed., VI, pt. 2, 593–96. Albert Michelson's brother, Charles, was director of publicity of the Democratic National Committee.

13. P. O. Ray, "Kahn, Julius," ibid., 1964 ed., V, pt. 2, 250–51; *Men of California* . . . (San Francisco and Los Angeles: Western Press Reporter, Inc., 1925), p. 16.

14. Leon L. Watters, *The Pioneer Jews of Utah* (New York: American Jewish Historical Society, 1952), pp. 126–27.

15. Joseph Gaston, "Aaron Meier," *Portland, Oregon, Its History and*

Builders . . . (Chicago and Portland: S. J. Clarke Publishing Co., 1911), II, 234. A son of Aaron Meier, Julius L. Meier, was Governor of Oregon, 1931-35.

16. *1864-1944. 80 Years of Service: Auerbach Company, Salt Lake City* (n.p., n.d.).

17. Registers of Marks and Brands (County Recorders' Offices). For additional information on Wangenheim and Rosenberg, see Edgar M. Kahn, "Simon Newman—and Newman, California," *Western States Jewish Historical Quarterly,* II (October 1969), 12-13; and Alice W. Heyneman, "A Backward Look at a Pioneer Grandfather, Sol Wangenheim," ibid., IV (January 1972), 86-100.

18. Frederick de Sola Mendes, "Agriculture," *Jewish Encyclopedia*, I (1902), 259.

19. Oscar Handlin, *Adventure in Freedom: Three Hundred Years of Jewish Life in America* (New York: McGraw-Hill Book Co., Inc., 1954), pp. 49-50, 83; Mark Wischnitzer, *To Dwell in Safety: The Story of Jewish Migration Since 1800* (Philadelphia: Jewish Publication Society of America, 1948), pp. 25, 289.

20. Jeffrey D. Salzman, "Between Two Worlds: Jewish Merchants in a Changing City" (Graduate seminar paper, Department of History, University of California at Berkeley, 1967), p. 3.

21. [I. J.] Benjamin, *Three Years in America, 1859-1862,* trans. Charles Reznikoff (Philadelphia: Jewish Publication Society of America, 1956), II, 26-96.

22. *Statistics of the Jews of the United States* . . . (Philadelphia: Union of American Hebrew Congregations, 1880), pp. 48-51.

23. Ibid., p. 48.

24. Levy, op. cit., pp. 12, 160-61.

25. Columbia *Tuolumne Independent,* July 4, 1874, p. 3.

26. Letter from Mrs. Morton V. Slater, Delano, California, July 31, 1966.

27. Interview with Harold L. Zellerbach, San Francisco, April 21, 1966; Martin A. Meyer, "Anthony Zellerbach," *Western Jewry,* . . . op. cit., p. 161; *The Years of Paper* [San Francisco?]: Crown Zellerbach Corp., 1941), p. 4.

28. Bob Paine, "Zellerbach Empire Had a Start in Nevada County," Nevada City *Nevada County Nugget,* November 23, 1965, p. 13.

29. See reference to the Fleishhacker family below.

30. Lawrence Kinnard, "James D. Zellerbach," *History of the Greater San Francisco Bay Region* (New York and West Palm Beach: Lewis Historical Publishing Co., Inc., 1966), III, 9-10; *The Years of Paper,*

op cit., p. 8; telephone conversation with Stephen A. Zellerbach, San Francisco, August 10, 1971. The Jennie B. Zellerbach Garden, located in the Strybing Arboretum in Golden Gate Park, San Francisco, was donated to the Recreation and Park Department of the City and County of San Francisco by Mrs. D. Stephen Coney in memory of her grandmother, Mrs. Isadore Zellerbach.

31. Kinnard, "Albert E. Schwabacher," op. cit., p. 246; Bailey Millard, *History of the San Francisco Bay Region* (Chicago: American Historical Society, 1924), III, 240–42; Martin A. Meyer, "Aaron Fleishhacker," *Western Jewry*, . . . op cit., p. 91; Nevada City *Nevada Journal*, July 14, 1854, p. 1; April 16, 1858, p. 1.

32. Later, in 1956, this consolidated bank merged with Crocker First National Bank to form Crocker-Anglo National Bank. In 1963, Crocker-Anglo merged with Citizens National Bank of Los Angeles to form Crocker-Citizens National Bank. The firm is now known as Crocker Bank. Herbert Fleishhacker, Sr., was a director of eighty-four corporations simultaneously. He was also chairman of the Fine Arts and Finance Committees of the 1939 World's Fair. The Fleishhacker Pool was named for him for his service as president of the San Francisco Park Commission. In honor of his mother, he donated to the city the Children's Playground located near the pool. Kinnard, "Mortimer Fleishhacker, Jr.," op. cit., p. 216; Michael M. Zarchin, *Glimpses of Jewish Life in San Francisco*, 2d ed. (Oakland: Judah L. Magnes Memorial Museum, 1964), pp. 59–60; Monroe A. Bloom, *A Century of Pioneering: A Brief History of Crocker-Citizens National Bank* (San Francisco [?]: Crocker-Citizens National Bank, 1970), pp. 12–14, 17, 26; "Just Plain Crocker," *San Francisco Chronicle*, July 1, 1971, p. 60; interview with Marshall H. Kuhn, San Francisco, May 15, 1972.

33. Ross L. Muir and Carl J. White, *Over the Long Term . . . the story of J. & W. Seligman & Co.* (New York: J. & W. Seligman & Co., 1964), pp. 39–43.

34. Martin A. Meyer, "Sigmund Steinhart," *Western Jewry*, . . . op. cit., pp. 151–52; Bloom, op. cit., pp. 11–12.

35. William Bronson, *Still Flying And Nailed To The Mast: The First Hundred Years of the Fireman's Fund Insurance Company* (Garden City, N.Y.: Doubleday and Co., Inc., 1963), p. 189; Zarchin, op. cit., pp. 71–74; Jacob Bertha Levison, *Memories for my Family* (San Francisco: John Henry Nash, 1933).

36. Bert Clinkston, *120th Anniversary Commemorative Edition: Congregation B'nai Israel, Sacramento, California* (Sacramento [?]: n.p., 1970),

n.p. See also Norton B. Stern, "The Life of Tzedakah—Isador Cohen of Sacramento," *Western States Jewish Historical Quarterly,* IV (October 1971), 25–34.

37. Oregon Legislative Assembly, *Journals of the Senate and House of the Twenty-Eighth Legislative Assembly* ... (Salem: State Printing Department, 1915), pp. 5–6; Julius J. Nodel, *The Ties Between: A Century of Judaism on America's Last Frontier* (Portland: Temple Beth Israel, 1959), pp. 48–50.

38. Letter from A. S. McSorley, Oakland, California, November 29, 1965; interviews with W. E. Hoskin, Sonora, September 11, 1963, and Mrs. Perry Tracy, Placerville, September 26, 1963.

39. Paul, op. cit., pp. 340–41.

BIBLIOGRAPHY

Primary Materials

Interviews

Baer, Alfred A., San Francisco, August 31, 1966.
Baer, Julius E., Sonora, September 14, 1963 and April 30, 1972.
———, July 24, 1967 (conducted by Norton B. Stern).
Bernheim, Lester, and Bernheim, Miss Hortense, Los Angeles, August 13, 1966 (conducted by Norton B. Stern).
Dinkelspiel, John Walton, San Francisco, March 9, 1966.
Drabkin, The Messrs. I. and I., Sonora, February 21, 1966.
Eastman, Barbara, Oakland, July 19, 1966.
Elkus, Ruth, San Francisco, May 13, 1966.
Furth, Victor L., Walnut Creek, California, September 8, 1966 (telephone conversation).
Gottheimer, Roy, San Francisco, July 13, 1966.
Gradwohl, Arthur, San Francisco, March 8, 1966, and telephone conversation, February 7, 1968.
Guggenheim, Mrs. Robert, San Francisco, August 16, 1966.
Hayman, Alvin, Jr., San Francisco, August 16, 1966.
Hirschfelder, Erwin M., San Francisco, July 14, 1966.
Hoskin, W. E., Sonora, September 11, 1963.
Jones, Oscar, Diamond Springs, January 21, 1966.
Kahn, Edgar M., San Francisco, December 21, 1965.
Kahn, Julius, Jr., San Francisco, November 11, 1965.
Kuhn, Marshall H., San Francisco, May 15, 1972.
Masters, Richard B., San Francisco, March 8, 1966.
Mierson, Augustus, San Francisco, March 9, 1966.

Putzel, Myron, Oakland, December 15, 1968.
Rosen, Mrs. David V., Oakland, March 7, 1966.
Rosenberg, Adolph, San Francisco, November 17, 1976.
Rosenberg, Rabbi Dr. Bernard D., Stockton, June 30, 1972 (telephone conversation).
Rothschild, August, San Francisco, March 9, 1966 (telephone conversation).
Salomon, Jerome, San Francisco, November 10, 1965.
Schrag, The Misses Irma and Ruth, San Francisco, December 2, 1971.
Schweitzer, Jeffrey, Jackson, January 31, 1966.
Tracy, Mrs. Perry, Placerville, September 26, 1963.
Vorspan, Rabbi Dr. Max, Los Angeles, March 17, 1966.
Weston, Julian W., San Francisco, March 9, 1966.
Zellerbach, Harold L., San Francisco, April 21, 1966.
Zellerbach, Stephen A., San Francisco, April 22, 1966, and telephone conversation, August 10, 1971.

Letters

Coan, Irving, San Francisco, July 26, 1965.
Coblentz, Zach B., M. D., San Francisco, February 10, 1968.
Eastman, Barbara, Oakland, November 16, 1966.
Ferguson, John A., San Francisco, June 30 and July 19, 1965.
Goldsmith, Arthur A., Portland, Oregon, June 15, 1965.
Gradwohl, Arthur, San Francisco, August 16, 1965, July 29, 1971, and August 9, 1971.
Heyneman, Mrs. George, San Diego, July 13, 1966.
Hibbard, Rene I., Lakeport, California, September 14, 1971.
Kelman, Rabbi Wolfe, New York, June 25, 1971.
Levy, Mrs. J. Aaron, Sumter, South Carolina, July 16, 1965.
Marks, Mrs. Milton, Jr., San Francisco, June 24, 1965.
McSorley, A. S., Oakland, November 29, 1965.
Myer, Arthur H., Berkeley, June 14, 1965.
Regner, Rabbi Sidney L., New York, February 7, 1968.
Schiller, Barry M., Northridge, California, February 11, 1971.
Simon, Estelle, San Francisco, August 24, 1966.
Slater, Mrs. Morton V., Delano, California, July 31, 1966.
Wise, Hazel L., San Francisco, August 10, 1965.

Archival Collections

Baer's Store, Records, and Baer Family Papers, Sonora.

Banks in California Outside San Francisco. Wells Fargo Bank History Room, San Francisco.
Biographical Files of Members. Society of California Pioneers, San Francisco.
Biographical Sketches: Utah (Frederick H. Auerbach). Bancroft Library, Berkeley, California.
Branch Historical Directory. Bank of America Archives, San Francisco.
[Congregation Emanu-El] Minutes, March 30, 1851. Congregation Emanu-El, San Francisco.
[Congregation Sherith Israel] Minutes, from April [13] 1851 [to October 19, 1856] and letters. Congregation Sherith Israel, San Francisco.
Index to People. Wells Fargo Bank History Room, San Francisco.
Livingston, Louis Lobenstein. "Memoirs Experiences Observations." California State Library, Sacramento.
Membership Roster, [Columbia] Engine Co. No. 2. Columbia State Park Museum, Columbia.
Minutes, Columbia Lodge No. 28, F. & A. M., in the possession of Tuolumne Lodge No. 8, F. & A. M., Sonora.
Receipts. National Hotel Museum, Nevada City.
Records of the Hebrew Cemetery, Sonora. Western Jewish History Center, Berkeley.
Zellerbach, Anthony, Papers. California Historical Society, San Francisco.

Jewish Newspapers

Cincinnati *Die Deborah*, 1856.
 Israelite, 1855–79.
Leipzig *Allgemeine Zeitung des Judenthums*, 1852.
London *Jewish Chronicle*, 1850–62.
Magdeburg *Israelitische Wochenschrift*, 1876.
New York *Asmonean*, 1850–57.
 Jewish Messenger, 1860.
Philadelphia *Occident*, 1852–66.
San Francisco *Hebrew*, 1865–69.
 Hebrew Observer, 1867–70.
 Jewish Bulletin, 1974.
 Jewish Progress, 1878.
 Weekly Gleaner, 1857–64.

General Newspapers

Angels [Camp] *Calaveras Californian*, 1975.
   Calaveras Mountaineer, 1872–73.
Columbia *Citizen*, 1852–67.
  Gazette (also called *Columbia Gazette, and the Southern Mines Advertiser*), 1853–57.
  Tuolumne Courier, 1858–61.
  Tuolumne Independent, 1874–92.
  Weekly Columbian, 1856–57.
  Weekly Times (also called *Columbia Times*), 1860–61.
Downieville *Sierra Advocate*, 1866–67.
   Sierra Age, 1871.
   Sierra Citizen, 1859–60.
   Sierra Democrat, 1857–64.
Grass Valley *Telegraph*, 1854.
   Union, 1965.
Jackson *Amador Dispatch*, 1864–72.
   Amador Weekly Ledger, 1856–73.
Los Angeles *Star*, 1857–60.
Mariposa *Chronicle*, 1854.
  Democrat, 1856.
  Star, 1859–60.
Marysville *Daily Evening Herald*, 1853.
Mokelumne Hill *Weekly Calaveras Chronicle*, 1851–70.
Nevada City *The Independent*, 1975.
   Nevada County Nugget, 1965.
   Nevada Daily Gazette, 1865–68.
   Nevada Daily Transcript, 1868.
   Nevada Democrat, 1863.
   Nevada Journal, 1851–59.
   Nevada Weekly Gazette, 1868.
   Weekly National Gazette, 1870–72.
New York *Herald*, 1851.
North San Juan *War Club*, 1872.
Placerville *El Dorado County Republican*, 1872.
   El Dorado News, 1852.
   Mountain Democrat, 1861–1902.
   American, 1856.
   Weekly Recorder, 1866.
Prescott *Weekly Arizona Miner*, 1877.

Sacramento Daily Union, 1855.
San Andreas *Calaveras Weekly Times*, 1863.
    Independent, 1856–60.
San Francisco *Californian*, 1848.
    Chronicle, 1971.
    Daily Alta California, 1856.
    Examiner, 1890.
    Pacific, 1852.
Sonora Herald, 1851–67.
  Tuolumne Independent, 1892.
  Union Democrat, 1855–98.
Stockton *San Joaquin Republican*, 1855–56.
Sutter Creek *Semi-Weekly Independent*, 1874.
Volcano Weekly Ledger, 1855–56.

Public Documents

Amador County

Articles of Incorporation. Clerk's Office.
Great Register, 1866, Amador County. Clerk's Office.
 Levi, Elias, deceased, estate of. Old Probate Index 182. Clerk's Office.
Record, A, Mining Claims. Recorder's Office.
Record, County Court Records, A. Clerk's Office.
Records, Judgment in District Court, B. Clerk's Office.
Register of Marks and Brands. Recorder's Office.
Register of Partnerships, 1. Amador County. Clerk's Office.
 Steckler, Charles, deceased, estate of. Probate Box 33. Clerk's Office.
Uncertified Index to Naturalizations. Clerk's Office.

Butte County

Book E, Deeds, Butte county. Recorder's Office.

Calaveras County

Abels, M., deceased, estate of. Probate Box 29. Recorder's Office.
Articles of Incorporation. Clerk's Office.
Assessment Roll, 1860, Sheriff's Office. Assessor's Office.
Calaveras County, Records. T. W. Norris Collection, Bancroft Library,
 Berkeley, California.
Great Register, Calaveras County. Clerk's Office.
Mining Claims, Calaveras County, A–F. Recorder's Office.

Register of Marks and Brands. Recorder's Office.
Register of Partnerships, 1, Calaveras County. Recorder's Office.
Uncertified Index to Naturalizations. Clerk's Office.

El Dorado County

Abraham, Marcus, deceased, estate of. Probate Box 2. Clerk's Office.
Articles of Incorporation. Clerk's Office.
Deeds, V and 62, El Dorado County. Recorder's Office.
Great Register, El Dorado County. Clerk's Office.
Mining Locations, El Dorado County, A. Recorder's Office.
Minutes of Judgment Book, B, County Court. District Attorney's Office.
Records, A. Recorder's Office.
Register of Marks and Brands. Recorder's Office.
Uncertified Index to Naturalizations. Clerk's Office.

Mariposa County

Articles of Incorporation, 1, Mariposa County. Clerk's Office.
Great Register, Mariposa County. Clerk's Office.
Quartz Claims, A. Recorder's Office.
[Quartz] Record, C. Recorder's Office.
Register of Marks and Brands. Recorder's Office.
Uncertified Index to Naturalizations. Clerk's Office.

Nevada County

Articles of Incorporation. Recorder's Office.
Deeds, 10, Nevada County. Recorder's Office.
Great Register, Nevada County. Clerk's Office.
Marriage Certificates, 1, Nevada County. Recorder's Office.
Mining Claims, 6, Nevada County. Recorder's Office.
Register of Marks and Brands. Recorder's Office.
Register of Persons and Partnership Under Fictitious Names, Nevada County. Recorder's Office.
Uncertified Index to Naturalizations. Clerk's Office.

Placer County

Articles of Incorporation. Clerk's Office.
Great Register, Placer County. Clerk's Office.
Register of Marks and Brands. Recorder's Office.
Uncertified Index to Naturalizations. Clerk's Office.

Sierra County

Articles of Incorporation. Clerk's Office.
Great Register, Sierra County. Clerk's Office.
Register of Marks and Brands. Recorder's Office.
Uncertified Index to Naturalizations. Clerk's Office.

Tuolumne County

Articles of Incorporation. Clerk's Office.
1855 Assessment Roll, Tuolumne County. County Archives.
[1856] Assessment Roll, Tuolumne County. County Archives.
Assessment Roll, Tuolumne County, 1860. County Archives.
Assessment Roll . . . Tuolumne County [1862]. County Archives.
Assessment Roll . . . Tuolumne County [1863]. County Archives.
Brands, 1, Tuolumne County. Recorder's Office.
Great Register, Tuolumne County. County Archives.
1 [and 2], Index, Marriage Certificates, Men, Tuolumne County. Recorder's Office.
Jacobs, A. and M., deceased, estates of. Probate Box 44. Clerk's Office.
Marriage Licenses, Tuolumne County. Recorder's Office.
Marriages, 1–4. Recorder's Office.
Separate Property of Wife and Sole Trader, VIII. Recorder's Office.
Uncertified Index to Naturalizations. Clerk's Office.

State of California

Governor's Message; and Report of the Secretary of State on the Census of 1852, of the State of California. Vallejo [?]: G. K. Fitch and Company, and V. E. Geiger and Company, 1853.
Muster Roll, Capt. Hopkins Company . . . 3rd Brigade, 1st Division. Secretary of State's Office, Sacramento.
Petitions for enactment of a Sabbath law. Archives and Central Records Depository, Sacramento.
Petitions supporting the Sabbath Observance Law. Archives and Central Records Depository, Sacramento.
Receipts for Foreign Miners License, and Schedule of Names . . . Archives and Central Records Depository, Sacramento.
Statutes of California . . . Second Session. n.p.: Eugene Casserly, 1851.
Statutes of California, Passed at the Sixth Session of the Legislature . . . Sacramento: B. B. Redding, State Printer, 1855.

United States Government

House of Representatives. *Compendium of the Tenth Census*. Washington: Government Printing Office, 1883.

Population of the United States in 1860; Compiled from the Original Returns of the Eighth Census . . . Washington: Government Printing Office, 1864.

Records of the Post Office Department, [Microfilm] Record Group 28, Records of Appointments of Postmasters, State of California, 1848–1930. Washington: General Services Administration, National Archives and Records Service, 1953.

The Seventh Census of the United States: 1850. Washington: Robert Armstrong, 1853.

U.S. Bureau of the Census. *Seventh Census of the United States, 1850*.

U.S. Bureau of the Census. *Eighth Census of the United States, 1860*.

Miscellaneous

Oregon Legislative Assembly. *Journals of the Senate and House of the Twenty-Eighth Legislative Assembly* . . . Salem: State Printing Department, 1915.

Theses and Dissertations

Goldmann, Jack Benjamin. "A History of Pioneer Jews in California, 1849–1870." Master's thesis, Department of History, University of California at Berkeley, 1940.

Holliday, Jaquelin Smith. "The California Gold Rush in Myth and Reality." Ph.D. dissertation, Department of History, University of California at Berkeley, 1954.

Kemble, John Haskell. "The Genesis of the Pacific Mail Steamship Company." Master's thesis, Department of History, University of California at Berkeley, 1934.

Kinsey, Stephen D. "They Called it Home: The Development of the Jewish Community of San Jose, California, 1850–1900." Master's thesis, Department of History, California State University, San Jose, 1973.

Levinson, Robert E. "The Jews of Jacksonville, Oregon." Master's thesis, Department of History, University of Oregon, 1962.

Salzman, Jeffrey D. "Between Two Worlds: Jewish Merchants in a Changing City." Graduate seminar paper, Department of History, University of California at Berkeley, 1967.

Vorspan, Max. "History of the Jews in Los Angeles, 1850–1900."

D.H.L. dissertation, Jewish Theological Seminary of America (University of Judaism), 1961.

Directories

Bean, Edwin F., comp. *Bean's History and Directory of Nevada County, California* . . . Nevada [City]: Daily Gazette Book and Job Office, 1867.

Brown, Nat. P., and Dallison, John K. *Brown and Dallison's Nevada, Grass Valley and Rough and Ready Directory, For the Year Commencing January 1st, 1856* . . . San Francisco: Town Talk Office, 1856.

Byrne, William S. *Directory of Grass Valley Township for 1865.* San Francisco: Charles F. Robbins and Company, 1865.

Fitch, Thomas and Company. *Directory of the City of Placerville and Towns of Upper Placerville, El Dorado, Georgetown, and Coloma* . . . Placerville: Placerville Republican Printing Office, 1862.

Heckendorn, J., and Wilson, W. A. *Miners & Business Men's Directory. For the Year Commencing January 1st, 1856* . . . Columbia: Clipper Office, 1856.

McKenney's District Directory for 1879–80, of Sacramento, City and County, Amador, Eldorado [sic], Placer and Yolo Counties. Sacramento and San Francisco: L. M. McKenney, 1879.

Thompson, Hugh B. *Directory of the City of Nevada and Grass Valley* . . . San Francisco: Charles F. Robbins, 1861.

Secondary Materials

Reference Works

Coffee, Rudolf I. "California." *Universal Jewish Encyclopedia.* Vol. II.

Learned, H. Barrett. "Michelson, Albert Abraham." *Dictionary of American Biography.* 1964 ed. Vol. VI, pt. 2.

Mendes, Frederick de Sola. "Agriculture." *Jewish Encyclopedia.* Vol. I.

Polk, James K. "Fourth Annual Message." *A Compilation of the Messages and Papers of the Presidents* . . . 20 vols. New York: Bureau of National Literature, Inc., 1897.

Ray, P. O. "Kahn, Julius." *Dictionary of American Biography.* 1964 ed. Vol. V, pt. 2.

Voorsanger, Jacob. "California." *Jewish Encyclopedia.* Vol. III.

Periodical Articles and Monographs

Atherton, Lewis E. "The Pioneer Merchant in Mid-America." *University of Missouri Studies*, XIV (April 1, 1939), 5–135.

Baron, Salo W., and Baron, Jeannette M. "Palestinian Messengers in America, 1849–79: A Record of Four Journeys." *Jewish Social Studies*, V (July 1943), 225–292.

Clar, Reva. "Samuel Sussman Snow: A Pioneer Finds El Dorado." *Western States Jewish Historical Quarterly*, III (October 1970), 3–25.

Cohn, Fritz Ludwig, trans. and ed. "St. Louis and Poker Flat in the Fifties and Sixties: From the *Jugenderinnerungen* of Henry Cohn," *California Historical Society Quarterly*, XIX (December 1940), 289–298.

Danziger, Gustav Adolf. "The Jew in San Francisco the Last Half Century." *Overland Monthly*, April 1895, pp. 381–410.

Dubow, Sylvan Morris. "Problems in Jewish Military Service Research." *Western States Jewish Historical Quarterly*, II (January 1970), 101–105; IV (April 1972), 146–148.

"Excerpts from the Scrap Books of Rev. J. J. Lyons." *Publications of the American Jewish Historical Society*, XXVII (1920), 499–517.

Fierman, Floyd S. "Peddlers and Merchants on the Southwest Frontier, 1850–1880." *Password*, VIII (1963), 1–17.

"The First Fund-Raisers for the Hebrew Union College in the Far West." *Western States Jewish Historical Quarterly*, VIII (October 1975), 55–58.

Gaines, Marlene S. "The Early Sacramento Jewish Community." *Western States Jewish Historical Quarterly*, III (January 1971), 65–85.

Glanz, Rudolf. "Where the Jewish Press Was Distributed in Pre–Civil War America." *Western States Jewish Historical Quarterly*, V (October 1972), 1–14.

Heyneman, Alice W. "A Backward Look at a Pioneer Grandfather, Sol Wangenheim." *Western States Jewish Historical Quarterly*, IV (January 1972), 86–100.

Higham, John. "Social Discrimination Against Jews in America, 1830–1930." *Publication of the American Jewish Historical Society*, XLVII (September 1957), 1–33.

Isaacs, Joakim. "Candidate Grant and the Jews." *American Jewish Archives*, XVII (April 1965), 3–16.

Jones, Fred Mitchell. "Middlemen in the Domestic Trade of the United States 1800–1860." *Illinois Studies in the Social Sciences*, XXI (1937), 61 ff.

Kahn, Edgar M. "Pioneer Jewish San Francisco Stock Brokers." *Western States Jewish Historical Quarterly*, I (January 1969), 47–65.

———. "The Saga of the First Fifty Years of Congregation Emanu-El, San Francisco." *Western States Jewish Historical Quarterly*, III (April 1971), 129–147.

———. "Simon Newman—and Newman, California." *Western States Jewish Historical Quarterly*, II (October 1969), 11–26.

Kaye, William. "Tale of a Scroll." *The Scroll*, 1975, p. 47.

Klauber, Laurence M. "Abraham Klauber—A Pioneer Merchant (1831–1911)." *Western States Jewish Historical Quarterly*, II (January 1970), 67–90.

Kohn, Abraham. "A Jewish Peddler's Diary." Translated by Abram Vossen Goodman. *American Jewish Archives*, III (June 1951), 81–111.

Korn, Bertram Wallace. "An American Jewish Religious Leader in 1860 Voices his Frustration." *Michael: On the History of the Jews in the Diaspora*, edited by Lloyd P. Gartner. Book 11 of Publications of the Diaspora Research Institute, edited by Shlomo Simonsohn. Tel-Aviv: Diaspora Research Institute and Haim Rosenberg School of Jewish Studies of Tel-Aviv University, III (1975), 42–47.

———. "Jews and Negro Slavery in the Old South, 1789–1865." *Publication of the American Jewish Historical Society*, L (March 1961), 151–201.

Kramer, William M., and Stern, Norton B. "A Search for the First Synagogue in the Golden West." *Western States Jewish Historical Quarterly*, VII (October 1974), 3–20.

Levinson, Robert E. "Julius Basinski: Pioneer Montana Merchant." *YIVO Annual of Jewish Social Science*, XIV (1969), 219–233.

———. "Ketubot From Early California." In *Michael: On the History of the Jews in the Diaspora*, edited by Lloyd P. Gartner. Book 11 of Publications of the Diaspora Research Institute, edited by Shlomo Simonsohn. Tel-Aviv: Diaspora Research Institute and Haim Rosenberg School of Jewish Studies of Tel-Aviv University, III (1975), 34–41.

Marcus, Jacob Rader, ed. "An Arizona Pioneer: Memoirs of Sam Aaron." *American Jewish Archives*, X (October 1958), 95–120.

[Marcus, Jacob Rader.] "Anti-Jewish Sentiment in California, 1855." *American Jewish Archives*, XII (April 1960), 15–33.

Narell, Irena Penzik. "Bernhard Marks: Retailer, Miner, Educator and Land Developer." *Western States Jewish Historical Quarterly*, VIII (October 1975), 26–38.

Pitt, Leonard. "The Beginnings of Nativism in California." *Pacific Historical Review*, XXX (February 1961), 23–38.

Schwartz, Mrs. David ("Bea"). "Oldest Jewish Cemetery in the

West—Stockton, California." *Western States Jewish Historical Quarterly*, I (January 1969), 66–74.

Shuford, Beth. "Report on Cemeteries and Lone Graves." *Covered Wagon* (1965), 40–42.

Smith, Timothy. "New Approaches to the History of Immigration in Twentieth-Century America." *American Historical Review*, LXXI (July 1966), 1265–1279.

Solis-Cohen, J[acob], Jr. "A California Pioneer: The Letters of Bernhard Marks to Jacob Solis-Cohen (1853–1857)." *Publication of the American Jewish Historical Society*, XLIV (September 1954), 12–57.

Stern, Norton B. "The Life of Tzedakah—Isador Cohen of Sacramento." *Western States Jewish Historical Quarterly*, IV (October 1971), 25–34.

———, and Kramer, William M. "The Major Role of Polish Jews in the Pioneer West." *Western States Jewish Historical Quarterly*, VIII (July 1976), 326–344.

Supple, Barry E. "A Business Elite: German-Jewish Financiers in Nineteenth-Century New York." *Business History Review*, XXXI (Summer 1957), 143–178.

"Trail Blazers of the Trans-Mississippi West." *American Jewish Archives*, VIII (October 1956), 59–130.

Turner, Justin G. "The First Decade of Los Angeles Jewry: A Pioneer History (1850–1860)." *American Jewish Historical Quarterly*, LIV (December 1964), 123–164.

Books

Asbury, Herbert. *The Barbary Coast* . . . New York: Pocket Books, Inc., 1947.

Atherton, Lewis. *Main Street on the Middle Border*. Bloomington: Indiana University Press, 1954.

Bancroft, Hubert Howe. *Works*. 39 vols. San Francisco: History Company, 1888.

Benjamin, [I. J.]. *Three Years in America: 1859–1862*. 2 vols. Translated by Charles Reznikoff. Philadelphia: Jewish Publication Society of America, 1956.

Billington, Ray Allen. *The Far Western Frontier, 1830—1860*. New York and Evanston: Harper and Row, 1956.

Birmingham, Stephen. *"Our Crowd": The Great Jewish Families of New York*. New York: Harper and Row, 1967.

Bloom, Monroe A. *A Century of Pioneering: A Brief History of Crocker-Citizens National Bank*. San Francisco[?]: Crocker-Citizens National Bank, 1970.

Book of Rates. No. 3. For the Use and Guidance of Fire Underwriters on the Pacific Coast. San Francisco: Pacific Insurance Union, 1886.

Borthwick, J. D. *Three Years in California*. Edinburgh and London: William Blackwood and Sons, 1857.

Bronson, William. *Still Flying And Nailed To The Mast: The First Hundred Years of the Fireman's Fund Insurance Company*. Garden City, New York: Doubleday and Company, Inc., 1963.

Buckbee, Edna Bryan. *The Saga of Old Tuolumne*. New York: Press of the Pioneers, Inc., 1935.

Buffum, Edward Gould. *Six Months in the Gold Mines*. Ann Arbor: University Microfilms, Inc., 1966.

Carson, Gerald. *The Old Country Store*. New York: Oxford University Press, 1954.

Carson, James H. *Early Recollections of the Mines, And a Description of the Great Tulare Valley*. 2d ed. Stockton: San Joaquin Republican, 1852.

Caughey, John W. *California: A Remarkable State's Life History*. 3d ed. Englewood Cliffs, N.J.: Prentice-Hall, Inc., 1970.

―――. *Gold is the Cornerstone*. Berkeley and Los Angeles: University of California Press, 1948.

Clinkston, Bert. *120th Anniversary Commemorative Edition: Congregation B'nai Israel, Sacramento, California*. Sacramento[?]: n.p., 1970.

Cohen, George. *The Jews in the Making of America*. Boston: Stratford Company, 1924.

Cohn, Henry. *Jugenderinnerungen*. Stettin: M. Bauchwitz, 1914.

Constitution and By-Laws of Congregation B'nai Israel Located at Jackson Amador County California. San Francisco: M. Weiss, 1873.

Credo Quia Absurdum: Being a Compilation of Historic Documents and Trivia Pertinent to a full Understanding of the Meaning and Purpose of the Ancient and Honorable Order of E Clampus Vitus. Placerville: n.p., 1949.

D'Ancona, David A. *A California-Nevada Travel Diary of 1876: The Delightful Account of a Ben B'rith*. Edited by William M. Kramer. Santa Monica: Norton B. Stern, 1975.

Dobie, Charles Caldwell. *San Francisco: A Pageant*. New York and London: D. Appleton-Century Company, Inc., 1933.

Dreyfus, A. Stanley. *Hebrew Cemetery No. 1 of Galveston*. Galveston: Congregation B'nai Israel[?], 1965.

Early, Raymond. *Columbia*. San Francisco: Fearon Publishers, 1957.//
1864–1944. 80 Years of Service: Auerbach Company, Salt Lake City. n.p.: n.d.//
Essays in American Jewish History . . . Cincinnati: American Jewish Archives, 1958.//
Ganzfried, Solomon. *Kitzur Shulchan Aruch*. Translated by Hyman E. Goldin. New York: Hebrew Publishing Company, 1927.//
Gaston, Joseph. *Portland, Oregon, Its History and Builders* . . . 4 vols. Chicago and Portland: S. J. Clarke Publishing Company, 1911.//
Gerstaecker, Friedrich. *California Gold Mines*. Oakland: Biobooks, 1946.//
Glanz, Rudolf. *The Jews of California From the Discovery of Gold Until 1880*. New York: Waldon Press, Inc., 1960.//
Glazer, Nathan. *American Judaism*. Chicago: University of Chicago Press, 1957.//
Goldstein, Israel. *A Century of Judaism in New York: B'nai Jeshurun 1825–1925, New York's Oldest Ashkenazic Congregation*. New York: Congregation B'nai Jeshurun, 1930.//
Hafen, Le Roy R.; Hollon, W. Eugene; and Rister, Carl Coke. *Western America* . . . 3d ed. Englewood Cliffs, N.J.: Prentice-Hall, Inc., 1970.//
Handlin, Oscar. *Adventure in Freedom: Three Hundred Years of Jewish Life in America*. New York: McGraw-Hill Book Company, Inc., 1954.//
Haney, Kenneth, ed. *From the Journal of Garrett W. Low: Gold Rush by Sea*. Philadelphia: University of Pennsylvania Press, 1941.//
Hansen, Marcus Lee. *The Atlantic Migration, 1607–1860: A History of the Continuing Settlement of the United States*. Edited by Arthur M. Schlesinger. Cambridge: Harvard University Press, 1940.//
———. *The Immigrant in American History*. Edited by Arthur M. Schlesinger. Cambridge: Harvard University Press, 1940.//
Heller, James G. *Isaac M. Wise: His Life, Work and Thought*. New York: Union of American Hebrew Congregations, 1965.//
Helper, Hinton Rowan. *The Land of Gold: Reality Versus Fiction*. Baltimore: Henry Taylor, 1855.//
Hirshler, Eric E., ed. *Jews From Germany in the United States*. New York: Farrar, Straus and Cudahy, 1955.//
History of Fresno County, California . . . San Francisco: Wallace W. Elliott Company, 1881.//
Howe, Octavius Thorndike. *Argonauts of '49: History and Adventures of the Emigrant Companies from Massachusetts 1849–1850*. Cambridge: Harvard University Press, 1923.

Hutchings, James Mason. *The Miner's Ten Commandments*. San Francisco: J. M. Hutchings, 1887.

Iser, Alexander, comp. *The California Hebrew & English Almanac, For the Year 5612, Corresponding with the Years 1851–2* . . . San Francisco: Albion Job Press, [1851].

The Israelites of Louisiana. New Orleans: W. E. Myers, 1904.

Jaffe, Bernard. *Michelson and the Speed of Light*. Garden City, N.Y.: Doubleday and Company, Inc., 1960.

Kemble, John Haskell. *The Panama Route, 1848–1869*. Berkeley and Los Angeles: University of California Press, 1943.

Kinnard, Lawrence. *History of the Greater San Francisco Bay Region*. 3 vols. New York and West Palm Beach: Lewis Historical Publishing Company, 1966.

Kinyon, Edmund. *The Northern Mines*. Grass Valley—Nevada City: Union Publishing Company, 1949.

Kip, William Ingraham. *The Early Days of my Episcopate*. New York: Thomas Whittaker, 1892.

Knopf, Adolph. *The Mother Lode System of California*. Washington: Government Printing Office, 1929.

Korn, Bertram W. *American Jewry and the Civil War*. Cleveland and New York: World Publishing Company, and Philadelphia: Jewish Publication Society of America, 1961.

———. *Eventful Years and Experiences: Studies in Nineteenth Century American Jewish History*. Cincinnati: American Jewish Archives, 1954.

Lamson, J. *Round Cape Horn. Voyage of the Passenger-Ship James W. Paige, From Maine to California in the Year 1852*. Bangor: Press of O.F.&W.H. Knowles, 1878.

Levison, Jacob Bertha. *Memories for My Family*. San Francisco: John Henry Nash, 1933.

Levy, Harriet Lane. *920 O'Farrell Street*. Garden City, N.Y.: Doubleday and Company, Inc., 1947.

Lewis, Oscar. *San Francisco: Mission to Metropolis*. Berkeley: Howell-North Books, 1966.

Lyons, Jacques J., and DeSola, Abraham. *A Jewish Calendar for Fifty Years* . . . Montreal: John Lovell, 1854.

Mack, Gerstle. *Lewis and Hannah Gerstle*. New York: Profile Press, 1953.

Marcus, Jacob Rader. *Early American Jewry: The Jews of New York, New England and Canada, 1649–1794*. Philadelphia: Jewish Publication Society of America, 1951.

———. *Memoirs of American Jews, 1775–1865*. 3 vols. Philadelphia:

Jewish Publication Society of America, 1955.

May, Philip Ross. *The West Coast Gold Rushes.* Christchurch, N.Z.: Pegasus Press, 1962.

McDonald, Frank V., comp. and ed. *Notes Preparatory to a Biography of Richard Hayes McDonald of San Francisco, California.* Cambridge [England?]: University Press, 1881.

McLeod, Alexander. *Pigtails and Gold Dust: A Panorama of Chinese Life in Early California.* Caldwell, Idaho: Caxton Printers, Ltd., 1947.

Men of California. San Francisco and Los Angeles: Western Press Reporter, Inc., 1925.

Messing, Aron J. *A Farewell Gift To His Friends From Aron J. Messing, Rabbi of Congregation "Beth Israel." July 1890-5650.* San Francisco: Francis, Valentine and Company, Printers, 1890.

Meyer, Henry O. "A Brief Account of the Family of Oser Meyer and Bertha Michelson Meyer and its Relationship to the Michelsons." South San Francisco: n.p., n.d.

Meyer, Martin A. *Western Jewry: An Account of the Achievements of the Jews and Judaism in California Including Eulogies and Biographies.* San Francisco: Emanu-El, 1916.

Mihm, Friedrich. *Interessante Berichte über die Reisen Abraham Abrahamsohns nach Amerika und besonders zu den Goldminen Kaliforniens und Australiens.* Ilmenau: Carl Friedrich Trommsdorff, 1856.

Millard, Bailey. *History of the San Francisco Bay Region.* 3 vols. Chicago: American Historical Society, Inc., 1924.

Muir, Ross L., and White, Carl J. *Over the Long Term . . . the Story of J. & W. Seligman & Company.* New York: J. & W. Seligman & Company, 1964.

Newmark, Maurice H., and Marco R., eds. *Sixty Years in Southern California, 1853-1913, Containing the Reminiscences of Harris Newmark.* 3d ed. Boston and New York: Houghton Mifflin Company, 1930.

Nodel, Julius J. *The Ties Between: A Century of Judaism on America's Last Frontier.* Portland: Temple Beth Israel, 1959.

Paden, Irene D., and Schlichtmann, Margaret E. *The Big Oak Flat Road: An Account of Freighting from Stockton to Yosemite Valley.* San Francisco: Lawton Kennedy, 1955.

Parish, William J. *The Charles Ilfeld Company: A Study of the Rise and Decline of Mercantile Capitalism in New Mexico.* Cambridge: Harvard University Press, 1961.

Paul, Rodman W. *California Gold: The Beginning of Mining in the Far West.* Cambridge: Harvard University Press, 1947.

———. *Mining Frontiers of the Far West, 1848–1880.* New York: Holt, Rinehart and Winston, 1963.

Perkins, William. *Three Years in California: William Perkins' Journal of Life at Sonora, 1849–1852.* Introduction and annotations by Dale L. Morgan and James R. Scobie. Berkeley and Los Angeles: University of California Press, 1964.

Peters, Charles. *The Autobiography of Charles Peters.* Sacramento: La Grave Company, 1915.

Phillips, A. Th. *Daily Prayers with English Translation.* New York: Hebrew Publishing Company, 1932.

Pomeroy, Earl. *The Pacific Slope: A History* . . . New York: Alfred A. Knopf, 1965.

Proceedings of District Grand Lodge No. 4, Independent Order of B'nai B'rith (1863, 1865, 1867, 1872, 1874, 1876–77, 1880, 1893, 1896).

Proceedings of the M[ost] W[orthy] Grand Lodge, Ancient Jewish Order Kesher Shel Barzel. San Francisco: Winterburn and Company, 1874.

Reinhart, Harold F. *Temple B'nai Israel and the Sacramento Jewish Community.* Sacramento: News Publishing Company, 1927.

Reznikoff, Charles, and Engelman, Uriah Z. *The Jews of Charleston: A History of an American Jewish Community.* Philadelphia: Jewish Publication Society of America, 1950.

Robertson, Priscilla. *Revolutions of 1848: A Social History.* Princeton, N.J.: Princeton University Press, 1952.

Rome, David. *The First Two Years: A Record of the Jewish Pioneers on Canada's Pacific Coast, 1858–1860.* Montreal: H. M. Caiserman, 1942.

Sargent, Mrs. J. L., ed. *Amador County History.* Jackson: Amador County Federation of Women's Clubs, 1927.

Scenes of Wonder and Curiosity in California. San Francisco: Hutchings and Rosenfield, 1860.

Sherman, C. Bezalel. *The Jew Within American Society: A Study in Ethnic Individuality.* Detroit: Wayne State University Press, 1961.

Shinn, Charles Howard. *Mining Camps: A Study in American Frontier Governments.* New York: Charles Scribner's Sons, 1885.

Shumate, Albert. *A Note on ECV in the Gold Fields.* San Francisco: Lawton Kennedy, n.d.

Soulé, Frank; Gihon, John H.; and Nisbet, James. *The Annals of San Francisco* . . . New York: D. Appleton and Company, 1855.

Statistics of the Jews of the United States . . . Philadelphia: Union of American Hebrew Congregations, 1880.

Stember, Charles Herbert, et al. *Jews in the Mind of America.* New York and London: Basic Books, Inc., 1966.

Stewart, Robert E., Jr., and Stewart, Mary Frances. *Adolph Sutro: A Biography.* Berkeley: Howell-North, 1962.

Storke, Yda Addis. *A Memorial and Biographical History of the Counties of Santa Barbara, San Luis Obispo and Ventura, California.* Chicago: Lewis Publishing Company, 1891.

Teggart, Frederick J. *Around the Horn to the Sandwich Islands and California 1845–1850: Being a Personal Record Kept by Chester S. Lyman.* New Haven: Yale University Press, 1925.

Tinkham, George H. *A History of San Joaquin County with Biographical Sketches* . . . Los Angeles: Historic Record Company, 1923.

———. *History of Stanislaus County, California* . . . Los Angeles: Historic Record Company, 1921.

Tuolumne County, California, Opportunities and Possibilities. Sonora: Union Democrat, 1909.

Upton, Charles Elmer. *Pioneers of El Dorado.* Placerville: Nugget Press, 1906.

Upton, Will O. *Churches of El Dorado County: Their History Covering a Period of Ninety Years from 1850 to 1940.* Placerville: Old Hangtown Press, 1940.

Voorsanger, Jacob. *The Chronicles of Emanu-El: Being an Account of the Rise and Progress of the Congregation Emanu-El Which Was Founded in July, 1850* . . . San Francisco: George Spaulding and Company, 1900.

Walling, A. G. *Illustrated History of Lane County, Oregon.* Portland: A. G. Walling, 1884.

Watters, Leon L. *The Pioneer Jews of Utah.* New York: American Jewish Historical Society, 1952.

Wells, H. L. *History of Nevada County, California* . . . Oakland: Thompson and West, 1880.

Wheat, Carl I. *Books of the California Gold Rush.* San Francisco: Colt Press, 1949.

Winther, Oscar Osburn. *Express and Stagecoach Days in California from the Gold Rush to the Civil War.* Stanford: Stanford University Press, 1936.

Wischnitzer, Mark. *To Dwell in Safety: The Story of Jewish Migration Since 1800.* Philadelphia: Jewish Publication Society of America, 1948.

Wolf, Simon. *The American Jew as Patriot, Soldier and Citizen.* Philadelphia: Levytype Company, 1895.

Wright, Richardson. *Hawkers and Walkers in Early America* . . . Philadelphia: J. B. Lippincott Company, 1927.

The Years of Paper. [San Francisco?]: Crown Zellerbach Corporation, 1941.

Zarchin, Michael M. *Glimpses of Jewish Life in San Francisco.* 2d ed. Oakland: Judah L. Magnes Memorial Museum, 1964.

Zucker, A. E., ed. *The Forty-Eighters: Political Refugees of the German Revolution of 1848.* New York: Columbia University Press, 1950.

INDEX

A

A. Block & Co., 157
A. Wolf & Bros., San Francisco, 151
A. Zellerbach & Sons, San Francisco, 134
A. Zellerbach, Paper Merchant, San Francisco, 134
Aaron, Sam, 33
Abels (or Abel), Michael, 48, 151
Abraham, Marcus, 48, 99
Abrahamsohn, Abraham, 145
Abrams, Jacob, 180
Abramson, E., 177
Agua Fria, CA., 158
　Jewish merchants in, 29
Alabama, 149
Alaska Commercial Co., San Francisco, 15, 34, 141
Albany, N. Y., 119
Allighanytown, CA., 105–106
Alsace, 146
Altdorf, Baden, 25
Amador City, CA., 164, 185–186
　Jewish merchants in, 57
Amador County, xvi, 24, 63–64, 142, 147–148, 163–164, 172
　Jewish merchants in, 29, 40, 47–48, 57
　mining claims in, 15
　travel to, 5
Amador County Labor Association, 67
Amador Lodge No. 65, F. & A. M., Jackson, 164
American River, 5, 173
American Southwest, 34
Amsterdam, 30
Ancient Jewish Order Kesher Shel Barzel, 101, 106–107
Ancient Order of United Workmen, 65
Angels, CA., 146
Anglo & London Paris National Bank of San Francisco, 134–135
Anglo California Bank, Ltd., 135
Anglo California National Bank of San Francisco, 135
Anglo-California Trust Co. of San Francisco, 135
anti-Semitism, 58, 69–84, 150, 169–170
　in San Francisco, 7
　in the gold rush, 13–14, 27–28, 69–84
　in California, 13–14
　in the U. S., 13
Applebaum, Rev. A. J., 118–119
Aramaic, 181–182
Argare Copper Mining Co., 20
Arizona, 52, 129, 152
　gold discovery in, 21
Aschheim, Mayer S., 158
Ashkenazic Jews, 185
Atlantic Ocean, 5
Atlantic states 49, 72–73
Auburn, CA., 55, 105–106, 164
auctioneers, 35, 152
Auerbach brothers, 129
　Co., 129

Frederick, 35
Samuel H., 35
Theodore, 35
Austin, Nev., 35, 129, 155–156
Austria, 140

B

Badt, Alexander, 171–172
Baer, Julius E., 116, 178–179
　Max, 84–85
　Mayer, 55, 112–113, 119, 121, 181–182
Baker, Ore., 128
bakers, 35, 152
Baltimore, Md., 184
Bank of America, 157–158
banking, Jews in, 53–55, 146
bankruptcies, 21, 40, 51–53, 156–157
Barbados, 30
Barkerville, B. C., 128
Barlow, Abraham, 55, 178–179
　family, Sonora, 98
　Francis, 97
Barman, Isaac, 158
　Leopold, 158
Bar Mitzvah, in Placerville, 119
Baruh, Aaron, 16, 117, 145, 166, 184
　family home, Nevada City, 184
　Jennie, 145
Baum, D., 72–73
Bear Valley, CA., 67
　Jewish merchants in, 55
Beavertown, CA., 145
Beer, Julius, 54
Bench Berith, 176
benevolent societies, 97–100, 111–112
Benhayon, J., 41
Benjamin, I. J., 131, 142–143
　in Diamond Springs, 103, 107
　in Folsom, 107
　in Grass Valley, 101, 109
　in Jackson, 110–111
　in Mokelumne Hill, 99–100, 103
　in Nevada City, 107
　in Placerville, 19, 111
　in Sonora, 109
Berg, Mrs. E., 20
　Emanuel, 103
Berkeley, CA., 179–180
Berliner, B., 113, 183
Bernheim, Jacob, 18
　Reuben, 18
Bien, Rev. Herman, 95
　Julius, 18
Big Oak Flat, CA., 83–84, 161
　Jewish merchants in, 29
Blackman, Abraham, 33
Block, A., 152, 157
　A. & Co., 42, 59, 157
　& Furth, 54, 157
　E., of Don Pedros Bar, CA., 83–84
　E., Jr., 152, 157
　family, Nevada City, 98
Blue Ledge Gold & Silver Mining Co., 147
Blum, Henry, 18
Blumenthal, A., 15, 45
　Joseph, 163
　M., 174
B'nai B'rith, 18, 101, 106–107, 140, 142, 154, 176–178
　in Grass Valley, 101, 106–107, 176–177
　in Marysville, 142, 154, 176, 178
B'nai B'rith Palestine Relief Fund, 107
Board of Delegates of American Israelites, 104–106, 131
Bodie, CA., 129
　Jewish merchants in, 57
book sellers, 37, 49–50, 155–156
Borowsky, Michael, 163–164
Borthwick, J. D., 143
Boston, Mass., 3, 96
branch merchandising, 31, 57
Brandenstein family, 31
Brazil, 30
brick buildings, 57–60, 146, 159–160, 162
Bridgeport, CA., 65
　Jewish merchants in, 57
Bridgeport Township, CA., 166

Brinn, Morris, 64, 147, 165
  Nathan, 112
British Columbia, 106
  gold discovery in, 21
  Jewish merchants in, 33
Brownstein, Charles, 173–174
Bruml, family, 51
  M. & Co., 56
  M. & S., 156
  Moses, 56, 164
Bruml's Celebrated Bohemian Bitters, 51
Buckeye, CA., 128
Buckeye quartz lode, 19
Buda Pesth, Hungary, 140
Bundes Brüder, 140
butchers, 35, 152
Butte Basin Mining Co., 147
Butte City Mining District, 147

C

Cahn, Ernestein, 99
Calaveras County, xvi, 129–130, 142, 146–148, 164
  assessment, 153
  Jewish merchants in, 32, 48
  Jewish tax-payers in, 38
  mining claims in, 15
  travel to, 5
Calaveras Gold Mining Co., 147
Calaveras Lodge, F. & A. M., 164
California, gold discovery in, xv, 1, 5–6, 21
  gold mining in, xv
  immigration to, xv, 1–2, 5–6
  Jews in, 3, 10
  militia, 166
  newspapers, 50
  overland to, 4
  population, 6, 25
  Senate and Assembly, 71–72
  ship transportation to, 1, 3–4
Californian (ship), 139
California State Division of Highways, 173–174
California Steam Navigation Co., 44

Campo Seco, CA., 25, 123, 128
Camptonville, CA., 105–106
Canada, 139
Capay, CA., 128
Cape Horn, 1, 3–4, 132, 139
Caribbean Sea, 30
Caro, Hartwig, 174
Carson Creek, CA., 158
Carson City, Nev., 134
cattle raising, 126, 129–130
cemeteries, 61, 97–101, 103–104, 106–107, 109–110, 123–124
  Galveston, Tex., 175
  Grass Valley, 98, 115
  Jackson, 98–99, 104, 175
  Marysville, 109, 142, 154
  Mokelumne Hill, 98–100, 103, 175, 177
  Nevada City, 98, 109, 155, 175
  Oroville, 142
  Placerville, 85, 98–99, 104, 175
  Sacramento, 98
  San Francisco, 98, 171–172
  Shasta, 173–174
  Sonora, 98–101, 109, 172, 174–176
  Stockton, 94, 98, 148, 174–175, 179–180
  Victoria, B. C., 175
census figures, 148, 172–173
Central California Colony, 80
Central Conference of American Rabbis, 182–183
Central Europe, 19, 30, 61, 66, 71, 88
chaplains, Jewish, 169
charities, Jewish, 104–105
charity, 104–110, 124
Charleston, S. C., 114
chazan, 94, 118–119
"Cheap John" (Samuel Haas of Nevada City), 31, 73–74
Cherokee (ship), 94
Chicago, Ill., 107, 184
Children's Playground, San Francisco, 189
Chileans, prejudice against, 62
Chinese, 7, 146, 162, 168
  prejudice against, 62, 70–71

Chinese Camp, CA., 98–99, 158, 160–161
Choynski, I. N., 178
Cincinnati, Ohio, 140, 158, 177, 182–183
cinnabar, 17
circumcision ceremonies, 117–119
  in Grass Valley, 185
  in Mokelumne Hill, 185
  in Nevada City, 118
  in Sonora, 113
Citizens National Bank, 189
Civil War, 13, 66, 74–79, 133, 145, 166–167, 169
Clinch Gold & Silver Mining Co., 147
clothing, 29–30, 35, 38, 150
clothing merchants, 37–42, 44–48, 51, 55, 57, 95, 126–127, 150, 158, 160
Coast Range, 142
Coblentz, A., 159
  David, 57
  family, 128
  Felix, 57, 64
  Gustave, 57
  Lambert, 57
  Lazard, 57
  P., 163
  Samuel, 57
Cody & Gatzert, 59
Coffee, Rabbi Rudolf I., 172–173
Cohen, A., 55
  & Levy, 153
  Benjamin, 136
  Isidor, 136
  Isidor, Elementary School, Sacramento, 136
  M., 175
  Morris, 146–147
  Morris, & Co., 17
  Moses, 164
  Samuels & Co., 158
  W. M., 50
Cohen's Old Stand, 47
Cohn, A., 65
  Alexander, 35
  Benjamin, 54
  Edward, 111–112
  Felix, 148
  Heiman (or Henry), 18, 152, 162
  J., 160–161
  Louis, 35
  N., & Co., Mariposa, 150
  Richard, 165
  Samuel, 168
Coloma, CA., 68, 72–73, 147, 164, 173
  1850 census, 91
  High Holidays in, 91–92
Colorado, 128
  gold discovery in, 21
  silver discovery in, 21
Columbia, CA., 43, 63–65, 67, 80–82, 109, 126, 128, 133, 154, 160–161, 163, 165–168, 181–182
  anti-Semitism in, 79
  brick buildings in, 58
  Engine Co. No. 2, 166
  High Holidays in, 90–91, 173
  Jewish bankers in, 54
  Jewish merchants in, 44–45, 50, 79
  Masonic Hall, 173
  mining in, 15
  schools in, 68
  synagogue, 173
  Terpsichorean Society, 67
Columbia Paper Co., 134
Commercial Hotel, San Francisco, 171–172
Commission for the Preservation of Pioneer Jewish Cemeteries and Landmarks, 176, 180–181, 186
Comstock Lode, Nev., 134
Coney, Mrs. D. Stephen, 188–189
Confederacy, 167
Confirmation, 119, 185
Congregation Beth Israel, Jackson, 102
Congregation Beth Israel, Portland, Ore., 185
Congregation Beth Israel, San Francisco, 107, 178
Congregation B'nai Israel, Galveston, Tex., 175

Congregation B'nai Israel, Jackson, 34, 102, 121–122
Congregation Emanu-El, New York, 184
Congregation Emanu-El, San Francisco, 90, 105, 179
Congregation Har Sinai, Baltimore, Md., 184
Congregation Rodeph Shalom, Philadelphia, Pa., 140
Congregation Ryhim Ahoovim, Stockton, CA., 178–179
Congregation Shearith Israel, New York, 140
Congregation Sherith Israel, San Francisco, 90, 105, 118–119, 121, 143, 171–172, 178, 181–182, 185–186
Congregation Sinai, Chicago, Ill., 184
Connecticut, 149
Constantinople, 30
Coon Hollow Road, Placerville, 85
Cosumnes Copper Mining Co., 20
Cosumnes Post Office, CA., 123
Cottonwood, CA., 33, 128
credit merchandising, 40, 55, 58, 60, 147, 154
Crocker-Anglo National Bank, 189
Crocker Bank, 189
Crocker-Citizens National Bank, 189
Crocker First National Bank, 189
Crown Paper Co., 134
Crown-Willamette Corporation, 134
Crown Zellerbach Corporation, 134

D

daguerreotypists, 35, 152
D'Ancona, David A., 176
Danielewicz, David, 99
  Gustav, 64
Davidson, B., 54
  Samuel, 148
  Samuel L., 163
Deep South, 182–183
Democratic National Committee, 187
Democratic Party, 63, 66, 74–79

Denver, Colo., 31
Diamond Springs, CA., 16, 99, 103–104, 152, 164–165
Diamond Springs Lodge No. 9, I.O.O.F., 165
dietary laws, 113
  in Georgetown, 185
  in Nevada City, 184
  in Sonora, 121
Dinkelspiel, L., 146
  Moses, 31, 128, 161
District Grand Lodge No. 4, B'nai B'rith, 18, 101, 106–107, 140, 142, 154, 176–178
Don Pedros Bar, CA., 83–84
Downieville, CA., 65–66, 70, 123, 129, 161–162, 168
  High Holidays in, 110, 122
  Jewish merchants in, 50, 52
  merchants in, 39
  Odd Fellows activities in, 65
  schools in, 68
Drachman, Samuel H., 152
Dreyfus, Julius, 152
Dreyfus (Dreyfuss), Louis Wendelin, 63, 152
drygoods, 29–30
Drytown, CA., 109–110
Durham, George, 64
"Dutch John" (pseudonym), 28–29
Dutch West India Co., 30

E

Eastern Prussia, 106
Eastern United States, 36
Eckman, Rabbi Julius, 95, 106, 115, 118, 122, 185
E Clampus Vitus, 65, 165, 187
Ehrenberg, Ariz., 34
Ehrenberg, T., 50
Eis, Max, 179–180
El Dorado (city),CA., 16, 99, 103–104, 113, 128, 156–157, 159
  Jewish merchants in, 57
El Dorado County, xvi, 24, 72–73, 80, 136, 145, 148, 163–164

Agricultural Society, 68
  mining in, 15–16, 20, 55
  travel to, 5
election officials, Jews as, 64
Elias, Edward, 45, 128, 163, 181
  Philip, 45, 128, 181, 187
  Sol P., 187
Elkus, L., 147
  Theodore, 72–73
Empire Clothing Depot, Nevada City, 20, 39
English Jews, 90
Episcopal church, 168
Eugene, Ore., 144
Eureka Benevolent Society, San Francisco, 90, 172
Eureka (Nevada County), CA., 17
Eureka Lake & Yuba Canal Co. Consolidated, 18
Eureka Lodge No. 16, F. & A. M., Auburn, 164
Eureka Social Club, Nevada City, 102
Europe, 2, 19, 22, 24, 30–31, 36, 39–40, 61, 66, 68, 71, 87–89, 94, 105–106, 125, 128, 130, 133, 140, 162, 171
express agents, 146

F

Falcon (ship), 139
Falk, Adolph, 134
Famine Fund, 106
farming, 22, 35, 126, 129–130, 150, 152
Feather River, 5
Fechheimer, L. W., 64
Ferguson, John, 113, 182
Fiddletown, CA., 105–106, 113, 163, 172
  Democratic Club No. 4, 163
  Jewish merchants in, 29, 57
fire insurance, 58–59, 159–160
Fireman's Fund Insurance Co., 135
fires, 38, 52, 57–60, 109–110, 133, 160–161
First Hebrew Benevolent Society, San Francisco, 90, 171–172
First National Bank of Sonora, 157–158
Fleishhacker, Aaron, 134
Fleishhacker & Co., Forest City, 160–161
Fleishhacker family, 31, 188
  Herbert, Sr., 134–135, 189
  Mortimer, Sr., 134–135
  Pool, San Francisco, 189
Fleishman, B. M., 20
  J., 164
foreign exchange, 68
foreign miners' tax, 19, 146
Forest City, CA., 134, 160–161
France, 146, 172
  Jews from, 6
Franco-Prussian War, 177
Frankl, Leopold, 67, 158
Fraser River, 33–34, 128
fraternal organizations, Jews in, 64–65, 164–165
Free and Accepted Masons, 64–65, 92–93, 119, 164–165
Freeport, CA., 44
freight, moved by railroad, 33, 43–44
  ship, 33, 39, 43
freighting, 6, 42–43
French (language) 50, 139
French people, prejudice against, 62
Fresno (city), CA., 85
Fresno (County), CA., 80, 142
Fridenberg, Charles, 164
Friedberger, Arnold, 84–85, 164
  Lotta, 84–85
Friedlander, Solomon, 94, 174
Friedman, A., 167
  S., 167
Friendly, S. H., 144
Frisbie's (Nevada City), 59
funerals, xvi, 112–113, 123
Furth, D., 166
  Daniel, 157
  Emanuel, 152
  S., 157
  Simon, 17

G

Gabriel, J., 113
Galveston, Tex., Hebrew Cemetery No. 1, 175
Garizim Lodge No. 43, B'nai B'rith, 101, 106–107, 176–177
Garotte, CA., 83–84
Gatzert, Bailey, 136, 150–151
general merchandise, 35, 45, 51
  merchants, 57
  sold by Jews, 126–127
Gentiles, as merchants, 127
  relations with Jews, 61, 67, 85, 136 (see also anti-Semitism)
Georgetown, CA., 5, 164–165
  dietary laws observed in, 185
  wedding in, 118
Georgia, 149
German Jews, 87
German (language), 50, 139–140
German Sanitary Commission, 177
German Sanitary Verein, 177
Germany, 2, 6, 66, 89–90, 132, 140, 172
Gerstle, family, 31
  Lewis, 15, 34, 145
ghetto occupations, 22
Giboth Olem, 121–122
Gibraltar, 105–106
Gibsonville, CA., 63, 163
Gilbert, Isaac, 83–84
  Michael, 161
gold coin, 35, 40, 152
  discovery, 1, 5
  economy, 13–22, 87
Gold Hill, CA., 72–73
goldminers, 13–22, 125–126
gold mining, 10, 13–22
Gold Mountain Water Co., 113
Golden Gate, 7
Golden Gate Park, San Francisco, 188–189
Goldberg, William, 54
Goldner, family, 99
  Herman, 63, 66, 163
  Mrs. Herman, 104

Julius, 85, 182
  Street, Placerville, 85
Goldsmith, Abraham, 63
Goldwater, family, 129
  Joseph, 156
  Michael (or Michel), 34, 51–52, 175
  S(am?), 156
  Sarah, 51, 109
Goodman & Co., 40
Gradwohl, Abraham, 66, 167
  Lazare, 181
  Marx, 181
  Cohen & Co., 146
Grant, Elder, 182
  U. S., 74–79
Grass Valley, CA., 26, 43, 65, 104, 106–108, 115–116, 119, 123, 134, 148, 159–161, 164, 166, 168–169, 174, 176–179, 181
  circumcision in, 185
  Hebrew benevolent society, 101
  Jewish bankers in, 53–54
  Jewish cemetery, 98, 106–107, 109, 175
  Jewish merchants in, 30, 32, 49, 57
  Masonic activities, 64
  mortuary house, 123
  Orthodox Judaism in, 115
  Passover in, 115
  riot in, 18
  synagogue, 101, 186
  Torah scroll, 179
Grauman, I., 92
  and Josephson, Nevada City, 160
Great Britain, 139
  Jews from, 6
Great Register of Voters, 14–15, 63, 148
Greenberg, Henry, 158
Greenebaum, family, 31
  Moses, 64
Greenwald, J., 177
Greenwood Valley, CA., 164
Griesman & Co., 150
Grizzly Flat, CA., 99
  Jewish merchants in, 48
Guggenheim family, 30

Gumpert, E., 175
Guthrie, S., 50

H

Haas, Samuel, 31, 42, 73–74, 152
Haines, Abraham, 103, 128, 156–157
   family, 147
   Rachel, 99, 104
Hamburg Reform Temple, 114
Hanauer, Moses, 55, 175
Hanover (Hanauer?), M., 172
Harris, Mr., 109–110
   Aaron, 117, 120, 129–130
   Abraham, 96
   H., 48, 177
   Levy & Co., Columbia, 153
   Samuel, 20, 155–156, 165
Hart, Mr., 105–106
Haxter, A. S., 52, 122
hay and barley merchants, 35, 152
Hayman, Alvin, Jr., 157
Hazan, 94, 118–119
   in Grass Valley, 115
Hearst, (Senator) George, 158–159
Hebrew benevolent society, 120, 124, 143
   Grass Valley, 101
   Marysville, 107–108
   Mokelumne Hill, 103
   Nevada City, 101–102, 108–109, 177
   Placerville, 102, 104, 108, 111–112, 178
   San Francisco, 53, 90
   Shasta, 173
   Sonora, 100–101, 172, 176
Hebrew Cemetery, Stockton, 148
   No. 1, Galveston, Tex., 175
Hebrew Congregation of Sonora, 100
Hebrew marriage contract, 100, 181–182
   Nevada City, 184
Hebrew Society, Nevada (City), 101–102, 108–109
Hebrew Union College, 136, 177, 182–183

Hecht family, 31
Hegarty, Charles, 134
Heilbronn, L., 92
   Leopold, 91–92, 173
Helbing, August, 140–141
Helena, Mont., 31
Hellman, family, 30
   Lewis M., 163
   Max, 163
Helper, Hinton R., 143
Hendelsohn, Moritz, 54
Henry, Rabbi Henry A., 143
Herman, Ida, 168
Hershman (or Hirschman), Henry, 42
Hexter, Kaufman, 152, 185
Heyman, Mr., 18
   Jacob, 53–54, 148, 157
   Solomon, 64
Hibbard, Rene I., 178–179
High Holidays, 87, 90, 110–113, 120, 124
   in Columbia, 90–91
   in Downieville, 110
   in Grass Valley, 112, 115–116
   in Jackson, 110, 113, 183
   in Marysville, 115–116
   in Mokelumne Hill, 181
   in Nevada City, 92–93, 112, 115–116, 184
   in Placerville, 93, 112, 119, 181, 183
   in Sacramento, 115–116
   in San Andreas, 110
   in San Francisco, 34
   in Sonora, 109–110, 113, 120–121, 123, 172–173, 182
   in Stockton, 115–116
Hills of Eternity Cemetery, Jackson, 121–122
Hirschfelder, Emanuel, 66
   Fannie, 168
Hirschman, Henry, 52
   H. & M., 59
   Moses, 52
Hochstein, F., 109, 112, 182
Holly Spring, Miss., 75
Honolulu, Hawaii, 57

Hornitos, CA., 25, 105–106, 180
  Odd Fellows activities in, 65
Horwitz, H., 148
hotel-keepers, Jews as, 35
Hughes, Seymour, 81
Humiston, Constable, 18
Hungarian (language), 139
Hungary, 140
Hutchings, James Mason, 82–83, 170
Hydraulic Hose Co. No. 1, Bridgeport Township, 166
Hydraulic Parlor No. 56, Native Sons of the Golden West, 184
Hyman Bros., 57
Hyman, Henry Wolf, 57
  Hyman Wolf, 57
  Michael S., 57
  Moses, 185
Hyneman, Moses, 163

I

Idaho, 21
immigration of Jews to the U. S., 13, 87
Independent Order of B'nai B'rith, 18, 101, 106–107, 140, 142, 154, 176–178
  in Grass Valley, 101, 106–107, 176–177
  in Marysville, 142, 154, 176, 178
Independent Order of Good Templars, 65
Independent Order of Knighthood, 65
Independent Order of Odd Fellows, 64–65, 119, 165
  in Big Oak Flat, 161
  in Columbia, 91, 173
  in Sonora, 109
Indian Diggings, CA., 63, 163
Indians, 28, 167
insolvency, 40, 51–52
insurance, fire, 159–160
Ione, CA., 164, 185–186
Ione Lodge No. 80, F. & A. M., 164
Iowa Hill, CA., 55

Irish immigration to the U. S., 2
Isaacs, B., 164
  Bernard, 164
  I. B., 64
Isidor Cohen Elementary School, Sacramento, 136
I. S. Rosenbaum & Co., 155–156
Italian Saloon, Columbia, 54
Italy, 30

J

J. M. Posner & Co., 158
J. Seligman & Co., 135
J. & W. Seligman & Co., 135, 165
Jackson, CA., 24, 33, 61, 63, 66, 68, 104–106, 109–110, 112–113, 128, 147–148, 152, 163–164, 172, 177, 185–186
  High Holidays in, 110–111, 113, 121–122, 176–177, 183
  Jewish cemetery, 98–99, 104, 175
  Jewish congregation, 177
  Jewish merchants in, 39–41, 47–48, 51, 56
  ladies' Hebrew benevolent society, 109
  Orthodox Judaism in, 121
  synagogue, 98, 102–103, 123, 177, 180–181
  synagogue regulations, 121–122
Jackson Street, San Francisco, 171–172
Jacksonville, CA., 83–84
Jacksonville, Ore., 33, 128
Jacobi, Albert, 165
  L., 67
Jacobs, Mr., 83–84
  Albert (or Aron), 151
  & Lewis, 59
  J., 166
  Julius, 182
  L., 172
  Mary, 73, 151
Jacobson, Mr., 26
Jacobson, Mr., 184
Jalumstein, L. (or Zelko), 153, 156

Jamestown, CA., 151
Jennie B. Zellerbach Garden, San Francisco, 188–189
Jenny Ledge (mining claim), 16
Jenny Lind, CA., 63, 161–163
Jerusalem, 107–108, 178
Jesu Maria, CA., 172
jewelers, 29–30, 50–51, 156
Jewell, Godfrey, 53
   Robert, 68
Jewish benevolent societies, 10, 61, 64, 88, 93, 97, 100, 108, 142 (see also Hebrew benevolent societies)
Jewish calendar, 93
Jewish cemeteries, xv, 10, 61, 84, 88, 97–101, 103–104, 106–107, 109–110, 175 (see also cemeteries)
   Galveston, Tex., 175
   Grass Valley, 98, 115
   Jackson, 98–99, 104, 175
   Marysville, 109, 142, 154
   Mokelumne Hill, 98–100, 103, 175, 177
   Nevada City, 98, 155
   Oroville, 142
   Placerville, 85, 98–99, 104, 175
   Sacramento, 98
   San Francisco, 98, 171–172
   Shasta, 173–174
   Sonora, 98–101, 109, 172, 174–176
   Stockton, 94, 98, 148, 174–175, 179–180
   Victoria, B. C., 175
Jewish chaplains, 169
Jewish charities, 104–108
Jewish community life in San Francisco, 7, 183
Jewish community life in the mines, 10
Jewish communities, 87ff.
Jewish congregations, 10, 88, 93, 100
Jewish education, 111, 119
Jewish family life, 8–9, 131
Jewish Friendship Club (Sonora), 176
Jewish funerals, xvi

Jewish New Year, in San Francisco, 34 (see also High Holidays and specific towns)
Jewish newspapers, xvi
Jewish organizations, xvi
Jewish prayer books, 171
Jewish religious practices, 113ff, 131
Jewish religious services, 61
Jewish synagogues, 90, 97–98
Jewish Theological Seminary of America, 182–183
Jewish weddings, xvi
Jews, as bankers, 54–56, 146
   as book-sellers, 37, 49–50, 155–156
   as civic leaders, 37, 63–68
   in the clothing business (see clothing merchants)
   emancipation of, 2, 88–89
   in Europe, 8–9 (see also Europe)
   as express agents, 146
   as farmers, 30, 150
   from England, 90
   from Germany, 89–90 (see also Germany)
   from Poland, 89–90
   immigration of to the U.S., 13
   as merchants, xv, 10, 13–14, 20–24, 26, 35, 37, 61, 85, 97, 126, 131–132, 146
   in Baker, Ore., 128
   in Barkerville, B. C., 128
   in Colorado, 128
   in Columbia, 44–45, 50, 79
   along Fraser River, B.C., 128
   in Jacksonville, Ore., 128
   in Los Angeles, 132
   in Mokelumne Hill, 32, 50
   in Montana, 128
   in Nevada City, 29, 31, 39, 42, 45–47, 49–50, 57, 59
   in Nevada (state), 128
   in the Northern Mines, 37
   in Oregon, 33
   at Orofino mines, Ida., 128
   in Oroville, 128
   in Phoenix, Ariz., 132

in Placerville, 19, 29-30, 47, 53, 55-56
in Portland, Ore., 132
in Sacramento, 132
in Salt Lake City, Ut., 132
in San Andreas, 31, 45, 49
in San Francisco, 6-7, 24, 132
in Shasta, 128
in Sonora, 29, 42, 46-47, 49, 51, 53, 55
in Stockton, 43, 132
in Yreka, 128
(see also specific cities & counties)
Jews, friendliness toward as merchants, 84
 in the gold economy, xv
 in the mining economy, 10, 13, 18, 21
 as miners, 13-15, 17-18, 21, 23, 30, 172
 mobility, 87
 participation by in town activities, xv, 63-68, 85
 as peddlers, 24-28, 136, 148
 as prospectors, 14-15, 21, 23, 145
 as postmaster, 146
 as recorders of mining districts, 20
 relations with Gentile merchants, 68
 relations with Gentiles, 61, 68
 as slave traders, 144
 as tobacco merchants, 37
Joseph, J., 175
Josephson, C., 59, 64
journalists, Jews as, 174
Judah L. Magnes Memorial Museum, 179-180, 186
Judaism, as nationality, 170
jurors, Jews as, 64

K

Kahn, Aaron, 47, 55-56, 104, 166
 Florence Prag, 129
 Isaac (or Ira), 57, 128
 Julius, 129
Katz, Frederick, 152

Katzenstein, Arthur, 142
Kauffman family, 132
Kaufman, H., 19
 J., 83-84
 M., 53
 Rose, 182
Kearny Street, San Francisco, 171-172
Kennedy Mining Co., Jackson, 147
Kentucky Store, Nevada City, 160
Kesher Shel Barzel, 101, 106-107
Kidd & Knox's brick building, Nevada City, 148
Kip, Rev. William Ingraham, 168
Klauber, A. & Co., 31
 Abraham, 31, 151
Klipstine, J., 163
Klondike gold strike, 34
Know-Nothing Party, 62-63, 79
Kohlberg, A., 43
 Rosenbaum & Co., 31
Kohlman, Jacob, 45, 63, 73
 Sol., 64, 155, 166
 Sol. & Bro., 59
Kohn, Abraham, 149
 D., 72-73
 Jacob, 85, 140, 145
 Nathan, 168
 Sarah, 168
Kol Nidre, 184
kosher meat, in Nevada City, 117
 in Sonora, 121
Koshland, Nathan, 33
Kossuth, Louis, 140
Kuhn family, 30
Kuppenheim, Baden, 129

L

Labatt, H. J., 95
Lachman, Mr., 108-109
 Benjamin, 152
 Davis, 152
La Grange, CA., 105-106
Lake Tahoe, 142
Lancha Plana, CA., 99, 177
Landecker, J. S., 33, 59, 150-151

L., 165
landsman, 92
Lane County, Ore., 144
La Porte, CA., 129
Laski, (Rev.) Samuel M., 117-118
Lasky, Marks, 103, 164
Latrobe, CA., 44
law, in San Francisco, 8
  in the mines, 9
Leake, Charles A., 167
Leeser, (Rev.) Isaac, 115-116, 122
Le Havre, France, 94
Lehman family, 30
Leiser, T., 48
Leo, (Rev.) Ansel, 93, 181
  H., 92-93, 173, 181
Levey (or Levy), J. M., 152, 166
Levi, Edward, 172
Levi (or Levy), Elias, 48
Levinsky, Mr., 109-110
  brothers, 39
  John, 33, 103
  Louis, 147
  Mark, 164
Levison, family, 31
  J., 41
  Jacob B., 135
  Louis, 132
  Mark, 135, 160-161
Levy, A., 16
  (Rabbi) A. M., 112, 182
  Abraham, 133
  Mrs. B. H., 187
  Brothers of Jackson, 47
  Charles, 41
  Daniel, 103
  David, 168
  E., 103
  Emma, 68
  Harriet Lane, 132
  Harris, 166
  Harris, & Co., 153
  Hyman, 133
  Isaac (of El Dorado County), 20
  Isaac (of Columbia), 91, 167
  J., 147
  Jacob, 41
  Joel, 53, 64, 112, 182
  Joseph, 72-73
  Lewis (of Jackson), 148
  Louis, (of Columbia), 163, 165
  M., 103
  (Rabbi) Myer S., 185
  N., 167
  Rachel, 133
  Raphael, 165
  S., & Bro., 160-161
  S. & H., 133
  (or Levey), Samuel, 47, 163-164, 185-186
  Sholom, 133
  (or Levey), Theodore, 24
  families, Columbia, 161
Lewis, Lewis, 33, 171-172
  M. & Co., 39
  & Rosenbaum, 59
  S. (of Nevada City), 166
  S. (of Placerville), 168
Lewisson, A., 167
Liebman & Co., 158
Lilienthal family, 31
Lincoln, Abraham, 66, 75, 77-78
Linoberg, Emanuel, 19, 35, 42, 58, 63, 79, 84, 114-115, 129, 152, 163-164, 167, 175
  Street, Sonora, 58, 84
Lippman, G., 103
  Louis, 165
liquor merchants, 41, 51
Loeb family, 30
Loewenthal, (Rev.) H., 182-183
London, England, 30, 70
  clothing manufactured in, 39
  Paris National Bank, 134-135
"Long Tom" saloon, Sonora, 47
Lord Mayor of London, 70
Los Angeles, CA., 34, 132, 151, 167, 189
Louis, Henry, 112, 118, 152, 164-165
  Pauline, 112
Louisiana, 149
  Co., 19
Low, Garrett W., 143
Lurch, Isaac, 99, 177

Index 223

Lubeck, D. W., 54–55, 164
Lundy, CA., 57
Lyons, A., 172

M

Madison, CA., 128
Magnes, Judah L., Memorial Museum, 179–180, 186
Mandelbaum, Francis, 31
Manifest Destiny, 2
Marcuse, Herman, 18
Margolis, (Rabbi) Elias, 113, 182–183
Mariposa (city), CA., 5, 158, 163
    mining in, 15
    Democratic Club, 163
Mariposa County, xvi, 25, 129–130, 148
    Jewish merchants in, 29, 39, 45, 50, 56
    mining in, 18
    travel to, 5
Marks & Co., 18, 54, 157
    & Jessel, 49
    Avenue, Fresno, 85
Marks, Bernhard, 72–73, 80–82, 85, 117
    Isaac, 168
    Jacob C., 115
    L., 73
    L. D., 63
    L. I., 64
marriage contract, Hebrew, 100, 184
marriages, xvi
Marshall, James W., 5, 91
Marysville, CA., 8, 26, 105, 107–108, 115–116, 143, 154, 176, 178–189
    B'nai B'rith in, 142, 154, 176, 178
    Hebrew Benevolent Society, 107–108
    Jewish Cemetery, 109, 142, 154
    Jewish merchants in, 41–42
    synagogue, 90
Masonic activities, 64–65, 119, 164
    in Columbia, 91
    in Nevada City, 64, 92–93
Masonic Hall, Columbia, 173

Jackson, 111, 123
Matuca chapter, E Clampus Vitus, 187
matzoth, 117, 121
Mayers & Coe, 59
    Simon (of El Dorado County), 73
    Simon (of Nevada County), 166
Meier, Aaron, 129, 161–162, 187–188
    Emanuel, 129, 161
    & Frank Co., 129
    Julius, 129, 161
    Julius L., 187–188
merchandising, 6, 23–59
    on credit, 8, 10, 32, 40, 60
merchants, Jews as, 23–59, 146 (see also Jews, as merchants and specific occupations)
Messing, (Rabbi) Aron J., 107, 178, 185
Mexicans, 66
    prejudice against, 62
Mexico, 1–2
Meyer, Bertha, 187
    Mathias, 182
    Oser, 161, 187
mezuzah, 184
Michelsen, M., 50
Michelson, Albert, 128–129, 187
    Charles, 187
    family home, Murphys, 187
    Samuel, 128, 187
Michigan Bluff, CA., 152
Michigan City, CA., 123
Middle West, 162, 182–183
Mierson, A. & Sons, 53
    A., Banking Co., 53
    & Jewell, 53
    Augustus, 53, 157, 164
    Max, 157
military service, Jews in, 66, 167
Miller, Bernhart, 21
miners, 7, 13–22, 40, 172
mining, xv, 1, 5–7, 13–22, 50, 125
    camps, 9
    claims, 10, 15
    congregations, 92
    corporations, 15, 17–18

partnerships, 18
stock, 20
stockholders, 20, 22
Minnesota (city), CA., 134
minyan, 89–90, 92, 110
Miriam Lodge No. 56, B'nai B'rith, Marysville, 142, 154, 176, 178
Mobile, Ala., 140
Mock, Rosalie, 113
Modesto, CA., 128, 187
mohel, 94, 185
Mokelumne Hill, CA., 25, 63, 66, 78, 99, 113, 116–117, 123, 148, 151–152, 163, 167, 177
   circumcision in, 185
   Hebrew Benevolent Society, 103
   High Holidays in, 181
   Jewish cemetery in, 98–100, 103, 175, 177
   Jewish merchants in, 32, 50
   ladies' Hebrew benevolent society, 109
   Passover in, 116–117
Molinari, Charles, 112
Momento Lodge No. 37, I.O.O.F., Georgetown, 165
Montana, 128
   gold discovery in, 21
Montefiore, Sir Moses, 107–108
Moore, Mr., 18
Moores Flat, CA., 18, 54, 133, 146
Mormon Bar, CA., 5
Mormons, 95
Morocco, 105–106
   Relief Fund, 105–106
Morris, family, 98–99
   George, 98–99
   Henry, 98–99
   J., 72–73
   Jacob, 159
   James, 98–99
   Minnie, 98–99
   Pauline, 98–99
   Saul, 98–99, 157–158
mortuary house, in Grass Valley, 123
   in Sonora, 123
Mother Lode, brick buildings in, 57–60, 146, 159–162
   Jews in, xvi, 10, 29, 32–33, 41, 43, 45, 55–57, 60–61, 63, 65, 77, 82, 84, 88, 90, 95, 98–99, 104–106, 109–110, 112–114, 116–119, 124–125, 128, 132, 142–143, 162, 174, 185
   location, 5–6
   Jewish population in, 6, 94, 148, 172–173
   mining in, 13–22
   Passover in, 116–117
   treatment of Jews in, 13–14, 27–28, 69–84
mule trains, 42–43, 150
Mulford's building, Nevada City, 58
Murphys, 15, 128–129, 145, 161, 187
Munckton, Justice, 69
Myers, D., 64

N

N. Cohn & Co., Mariposa, 150
Nachman, Flora, 168
   Jacob, 168
   Sarah, 168
Nathan, David, 159
   Morris, 159
   Nathan, 159
National Exchange Hotel, Nevada City, 178
National Hotel Museum, Nevada City, 157
Native Sons of the Golden West, 184
naturalization, 62–63
   records, 57
Netherlands, 6
Nevada City, CA., 24, 26, 33, 61, 63, 65, 67, 73, 97, 104–109, 115–116, 123, 136, 148, 150–152, 156–157, 160, 165–166, 175–176, 178–179, 181
   brick buildings in, 58
   circumcisions in, 118
   dietary laws in, 184

fires, 59
Hebrew Cemetery, 98, 109, 155, 175
Hebrew marriage contract, 184
Hebrew Society, 101–102, 108–109, 177
   High Holidays in, 92–93, 184
   Jewish bankers in, 54
   Jewish merchants in, 29, 31, 39, 42–43, 45–47, 49–50, 57, 59
   Jewish Sabbath in, 120
   Library Association, 156
   Masonic activities in, 64, 92–93
   merchandising in, 21
   mezuzah in, 184
   Nevada Rifles, 166
   Passover in, 117
   Sunday closing law in, 95–96
   synagogue, 108–109
Nevada County, CA., xvi, 54, 63, 73, 163
   branch merchandising in, 57
   Jewish merchants in, 29
   Masonic activities in, 64–65
   mining in, 16–17
   travel to, 5
Nevada (state of), 57, 128, 134, 146, 176
   gold discovery in, 21
   silver discovery in, 21
Newbauer & Co., 49
   David, 156–157
New England, 38, 153
Newhouse, Moritz, 163
Newman, G., 64
   Jacob, 148
New Mexico, 21
New Orleans, La., 3, 109, 139, 145, 155
New Orleans Wholesale & Retail Clothing Depot, Nevada City, 155
Newport, R. I., 30
newspapers, xvi, 5, 21, 32, 37, 44–45, 47, 50, 52, 56, 59–60, 65, 68–71, 73, 82, 89, 95–97, 104, 133, 160
Newstadt, Mr., 105–106

New York City, N. Y., 18, 30, 39, 45, 135, 139–140, 157, 165, 181, 184
   clothing manufactured in, 38–39
New York State, 149
New York Bakery & Saloon, 56
Nicaragua, 1, 39
Nieman, F., 18
Northern Mines, 41, 61, 63, 74, 84, 90, 98, 108, 110, 124–125, 134, 140, 142, 154
   Jewish merchants in, 29, 32, 45, 60
   location of, 5–6
Nobel Prize, 128–129
North California Mining Co., 20
North Carolina, 149
North San Juan, CA., 157
   Jewish bankers in, 54
   Jewish merchants in, 29
North Star Lodge No. 12, Ancient Jewish Order Kesher Shel Barzel, Nevada City, 101, 106–107
Northern Europeans, 71, 88
Notkin, (Rabbi) Nathan, 107–108
Novitzki, Mrs. Ray, 119

O

Oakdale, CA., 128
Oakland, CA., 179–180
Oberfelder, Max, 34
   Tobias, 34
Odd Fellows, 64–65, 109, 119, 161, 165, 173
Ohio, 149
Old South, 10, 144
Openheim, P. B., 163
Oppenheim, B., 55–56
Oppenheimer, H., 49
   Helena (or Helene), 181–182
   L. & J., 49
Order No. 11, 75, 169
Oregon, 136, 139, 182, 187–188
   gold discovery in, 21
   Jewish merchants in, 33
organizations, Jewish, xvi
Orleans Flat, CA., 145
Orleans Hotel, Placerville, 152

Orofino mines, Idaho, 128
Oroville, CA., 107–108, 128
  Jewish cemetery in, 142
Orthodox Judaism, 88, 94, 113–115, 117, 119, 122, 183
Oser Meyer & Friedlander, store, Murphys, 161

P

Pacific Hebrew Orphan Asylum & Home Society, 107
Pacific Mail fleet, 139
Pacific Northwest, 10, 136
Pacific Street, San Francisco, 171–172
Palestine, 95
  Fund, 178
  Relief Fund, 107
Panama, 1, 3–5, 123, 139–140
Panama-Pacific Exposition, 41
Paris, France, 39
partnerships, 56–57
Passover, in Grass Valley, 115
  in Mokelumne Hill, 116–117
  in the Mother Lode, 116–117
  in Nevada City, 117
  in Placerville, 117
  in Sonora, 116, 121, 178–179
  in Yosemite Park, 117
Pawbroch, Mr., 115, 184
peddlers, 24–26, 87, 136, 148–149
  regulations against, 25
Pentecost, 91
Perham, Dr., 19
Peyser, A., 50, 148
  I., 47
Philadelphia, Pa., 80, 117, 140
Phoenix, Ariz., 132
Phoenix Quartz Mining Co., 20
Pine (city), CA., 148
Pinto, Adolph, 112, 181–182
Piny Hill Quartz Ledge, 18
Placer County, xvi, 148
  travel to, 5
  Bank, 55
Placerville, CA., 27, 55, 61, 63, 65, 67–68, 72–73, 80, 84–85, 103, 113, 118, 135, 140, 145, 148, 152, 155–157, 160–161, 165–166, 168, 182
  Bar Mitzvah in, 119
  Hebrew Benevolent Society, 102, 104, 108, 111–112, 178
  High Holidays in, 93, 112, 119, 181, 183
  Jewish cemetery, 85, 98–99, 104, 175
  Jewish merchants in, 19, 29–30, 47, 53, 55–56
  ladies' Hebrew Benevolent Society, 109
  Masonic activities in, 64
  mining by Jews in, 19
  mining near, 20
  Passover in, 117
  schools in, 68
  synagogue, 98, 102, 104, 111–112, 123, 176
  & Sacramento Valley Rail Road, 43
  Gold & Silver Mining & Tunnel Co., 147
Plymouth, CA., 57
  Jewish merchants in, 57
Poker Flat, CA., 35, 152, 162
Poland, 89–90, 106, 132, 172
Polish minhag, 90, 115, 121–122
politics, Jews in, 63
Polk, President James K., 1
population figures, 25, 31, 127, 131–132, 142, 148, 172–173
Portland, Ore., 31, 33, 57, 129, 132, 136, 185
Portuguese, 185
  ritual, 140
Posner, J. M., & Co., 158
Postmaster, Jews as, 63, 146
Prag, Conrad, 35, 65, 129
Prager, Simon, 24
prayerbooks, Jewish, 171
prejudice against foreigners, 15, 62, 70–71
Prescott, Ariz., 34
Price, William, 41
  & Co., 41

Pringle, Miss, 111
probate records, 41, 47–48
property assessment, 83–84
  tax payments, 162
prospectors, 13–22, 40, 125–126, 145
Protection Hose Co. No. 1, Grass Valley, 166
Protestants, 71
Prussia, 106, 172
Prussian Poland, Jews from, 6
public schools, 62, 68, 80–82
  in Columbia, 80–82
Purim, in Grass Valley, 115

Q

quartz mining, 19
  veins, 16

R

Rabbinical Assembly of America, 182–183
rabbis, xvi, 112, 117–118, 182
Rabbit Creek, CA., 35, 129
railroad transportation, 43-44, 130
railroads, 150
Ransohoff, N. S. & Co., 35, 129
Raphael, Henry D., 47, 55–56, 64, 163–164
  M., 163
Recreation & Park Dept., San Francisco, 188–189
Reeb, Melanie, 99
  Moses, 99, 156–157
  Moses & Brother, 47
Reform Judaism, 113–115, 119–120
Reformed Society of Israelites, 114
religious services, Jewish, xvi
Reno, Nev., 159
  Jewish merchants in, 57
Republican Party, 78–79
Rhine, Nathan, 16, 103
Richmond, Va., 112
"Riffle" Saloon, Sonora, 49
Ritzwoller, Selig, 53
Rosenbaum, I. S. & Co., 155–156

Rosenbaum, Mr., 174
Rosenberg, Alfred, 148
  (Rabbi) Bernard D., 178–179
  building, Jenny Lind, 161
  Louis, 129, 163
  M., 184
  M. J., 147
Rosenblum building, Chinese Camp, 161
Rosenfield, Mr., 170
  A., 50
Rosenheim, Mr., 67
  A., 92, 166
  A. S., 50
  M., 50
  & Bro., 45, 59
Rosenstock, S. W., 33
Rosenthal, A., 47
  Davis, 65, 129–130
  Joseph, 25, 148, 180
  L., 65
  (Rev.) S., 176
  Simon, 108–109
  Simon & Brother, 39, 46, 58–59
Rosentorff, Simon, 97
Rosenwald, Alexander, 57
  family, 30
Rosh Hashanah, 91, 110–116
  in Columbia, 173
  in Jackson, 121–122
  in San Francisco, 34
  in Sonora, 120–121
Rosner, Mr., 53
Rothschild, Henry, 20, 39
  S., 120
  The Messrs., 54, 95
Rough & Ready, CA., 29
Round Tent Store, Placerville, 55
Royal Arch Masons, 164
Russia, 106, 172
  Jews from, 6
Russian Steam Baths, near Sonora, 35

S

S. Levy & Brother, Columbia, 160–161

S. & H. Levy, Columbia, 133
Sabbath, 113
  in Nevada City, 120
  in Sonora, 121
  in Yosemite Park, 120
Sachs brothers firm, 33
Sachs, Robert, 50
Sacramento (city), CA., 15, 31, 33–34, 39, 41–43, 98, 102, 115–116, 118, 132, 134, 136, 143, 185
  travel to, 8
Sacramento River, 5, 8, 43, 154
  Valley, 5, 132
Sacramento Valley, Jewish merchants in, 32
Salomonson, Julius, 158
saloon-keepers, 35, 152
Salt Lake City, Ut., 31, 35, 129, 132
San Andreas, CA., 35, 65, 84–85, 129, 146, 155–156, 164, 180
  High Holidays in, 110
  Jewish merchants in, 31, 45, 49
  fault, 41
Sanders, Mr., 109–110
  A. A., 177
  S., 103
Sandias, CA., 19
San Francisco, CA., 15, 17–18, 25, 30–31, 36–37, 42–46, 53–55, 57, 62, 70, 82, 89–90, 94–95, 98, 102–104, 106–107, 110–111, 113, 117–118, 122–124, 129–135, 139–140, 142–143, 146, 150–152, 158, 171, 176, 178–179, 181–182, 185–189
  anti-Semitism in, 7
  as trading center, 30, 32
  branch merchandising, 32
  clothing manufactured in, 39
  credit merchandising in, 35
  earthquake and fire in, 41
  High Holidays in, 34
  Jewish community life in, 7, 183
  Jewish merchants in, 6–7, 24, 132
  Jewish newspapers in, xvi
  Jews in, 6
  Jews naturalized in, 63

law and order in, 8
merchandising in, 7
overland to, 4
Park Commission, 189
population, 8, 31
ship transportation to, 3, 7
synagogues, 105
transportation from, 6, 8
vigilance committees in, 66
wholesale merchandising in, 21, 31, 33, 35, 38–41, 52–53, 58–60
San Joaquin River, 8, 43
  Valley, 132
  Jewish merchants in, 32
San Jose, CA., 142, 185
San Simeon, CA., 158–159
Santa Cruz (city), CA., 31
Santa Cruz County, 72
Sattley, CA., 5
Sarah Lodge No. 4, Ancient Jewish Order Kesher Shel Barzel, 106
Scharff, Emanuel, 156–157
Scheeline, Alexander, 163
  Nathan, 163
Schiff family, 30
Schiller, Henry, 66, 145, 166
Schloss, M., 171–172
School Hill, Placerville, 111
School of Inquiry, 67
Schwab, Moses, 18
Schwabacher, Ludwig, 134
Schwartz, Daniel, 165
Schwartz, Philip, 44, 64
Schweitzer, Bernard, 25
  Sam, 25
Seattle, Wash., 136, 151
Second Cavalry Regiment, 166
Seder, Passover, 116
Seeligsohn, M., 155–156, 175
Seldner, Louis, 45
Selig, A. & Co., 45
Seligman, Abraham, 65, 135, 165
Seligman Block, Placerville, 165
  family, 30
  Henry, 135
  J. & Co., 135
  J. & W., & Co., 135, 165

James, 135
  Leopold, 135, 165
Selling, Ben, 136, 182
  Isaac, 136
  Jeanette, 182
  Philip, 136, 160–161
Sephardim, 30, 140
Seymour, Horatio, 77
Shaar Zedek Hebrew Society, Grass Valley, 179
Shasta (city), CA., 5, 128
  Hebrew Benevolent Society, 173
  Jewish cemetery, 173–174
Shaurey Shomagin Cemetery Association, 16, 103–104, 177
Shaw's Flat, CA., 83–84, 156, 182
Shinn, Charles, 144
ship transportation to the mines, 8
Shirpser, D., 33, 43, 59
  Herman, 33
shochet, 94
  in Nevada City, 117
shofar, 108–109, 113
  in Grass Valley, 115
Sierra County, xvi, 35, 148, 152
  travel to, 5
Sierra Nevada Mountains, 5, 8, 15, 42, 132
Silbermann, Mrs., 68
  C., 158, 166
  P., 47, 55–56, 158
  P. & Co., 47, 56
Silberstein, S., 147
Silvester, Henry, 166
Simon, Albert, 85
  & Bro., 58
  Drive, Placerville, 85
  Michael, 102, 111–112, 158
Simons, Hiram C., 18
"Sinbad" (pseudonym), 102, 176
slavery, 2, 13, 66
slave-traders, Jews as, 144
Sloss & Co., 34
Sloss, family, 31
  Louis, 15, 34, 141
Snow, Samuel S., 85, 111–112, 152
Snows Road, 85

social events, 67
Solis-Cohen, Jacob, 80, 117
Solomon, N., 40
Solomons, Lord Mayor, 70
Sonora, CA., 34–35, 43, 61, 63, 65, 70, 79, 84, 91, 94, 105, 109, 112–113, 116, 119, 123, 136, 151–153, 155–157, 160–161, 164, 167, 172–173, 181–182
  brick buildings in, 58
  census in, 90
  dietary laws in, 121
  Hebrew Benevolent Society, 100–101, 172, 176
  High Holidays in, 109–110, 113, 120–121, 123, 172–173, 182
  Jewish cemetery, 98–101, 109, 174–176
  Jewish Friendship Club, 176
  Jewish merchants in, 29, 42, 46–47, 49, 51, 53, 55
  kosher meat in, 121
  matzoth in, 121
  merchants in, 27
  mining by the Jews of, 19
  mortuary house, 123
  Passover in, 116, 121, 178–179
  peddling ordinance, 25
  religious services, 178–179
  Sabbath in, 121
  synagogue, 90, 100
  Torah scroll in, 178–179
  Yahrzeit observance in, 178–179
Sonora & Columbia Hebrew Benevolent Society, 82, 100, 105–106, 177
Sons of Temperance, 65
South America, 4
Southern Mines, 19
Spanish language, 50, 139
  ritual, 140
Spokane, Wash., 99
Springfield, CA., 65, 165
Squarza punch, 156
Stamper, Mr., 83–84
  Rev., 118
State Highway 49, 5

stationery sellers, 155–156
steamboats, 150
Steckler, Charles, 40–41, 56, 152
   Martin, 68
Steinhart Aquarium, San Francisco, 135
   Frederick, 135
   Ignatz, 135
   Sigmund, 135
Stiefel & Cohn, 59
St. Louis, CA., 152, 162
   MO., 140
Stockton, CA., 31, 33, 98, 105, 113, 115–116, 118, 132, 154, 182
   Jewish cemetery, 94, 98, 148, 174–175, 179–180
   Jewish merchants in, 43, 132
   transportation to, 8
Stoutenburgh, CA., 144
Stow, William W., 71–72
Straus family, 30
   J., 50
Strauss, Ben, 164
   L., 147
   Levi, 35, 89
Street, C. L., 182
Strouse (or Strauss), Bertha, 99
Strybing Arboretum, San Francisco, 188–189
Stursberg, Herman, 18
suicide, 53
Suisun City, CA., 128
Sukkoth, in Sonora, 116
Sunday closing law, 67, 71–74, 80, 82–83, 95–96, 168–170
sureties, Jews as, 64
Sutro, Adolph, 146
   Emil, 33
   Gustave, 33
Sutter Chapter No. 11, Royal Arch Masons, 164
   John, 92
Sutter Creek, CA., 67, 99, 105–106, 112–113, 148, 164–165, 168, 177, 185–186
   circumcision in, 118
   Jewish merchants in, 57

schools in, 68
Sutter Creek Lodge No. 31, I.O.O.F., 165
synagogues, 90, 97–98, 100
   in Columbia, 173
   in Grass Valley, 101, 186
   in Jackson, 98, 102–103, 110–111, 123, 177, 180–181
   in Marysville, 90
   in Nevada City, 108–109
   in Placerville, 98, 102, 104, 111–112, 123
   in San Francisco, 105
   in Sonora, 90

T

tailors, 96
Tannenwald, L., 158
tax payments, 38
teamsters, 35, 152
Tehama Quartz Mining Co., 20
Temple Israel, Stockton, 178–179
   Cemetery, 174
   (see also Stockton, Jewish Cemetery)
Tennessee, 75
Texas, 167
Thann, Haut Rhine, 181
theft of merchandise, 26, 43
Thompson Building, Murphys, 161
Three Brothers Store, Columbia, 133
Tienda Mexicana store, Sonora, 35
Tiger Hook & Ladder Co. No. 1, 166
tobacco, 29–30
   merchants, 48–51, 155–156
Toby Street, Sonora, 84
Tombstone, Ariz., 34
Torah scrolls, 94, 108 111
   in Grass Valley, 115, 179
   in Sonora, 178–179
transportation, 125
   to the mountains, 155
   by freight wagon, 43, 46
   by mule train, 150
   by pack trains, 42, 46
   by railroad, 43, 46, 150

Index

by ship, 57
by steamboat, 43, 149–150
Tucson, Ariz., 34
Tuolumne County, xvi, 42, 45, 51, 66, 114–115, 126, 129, 148, 163–164, 184–185
   anti-Semitism in, 79–84
   assessment, 153
   Jewish merchants in, 29, 83–84
   Jewish taxpayers in, 38
   peddling in, 26
   travel to, 5
Tuolumne Lodge No. 21, I.O.O.F., Columbia, 165
Tuolumne National Guard, 166

U

Uncle Sam (ship), 39
Union of American Hebrew Congregations, 131
United States Bakery, Nevada City, 152
United States Naval Academy, 128–129
United States, Jewish settlement in, 3
Utah, 35
urban society, 22

V

Vallecito, CA., 128, 146, 153, 161
   mining in, 16
   Flat, 17
   Tunnel & Mining Co., 17
Vertimer, P., 56
Victoria, B. C., 33, 123
   Jewish Cemetery, 175
vigilance committees, 66–67, 79
Virginia (state), 149
Virginia City, Nev., 31, 57, 84, 99, 128, 134–135, 159
Volcano, CA., 69, 113, 152
   Jewish merchants in, 31, 45
   mining by Jews in, 19
volunteer fire departments, 65, 67, 119, 165–166
Volunteer Rifle Co., 166
Voorsanger, (Rabbi) Jacob, 89, 172

W

Wangenheim, Sol, 129, 162
   & Rosenberg, 188
Warburg family, 30
Washington Hall, Sonora, 113
   Mining District, 147
Washington (state), gold discovery in, 21
   Jewish merchants in, 33
watchmakers, 50
Watkin, (Rabbi) Nathan, 107–108
weddings, xvi, 117–118, 181–182, 184
Weekly Gleaner (newspaper), 178, 181–182
Weil, Aaron (or Aron), 164
   Henry, 18
Weis, Jacob, 166
Weissbein, Jacob, 53–54, 157
   Joseph, 53–54
   Brothers & Co., 53
   Brothers & Co. Broking & Business Corp., 54
Weldman, Lena, 168
Wells Fargo & Co., 43
   agents, 157, 161
   Bank History Room, San Francisco, 157–158
West, gold discovery in, 21
Western Clothing Depot, 39
Western Jewish History Center, 179–180
Western United States, 10, 33
Weston, Julian W., 157
wholesale merchandising, 21, 31, 33, 35, 38–42, 52–53, 58–60, 155
Willamette Paper Co., 134
Wilson, Henry, 78–79
Wilzinski, family, 98
   Tobias M., 84
Wise, (Rabbi) Isaac Mayer, 119, 123
Wolf, A., & Bros., San Francisco, 151
   & Co., Chinese Camp, 160–161
   Brothers, Sonora, 46

H., 151, 175
Herman, 166
Jacob, 163
M., 165
Rosalie, 184
Wolfe, Henry M., 168
　Herman, 67
　P. H., 73
women, 109
　merchandising by, 51
Woodland, CA., 128
Woolf, Israel, 40
Woolf's Shirt Depot, 40
World's Fair, San Francisco, 189
Wulff, General D. W., 59
　Henry, 168
"W. Y. O. D." mine, Grass Valley, 157

Y

Yahrzeit observance, 178–179
Yom Kippur, 89, 93, 110–116
　in Columbia, 173
　in Downieville, 122
　in Jackson, 121–122
　in Nevada City, 184
　in San Francisco, 171–172
Yo Semite Lodge No. 97, I.O.O.F., 161
Yosemite Mining Co., 18
Yosemite Park, 117
　Sabbath in, 120
Yreka, CA., 33, 128
Yuba County, 146, 156–157
　River, 91

Z

Zacharias, L., 166
　P., 65
Zellerbach, A. & Sons, 134
　A., Paper Merchant, 134
　Anthony, 133–134, 146
　Isadore, 133, 145
　Mrs. Isadore, 188–189
　Jacob, 133
　James D., 134
　Jennie B., 188–189
　Marks, 18, 54, 133, 145–147
　(Zellerbach), Marks & Co., 157
　Paper Co., 134
Zerker, H., 48
Zeta Encampment No. 5, I.O.O.F., Placerville, 165
Zuckerman, Jacob, 156
　Lisette, 156